HEBREW: THE ETERNAL LANGUAGE

WILLIAM CHOMSKY

HEBREW:

THE ETERNAL LANGUAGE

PHILADELPHIA
THE JEWISH PUBLICATION SOCIETY OF AMERICA

Copyright © *1957 by*
THE JEWISH PUBLICATION SOCIETY OF AMERICA
All Rights Reserved
Fifth Printing, 1975

ISBN 0-8276-0077-1
Library of Congress Catalog Card No.: 57-8140
PRINTED IN THE UNITED STATES OF AMERICA

To
My Children

PREFACE

There has long been need for a book on the origin of the Hebrew language, its struggle for survival in the face of almost insurmountable obstacles, and its survival as a spoken vernacular in our own day. I confess to having for many years cherished the hope that it would some day be given me to write this story. At the same time, I shrank from undertaking a task so vast and important, so basic to the Jewish cultural heritage, and involving so many aspects of Jewish life and history. When, therefore, the Zionist Organization of America approached me several years ago with the request that I prepare a pamphlet on the subject, *Hebrew, The Story of a Living Language*, I allowed myself to be persuaded for the very reason that the discussion would be brief and tentative. Yet some of my friends at once began urging me to expand that pamphlet into a full-sized book, and this is the result.

The account is far from exhaustive. It is designed primarily for the intelligent reader rather than for the scholar. In the process of popularization much had to be diluted, omitted or condensed. In many areas the presentation is very sketchy, though, I hope, authentic and accurate. A more comprehensive account will have to await more auspicious circumstances.

In the writing of this book I had to resort to various sources of information and to the help of individuals who are expert in certain specific areas, and I herewith wish to pay grateful acknowledgment. I am, of course, primarily indebted to Dr. Solomon Grayzel for his stimulation and encouragement, criticism and advice, in the preparation of this book. My thanks are due to the following individuals for helpful counsel and information: Judah Lapson, Chairman of Hebrew Culture Service Committee for American High Schools and Colleges; A. Leo Oppenheim, Oriental Institute, University of Chicago; Cecil

vii

Roth, Oxford University, England; E. A. Speiser, Chairman, Department of Oriental Studies, University of Pennsylvania.

I also wish to make appreciative acknowledgment of the following publications from which illustrative materials were taken: *The Hebrew Scripts,* S. A. Birnbaum; *Millon ha-Lashon ha-Ibrit,* Eliezer Ben Yehudah; *The Field of Yiddish,* edited by Uriel Weinreich, Linguistic Circle of New York; *Semitic Writing,* G. R. Driver, Oxford University Press; *A Study of Writing,* I. J. Gelb, University of Chicago Press. Recognition is also due to *Historische Grammatik der Hebraischen Sprache,* Hans Bauer and Pontus Leander, Verlag von Max Niemeyer, which provided a model for the illustration of Branches of the Semitic Languages, on page 22.

It is my hope that this volume will stimulate new interest in the Hebrew language among those who know it as well as those who do not. May the story of the ancient tongue prove as fascinating to my readers as it has always been to me.

W. C.

March 1, 1957

CONTENTS

LIST OF ILLUSTRATIONS

xi

Between pp. 242 and 243

HEBREW: THE ETERNAL LANGUAGE

INTRODUCTION
THE ROLE OF HEBREW IN JEWISH LIFE

Hebrew as a Modern Vernacular

Barely a decade or two ago there were people who maintained that Hebrew was not a living language. Now, the "sacred language" of the past is the daily vernacular of hundreds of thousands of Jews in Israel. There the language lives in the mouths of school children, bootblacks, busmen, cab drivers, cabaret singers, lawyers, doctors and officials, of the religious, irreligious and anti-religious—indeed, of everyone. The thick horizontal strokes and thin verticals of the Hebrew alphabet are blazoned all over the country on posters, advertising signs, stamps and coins; on highways, shops, stores and hotels. Hebrew slang, colloquialisms and even curses are freely coined; while the Hebrew Language Academy (formerly, Vaad ha-Lashon), composed of outstanding scholars and writers and sponsored by the Israel government, is vigilantly on guard against the intrusion of any solecisms or barbarisms that might impair the purity of the language. From time to time, moreover, this Academy publishes lists of technical terms covering every branch and aspect of science, industry, technology and the like: some ten thousand new words have gained currency since the establishment of the State of Israel. At least four theatrical companies offer regular performances—all, of course, in Hebrew. Thousands of

1

books, magazines, newspapers and brochures on every conceivable topic are in daily circulation. Close to two hundred periodicals are published there in Hebrew, including fifteen dailies and the rest weeklies, monthlies, quarterlies and annuals. Hebrew books are published in Israel at the rate of more than three a day. The air waves of Israel vibrate to the rhythm of the classical tongue.

Outside of Israel, the most significant center of Hebrew culture is America. The language is read, understood and spoken by thousands of American Jews. There are Hebrew periodicals of popular as well as scholarly character; Hebrew books, fictional and scientific; Hebrew language instruction on elementary and college level. Schools, camps and clubs encourage the speaking of Hebrew.

Can there be any question as to the vitality of the Hebrew language? None of the modern attempts to revive old languages, such as Gaelic, Welsh and Indi, can boast of anything approximating the progress made by Hebrew. Yet the Irish, Welsh and Indians have been rooted on their own soil and are free from political, physical and economic difficulties with which the young struggling Jewish community in Israel has had to cope.

Sources of Vitality of the Hebrew Language

How was the Hebrew language able to exist and function as an effective instrument of creative self-expression and inter-communication for about two thousand years, without such an essential ingredient for survival as a state or territory? How could Hebrew retain its vitality and elasticity over such a long period of time in the face of such adverse conditions?

The answer to these questions may be discovered by considering the unique character of Judaism and its relation to the Hebrew language. Hebrew has not been a denationalized universal tongue, the medium of a specific religion, in the sense that Latin has been the official language of the Roman Catholic Church. Nor has it been merely a folk tongue like other living languages. As a matter of fact, it has persisted as a living language for many centuries after it had ceased to be a spoken vernacular in the accepted sense of the term, as will be demonstrated in a later chapter in this volume. Hebrew has been the *sacred language* of the Jewish people—the language of its religion, culture and civilization. It has been, in sum, the language of Judaism and intimately identified with the national and religious experiences of the Jewish people throughout the generations. The Jewish people can no more be dissociated from Hebrew than they can be dissociated from their own spiritual identity—Judaism.

Relationship between Language and Culture

An analysis of the nature of language and of Judaism may help to clarify this point. Language is not merely a means of expression and communication; it is an instrument of experiencing, thinking and feeling, as well as a means of self-expression and personal growth. In investigating the origin of language and "after tracing back its history as far as we can, we see that the earliest language was anything but intellectual, that it was indeed a sort of half-way house between singing and speech with long almost conglomerations of sounds, which served rather as an outlet for intense feelings than for an intelligible expression of them . . ."[1] Indeed, even in modern days language is employed "by children (and often by grown people), not so much to formulate and express thoughts as to give vent to feelings . . ."[2]

Our ideas and experiences are not independent of language; they are all integral parts of the same pattern, the warp and woof of the same texture. We do not first have thoughts, ideas, feelings and then put them into a verbal framework. We think in words, by means of words. Language and experience are inextricably interwoven, and the awareness of one awakens the other. Words and idioms are as indispensable to our thoughts and experiences as are colors and tints to a painting. Our personality matures and develops through language and by our use of it. Defective linguistic growth is known to go hand in hand with stunted intellectual and emotional development. Deaf and dumb people are, as a rule, intellectually retarded and, in some degree, even callous, unless given means of adequate communication.

What is true of language in relation to individual growth is equally true in the case of the cultural growth and development of a people. Indeed, students of language have come to recognize that the experiences of a group, its mental and emotional habits, its modes of thoughts and attitudes are registered and reflected in the words and idioms of the group's language. Thus, for example, the word *shalom,* usually rendered by "peace," has in effect little in common with its English equivalent. *Shalom* does not have the passive, even negative, connotation of the word "peace." It does not mean merely the absence of strife. It is pregnant with positive, active and energetic meaning and association. It connotes totality, health, wholesomeness, harmony, success, the completeness and richness of living in an integrated social milieu. When people meet or part they wish each other *shalom,* or they inquire about each other's *shalom.*

Similarly, the Hebrew words *ruah* (spirit) and *nefesh* (soul) do not have the implications of a disembodiment, such as are indicated by their English equivalents. There is no dichotomy in the Hebrew mind between body and spirit or soul. One is not the antithesis of the other. These Hebrew words have dynamic, life-giving and motor-urgent connotations. Every living being has a *ruah,* even the beast possesses a *ruah* (Ecclesiastes 3. 21). The same is true of the synonym *nefesh,* which is generally rendered by "soul." But *nefesh,* too, is the property of all living beings (Job 12. 10), including the beast (Proverbs 12. 10). Even the netherworld has a *nefesh* (Isaiah 5. 14). Furthermore, every living creature, man as well as animal, is designated as *nefesh* (Genesis 1.20, 21, 24, 12.5, 14.21, etc.). Both *nefesh* and *ruah* often signify strength and vigor, both in a material and a spiritual sense. Voracious dogs are said to possess a strong *nefesh* (Isaiah 56. 11); and the ·horses of Egypt, the prophet warns, are weak: they are "flesh and no *ruah*" (*ibid.,* 31. 3).

There is likewise a far cry between the Hebrew word *tzedakah* (from the stem *tzadak,* to be just or righteous), with its implications of social justice, and the English word "charity." In the case of "charity" the recipient sees himself beholden to the donor, whose action is voluntary. *Tzedakah,* on the other hand, has to be performed as a matter of obligation and the recipient is in no way indebted to the donor. The needy have a right to *tzedakah,* while those possessing means have a duty to give it. Indeed, even a poor person who receives *tzedakah* must in turn give *tzedakah* (Gittin 7b).

There is, likewise, a wide semantic gulf between the Hebrew *rahamim* or *rahmanut* and the English equivalent "pity" or "mercy." The Hebrew word connotes love, family feeling (see Genesis 43.30, etc.), even motherliness, since it is related to *rehem* (mother's womb) of the same stem. None of these connotations is implied in the English equivalents. Similarly, the richly meaningful and historically hallowed implications of the Hebrew *torah* are totally absent in the English equivalent "law." The Hebrew term *torah* embraces the totality of Jewish creative labor throughout the ages. Just as inadequate is the English translation "commandment" for the Hebrew *mitzvah.*

In one of his *hasidic*[3] stories, the Hebrew writer Yehudah Steinberg depicts a *hasid* expressing astonishment at the ignorance and stupidity of the *resha'im* (the wicked or the disbelievers). The main motive for committing wicked deeds, reasons the *hasid,* is the search and pursuit of pleasure and enjoyment. But is any greater pleasure or joy conceivable than that of performing a *mitzvah?* Hence, he continues, if the *resha'im* were sufficiently wise to realize this, they would abandon their wickedness and would all become *tzaddikim* (righteous or strictly observant Jews), just for their pleasure's sake.

This type of reasoning was not unique among traditional Jews. *Simhah shel mitzvah,* the joy of performing a *mitzvah,* constituted an integral element in the pattern of the Jewish way of life. To be sure, the word *mitzvah* originally meant no more than a *command* in the accepted sense. But the specific religious experiences of the Jewish people, their feeling of exultation in the performance of religious responsibilities, invested this word with a cluster of associations and connotations not originally inherent in it. Is it conceivable that one could get a thrill out of performing a *mitzvah* if it were merely a "commandment"?

Every language, including English, has a stock of words which are charged with the emotional and intellectual experiences of the people employing it. To illustrate, within our own experiences, the English word "fireside" came to assume a new connotation as a result of listening to the fireside chats inaugurated by the late president, Franklin D. Roosevelt. Similarly, the word "filibuster," originally signifying a freebooter or pirate, is now employed in the United States in the sense of hindering legislation by means of long speeches or other parliamentary tricks. One may also add, as examples, such expressions as "go to bat," "strike out" and the like. The richer and the more intense the historical experiences of a people, the greater is the number of such words in its language and the more emotionally charged they are. When translated into another language, they become devitalized and almost meaningless.

Such words are not mere linguistic units; they are cultural deposits. But they cannot be transmitted in isolation. They take on their meaning and gain in richness of association and connotation only through the context of experience. In the past some Hebrew words and expressions survived in the vernacular of the people long after the Hebrew language had ceased to be popularly spoken. They were kept alive by the intimate contact which the majority of the people continued to maintain with the Hebrew literary sources and by the persistence of Jewish forms of living and habits of thinking.

Furthermore, one can readily quote a host of expressions and idioms which, though composed of words in the vernacular, encase, in effect, Hebraic thought-patterns. It would seem that as long as the Jews were rooted in their traditional patterns of life, they were sensitive to the inadequacy of the vernacular in expressing and conveying the emotionally charged meaning of certain Hebrew words. They therefore persisted either in retaining the original words and expressions, or in investing the Hebraic mental pattern or idiom with the garb of the vernacular. In this manner a great many words and expressions, as well as idioms, found their way into the various vernaculars employed by the Jews throughout the history of their dispersion. Such dialects arose as Judaeo-Greek, Judaeo-Arabic, Judaeo-Persian and the like. The best known of these dialects, surviving to this day and incorporating a considerable proportion of these Hebraic elements, are Ladino, a Judaeo-Spanish dialect employed by the Jews in the Balkan States and Morocco, and, especially, Yiddish.

At present, however, especially in this country, Jewish patterns of life no longer provide a suitable functional context for these words and expressions. The distinctive features of the Jewish climate characteristic of traditional Jewish ghettos, especially those of Eastern Europe, have almost completely disappeared. The specific vocabularies and idioms of Jewish life no longer function; they have been translated into English equivalents. *Yamim nora'im* are High Holy Days, a *siddur* is a prayerbook, a *mahzor* is a High Holy day or Festival prayerbook. *Yom tov* has been replaced by *holiday*. Such traditional Hebrew terms as *hazzan* (cantor), *shammash* (sexton), *'aron kodesh* (holy ark), *menorah* (candelabrum), *sefer torah* (scroll of the Torah), *gabbai* (an elder in the synagogue), etc., once commonly employed, have fallen into desuetude. A good Jew is no longer *mekayyem* a *mitzvah*, or is a *shomer shabbat*. Instead, he is *performing a command* or *good deed* and is a *Sabbath observer*. He does not drink *le-hayyim* (to life or health); he drinks *to happy days*, and so on. The contact with the literary Hebraic sources remains, therefore, the only avenue to these cultural deposits.

The Meaning of Judaism

The meaning of the terms "Jews" and "Judaism" has, likewise, been a source of confused thinking. Are the Jews a race, a nation, a religious group, or what? Is Judaism only a body of beliefs and practices, or of nationalistic symbols and slogans, or of cultural ideas and literary compilations, such as could be conveyed by one linguistic vehicle or another? Much futile argumentation relative to these matters may be found in our recent literature. The disputants seem to ignore the fact that a feeling of kinship exists among Jews of all "races" and colors, of all parts of the world, regardless of whether they are orthodox, reform or even atheistic.

To be sure, some or all of the elements mentioned above may be found in the Jewish group or in Judaism, as the case may be, not in an additive sense, but rather in an integrative or chemical sense. Hence, the whole is not like any of the parts, just as common salt is not in the least like the sodium and chlorine of which it is compounded; or just as water is nothing like its elements, oxygen and hydrogen, of which it is a compound. The compound ABC is larger than the sum of the parts and different in character from each of them as a result of their integration and reciprocal influence. In such a compound the individual component elements are changed and modified. Removing one of these elements or substituting one for another will destroy or change the whole compound. All this is equally true of the cultural, national and religious elements that make up Judaism. Jewish religion is, in effect, a distinctive, dynamic life-pattern, constantly and progressively adapting itself to changing needs and circumstances; it is accordingly intimately bound up with the Jewish people, their history, culture and civilization.

It is in this vein that Judah Halevi interprets the very first Commandment, where the Lord is referred to as "thy God, who brought thee out of the land of Egypt," and not as the God who created the universe and humanity. This purports to emphasize, Halevi asserts, the close identification of the Torah with the Jewish people and their historical experiences.[4]

It is significant that neither biblical nor mishnaic Hebrew possesses a term for either "religion" or "Judaism." To this day no specific term for "religion" is to be found in Hebrew, while the concept "Judaism" (Greek *Judaismos*) stems from alien soil. It was invented by the Jews of the Hellenistic Diaspora to indicate the contrast between their faith, or way of life, and "Hellenism" (*Hellenismos*).[5] The Hebrew term for this concept (*yahadut*) was probably coined by Rashi (1040-1105). The traditional term for this concept, employed in the Bible and in the Talmud, is "Torah." Now this term, as has been said, embraces the totality of Jewish beliefs and practices, ideals and ideas, in fact, all the products of the Jewish creative genius through the centuries. "The Commandments," according to one source, "imply all that is included in the Bible, the Mishnah, the Talmud, whether legal or homiletic in character. In fact, any interpretation which at any time a faithful student is likely to offer before his teacher was already presented to Moses on Mount Sinai."[6] When the rabbis were in doubt about the legality of certain rituals and practices, they would say: "Go and see how the people conduct themselves."[7] The conduct of the people in a normal traditional environment served as a guide for establishing and codifying certain laws and rituals; indeed "a custom may nullify a law."[8] No religion in the accepted sense of this term would permit such latitude. Significantly, the Hebrew term for law, whether ritual, ethical, criminal, or civil, is *halakhah,* a word which signifies "conduct."

Peculiar historical circumstances, the analysis of which is outside our province, have operated in the case of the Jewish people in such a manner as to merge race, nationality, culture and religion into a composite unit, which is articulated in a distinctive language, with the result of modifying the individual characteristics of each of the components. Hence, the laws applying to each of them in isolation will not apply to any or all of them in integration. Thus, although Christianity may continue to function without a distinctive language, the Jewish religion cannot do so, because it is too intimately fused with elements of race, nationality and culture, all of which are in turn rooted in the Hebrew language. It is inconceivable that any of the traditional Jewish prayers, in translation, could evoke the same historical associations, cultural allusions and national memories, as they do in the original Hebrew. Because Jews of old wanted those associations they continued to pray in Hebrew and study their literary sources in Hebrew. They preserved the language and the language preserved them.

Hebrew as the Language of Judaism

In sum, Judaism may be defined as the ongoing historical experience of the Jewish people, in which are compounded religious, national and cultural elements. This unique historical experience has been articulated in distinctive words and idioms of the Hebrew language, with which it has become inextricably blended. Disassociate this historical experience from the Hebrew language, and the result is a pale, anemic reflection, a dilution and sometimes even an adulteration of the original experience.

Indeed, some Jewish scholars maintained that the deviations of Christianity from Judaism may be directly traceable to the translations of the Bible into Greek. The original Hebrew words took on, in the Greek translation, connotations which were not intended by the Hebrew authors, with the result that they suggested views and ideas entirely alien to the Jewish spirit. One of the many glaring examples is the origin of the virgin-birth dogma in Christianity, a concept which was associated with the mistranslation of the word *'almah* (Isaiah 7. 14). In Hebrew the word merely means "young woman"; in the Greek translation it was rendered by *parthenos* which means "virgin." Another example is the word *ruah,* which in the Greek translation connoted the un-Jewish concept of spirit-versus-body.

In the course of their long and rich history, the Jewish people have gone through intensive intellectual and emotional experiences. They have experimented with life and its problems; problems of the relationship of man to man, of man to God, problems of human destiny and of the impact of cosmic forces upon mankind. They have known joys and suffering, hope and despair. They have given voice to all these experiences in their own distinctive Hebrew idiom. Language and experience have become intertwined so that one cannot be fully mastered without the other.

Who can render in suitable translation the overtones, the cluster of associations and allusions attached to such expressions as *shema' yisrael, kiddush ha-shem, hillul ha-shem, mesirut nefesh,* and a host of others? It cannot be done. Yet such expressions symbolize the warp and woof of our historical religious and national experiences. These expressions stir in every conscious Jew feelings and images such as could never be evoked in any other language. In the words of *Shema' Yisrael,* for example, we hear echoes and reverberations of the agonized cries of our martyrs from the days of Akiba down to the "rebels" of the Warsaw Ghetto. In comparison the English equivalent, "Hear, O Israel," sounds flat and insipid.

Similarly, the terms *kiddush ha-Shem* (sanctification of the Name) and *hillul ha-Shem* (profanation of the Name) are the obverse and reverse of a concept which epitomizes Jewish martyrology throughout the ages. This concept has been a mainspring of traditional Jewish conduct, by word or act, with the view of hallowing God's name, even at the risk of death, through proper conduct and avoiding deeds which might profane the name of God. The term *mesirut nefesh,* likewise, connotes the idea of self-sacrifice and readiness to devote one's life to an ideal. The English equivalents of these terms fail completely to convey even a shade of the meaning of these repositories of Jewish experiences.

Language is, of course, the symbol of meaning, or the expression of ideas by means of articulate sounds or graphic representations of these sounds. Yet, meaning is not inherent in the sounds or the words, but rather in our personal and group experiences which are fused with the particular words. In themselves words have no meanings; it is our reactions to them or our experiences with them that lend them their meaning. What the words "mean" or convey to us depends on the nature, extent and intensity of our experiences, direct or vicarious, with them. The word "democracy," for example, means one thing to an American, and something entirely different to a Russian communist. The term "crusade" awakens in the minds of Jews clusters of historical memories and associations totally at variance with those in the minds of Christian peoples. Words are set in the orbit of the experience of the people employing them. When transposed from one experiential orbit into another by means of translation or borrowing, the words change their "meaning."

Sometimes our experiences are blended and associated with specific forms of the word, with its particular pronunciation or configuration, and only these forms will convey to us meaning to its fullest extent. A radical change in the form, even of the same word, such as a difference of pronunciation or spelling, may at the outset fail to evoke our experiences associated with the particular word. Hence there is often resistance to spelling reforms or to changes in pronunciation, as for example, in the case of Hebrew, from Ashkenazic to Sephardic, and vice versa. An attempt by Itamar Ben Avi and others, several years ago, to change the Hebrew to Latin script proved abortive in the face of serious opposition.

It should therefore be clear that language cannot be taken as a sort of currency or medium of exchange. Words in one language cannot be rendered by their equivalents in another language without losing something vitally and essentially peculiar to the mentality and genius of the people employing the tongue. It is a delusion to assume that one can fully understand the essence of Judaism in any language but Hebrew. As indicated previously, one cannot get the pristine and genuine message of the Bible in a translation, however effectively executed. Our Sages likened the day on which the Bible was translated into Greek to the day when the Golden Calf was made, "for the Torah does not lend itself to an adequate translation." Dr. Max L. Margolis, editor of the Jewish Publication Society Bible translation, asserted: "It frequently happens that the translator, vainly seeking an equivalent for a Hebrew word or phrase, realizes that translation deals not so much with words as with civilizations."

Consequently, some of the most significant and indispensable sources of Judaism must remain in a certain sense "sealed books" to those who do not know Hebrew. The wisdom of the Sages, the poetry of Ibn Gabirol, Judah Halevi, Bialik and Chernichovski; or the prose of Mendele, Peretz and Agnon can never be rendered adequately in English or any other language. Nearly every word, every turn of expression or locution employed by these masters of Hebrew literature, springs from the bed-rock of Jewish experiences, literary sources and Jewish folklore, and stirs within us memories, associations and images, such as no translations, however artistically done, can duplicate.

PART ONE

How the Language Began to Be Spoken

CHAPTER ONE
HEBREW AND THE LANGUAGES
OF MANKIND

Ancient Attempts to Identify the Original Language

How many languages are there in the world? How did these languages arise? Did they evolve from one primeval language, or are they to be traced to several basic languages? What was this primeval language, or which were the basic languages?

These questions have attracted wide attention among the inquisitive minds of the ancients as well as of modern scholars. The Greek historian Herodotus reports an experiment conducted by Psammetichus, king of Egypt (sixth century B.C.E.), with the object of discovering what race of men was first created or evolved. He took two newborn babes, haphazardly selected, and placed them in the charge of a goatherd with strict instructions to bring them up on goat's milk and to isolate them from any human contacts, so that no word of human speech might reach their ears. In this manner, the king hoped, the children would eventually yield to the promptings of nature and break out into human speech representing the primeval language of the original human race. The experiment succeeded, according to Herodotus. One day, after two years had passed, as the goat-

17

herd opened the door of the lonely hut to serve the children their daily portion of milk, they cried out "Bekos!" and held out their hands. The goatherd reported this to the king, and upon investigation the king discovered that *bekos* was the Phrygian word for bread. He thereupon concluded that the Phrygians were the first race of men.

The story bears, of course, the earmarks of pure racial propaganda. It is calculated to demonstrate the superiority of the Grecian race, the kinsmen of the Phrygians according to Greek tradition, by attributing to them a higher rank in antiquity than that of the Egyptians. But this experiment was not unique. Similar experiments are said to have been conducted in later ages: by the Mongol emperor Akbar Khan (sixteenth century), the German emperor Frederick the Second (thirteenth century), and King James IV of Scotland (fifteenth century). The last-named is reported to have shut two infants up with a dumb woman on the island of Inchkeith and ordered them kept there until they were old enough to speak perfectly. These children are said by some to have spoken a pure Hebrew, although the chronicler himself entertained some doubts on the subject.

Hebrew—the Mother of Languages

There was, indeed, a time when Jews as well as Christians believed that all the languages of mankind derived from Hebrew, the language spoken by Adam and Eve in the Garden of Eden. This is, of course, to be inferred from the biblical accounts. Thus Eve was called *Hawwah* "because she was the mother of all living" (*hai,* Genesis 3.20). Similarly, the woman was called *ishshah* "because she was taken out of man" (*ish, ibid.,* 2.23).[1] In no other language besides Hebrew, the rabbis argued, do we find the terms for man and woman derived from the same root. The Hebrew language, it is therefore to be assumed according to them, was created simultaneously with the world and was the language employed by God in his conversations with Adam and Eve.[2] When Abraham was born, all the dignitaries of Nimrod's court wanted to destroy him, says an old midrashic account, and he was hidden in a cave for thirteen years. When he came out of the cave he spoke Hebrew.[3] "It (Hebrew) is, according to tradition, the language in which God spoke to Adam and Eve and in which they spoke between themselves" (Judah Halevi).

This traditional view is reiterated time and again during the Middle Ages and later by both Jews and non-Jews. Among the theses offered by the first class of Harvard graduates in 1642 was one entitled *Hebrea est Linguarum Mater* (Hebrew is the mother of the languages). Non-Jewish sources resorted to all sorts of whimsical etymologies to prove that the origin of European languages is to be found in Hebrew.[4] In his introduction to the Pentateuch, Moses Mendelssohn restates the view of the primacy of Hebrew and attempts to adduce additional proof in its corroboration. It was only after the fiasco of the Tower of Babel, according to the biblical tradition, that "the Lord did there confound the languages of the earth; and from thence did the Lord scatter them abroad upon the face of all the earth" (Genesis 11.9). Thus, says rabbinic tradition, evolved the languages of mankind, numbering seventy-two (or seventy), twenty-two of which were spoken by the descendants of Japheth, twenty-four by the children of Ham, and twenty-six by the children of Shem.[5]

Modern Studies of Indo-European Languages

Toward the end of the eighteenth century the study of linguistic science was given strong impetus by the discovery of Sanskrit and the recognition of the relationship of this language to Greek and Latin. It was then and during the major part of the nineteenth century that the Aryan or Indo-European languages were identified and subjected to careful study and scrutiny.

No one knows how many languages there are in the world. They certainly can be counted in the thousands. Many of them are unrecorded in writing and may disappear without leaving a trace, as many unrecorded languages have undoubtedly disappeared already, while others are known from very scanty records. The majority of the languages of the world are probably those which have never been committed to writing by any of their native speakers.

The most thoroughly investigated language family is the Indo-European. This family includes such languages, and language groups, as Sanskrit, Latin, Greek, Armenian, Albanese, Celtic, Slavic, Baltic and Germanic. The Germanic group, to which English belongs, is probably the most widely employed, and English is now the most widespread of all languages in the world. However, the language which is known to have retained the greatest number of original forms of the Germanic dialect is Icelandic, a language spoken today by about 100,000 persons. Similarly, Lithuanian, one of the two surviving languages of the Baltic branch, spoken by several million people who live on the borders of Prussia and Russia, is said to have "preserved many of the forms of Indo-European speech in a less corrupted condition than any of its European cogeners, aye, than any dialect of the entire family which is not at least *two* thousand years older."[6]

All these language groups have been identified as divergent forms of a single prehistoric language, hypothetically named Primitive Indo-European. No records of this primitive language are available, but this may be a mere historic accident. One of the oldest known member, or near relation, of this family is an extinct language, spoken by the Hittites, a people widely mentioned in the Bible and even regarded by the prophet Ezekiel as among the ancestors of the Hebrew people (Ezekiel 16.3, 45). The available documents in that language already deciphered are written in a form of the cuneiform syllabary—a wedge-like form of characters having syllabic rather than alphabetic value. These documents date back to about the fifteenth century B.C.E. Other Hittite documents, written in hieroglyphic script, have already been virtually deciphered.

Hittite Hieroglyphic Writing

From I. J. Gelb, *A Study of Writing* (University of Chicago Press), 1952, page 83.

Semitic Languages

The language family which concerns us most at this time is that designated since 1781 as Semitic. The origin of this designation is the genealogical record of Genesis 10. 21-31, according to which the peoples employing these languages were descendants of Shem, son of Noah. These peoples occupied a territory extending from the Mediterranean to the other side of the Euphrates up to the Tigris, or Mesopotamia, and from the mountains of Armenia to the southern coast of Arabia. Through conquests and migrations these languages spread also to parts of Africa and Europe. The Canaanites (Phoenicians, etc., Genesis 10. 15-20) are traced in the Bible back to Ham, probably on account of their being a mixed race and also because, owing to their paganism, they were regarded with contempt by the biblical writers. However, their language is clearly a branch of the Semitic family, and the prophet Isaiah (19.18)

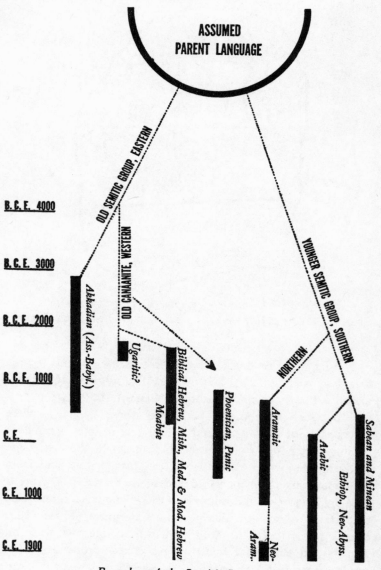

Branches of the Semitic Language

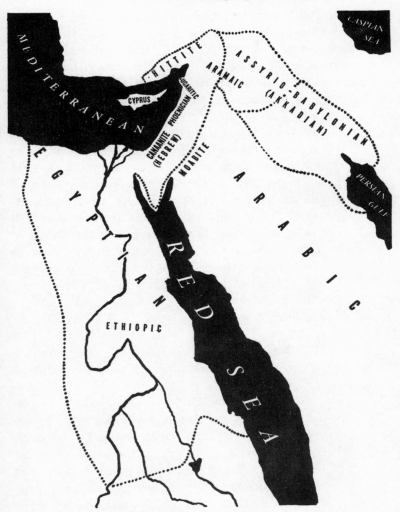

Geographical Distribution of the Semitic Languages

refers to Hebrew as the language of Canaan (*sefat Canaan*).

Most of these languages are now dead, some having left important literary legacies. The only languages of this family still spoken, besides Hebrew, are: Arabic, Ethiopic, and, to a limited extent, Syriac or Aramaic.

The Semitic languages are generally divided into the following branches:

A. East Semitic: Assyrian-Babylonian or Akkadian. This language is known now from inscriptions on stone and clay, in cuneiform writing, dating back to about 2500 B.C.E. In this language were written the Code of Hammurabi (around 1800 B.C.E.), the Amarna letters (1400 B.C.E.) and other important documents. It was at one time widely in vogue in the Orient in official circles. It was there a sort of *lingua franca,* an international language. Later, around the middle of the first half in the first millennium B.C.E., it was superseded by Aramaic.

B. Northwest Semitic
  1. Aramaic Branch.
     a. *Eastern Aramaic* or *Syriac,* of which the Aramaic of the Babylonian Talmud is a Jewish modification.
     b. *Palestinian* or *Western Aramaic,* which is represented by portions of the Palestinian Gemara and the Targumim (Bible translations generally included in the traditional Jewish editions of the Bible). The Aramaic portions of the Bible may also belong in this category, although some modern scholars challenge the possibility of establishing the local identity of these portions. At that early period, when these documents were written, no distinction between Eastern and Western Aramaic existed, according to these scholars.

The oldest documents in the Aramaic language date from the eighth century B.C.E. A few centuries later, especially around the beginning of the Christian Era, Aramaic gained wide currency over large tracts of Western Asia, superseding several languages, among them Assyrian, and to a considerable extent also Hebrew. The theory held by some Jewish and non-Jewish scholars that Aramaic had completely displaced Hebrew is without any foundation and has been effectively disproved. But Aramaic undoubtedly exercised a tremendous influence on the evolution of the Hebrew language, and left its impress upon it.

For about a millennium (from about 700 B.C.E. to around 650 C.E.) Aramaic was employed as the official language of the Near East, until it was replaced by Arabic as one result of the Mohammedan conquests (of the seventh century C.E.). When Assyria conquered the Aramean states and incorporated them into its empire, it adopted the language of the vanquished. The spread of this language was facilitated especially by the Persian Empire which flourished during the fifth to third centuries B.C.E. The imperial policy of Persia was generally favorable to the preservation of the national mores and culture of its subject peoples. The Persian chancery accordingly chose to correspond with the provinces of Western Asia in their own peculiar dialect, Aramaic.

Aramaic is still spoken by a few thousand Syrian Christians and Jews in Kurdistan, and various other isolated localities in the Orient on the borders of Persia, Iraq, Turkey and in Syria near Damascus. A considerable number of the Aramaic-speaking Kurdish Jews have recently immigrated into Israel.

> 2. Middle Semitic or Canaanite Branch.
>> a. *Moabitic,* known especially from the famous inscription of King Mesha, ninth century B.C.E. The character and significance of this inscription will be discussed in a subsequent chapter.
>> b. *Phoenician,* the language spoken in Phoenicia, as well as in the Phoenician colony of Carthage in North Africa, close to the present site of Tunis. The Phoenicians continued to identify themselves as Canaanites down to the Roman period. Its oldest known inscriptions are of the

twelfth or fourteenth century before the Christian Era. Around the early part of the first millennium B.C.E., Phoenician enjoyed the status of an international language in Syria and nearby coastal Asia Minor, until it was replaced by Aramaic by the end of the eighth century. It continued to flourish in Carthage until several centuries into the Christian Era, and was still spoken in the time of Augustine in the fifth century C.E.

c. *Hebrew.* The oldest portions of the Hebrew Bible probably date back to about 1300 B.C.E., and the language has never ceased to be employed in most Jewish localities as a literary medium, as well as for purposes of written (if not spoken) intercommunication. In oral use it has been restricted largely to houses of worship and study, although there is ample evidence to prove that even for conversational purposes oral Hebrew has been employed, in a limited degree and in certain localities, throughout the history of the Jewish people. Furthermore, many words and expressions dealing with intimate personal and national experiences have been incorporated into the various languages spoken by the Jewish people in the lands of their dispersion. Similarly, many Hebrew idioms have infiltrated, in translated forms, into the various Jewish dialects, such as Yiddish and Ladino (a Judaeo-Spanish dialect), and have persisted there to this day. In modern times the vitality and adaptability of the Hebrew language have been demonstrated to a remarkable degree, as a spoken language in Israel, and in many Jewish communities outside of Israel.

d. *Ugaritic.* A rich and significant literature has

been unearthed since 1930, shedding much light on biblical literature and language, in modern Ras Shamra, on the coast of Syria, opposite Cyprus. This Canaanitic literature was written in an alphabetic cuneiform script, indicating consonants and even some vowels. It contains epic poems typical of ancient Canaanite religion and civilization during the Late Bronze Age, when Ras Shamra was the site of Ugarit, the wealthiest Canaanite city. In language and style, this literature resembles to a remarkable degree the poetic portions of the Bible. Biblical literature and language must have been influenced tremendously by the highly developed culture and civilization of Ugarit.

C. South Semitic.
  a. *Arabic and its various dialects.* The earliest records of Arabic are of the third century B.C.E. Since the seventh century C.E. the territory of the language has extended, as a result of the Mohammedan conquests, to embrace large tracts of Asia and Africa. It is now in oral and written use by nearly forty millions of people, besides serving as the sacred and official language of Islam.
  b. *Ethiopic and its dialects.* This language is used on the east coast of Africa (Abyssinia). It emerged into the light of history towards the beginning of the fourth century C.E., immediately after the conversion of the Abyssinian Kingdom to Christianity. The language is still used in Abyssinia in modern dialects.

Uniformity vs. Diversity in Languages

Attempts were made by students of language to discern relationships between the Indo-European and the Semitic languages. These attempts stem from the assumption that both these language families evolved from the same parental stock. In proof of this assumption scholars adduce the examples of the Hebrew *banah* (built) and the Latin *pono* (compare English "exponent," "expound"); also *ba'ar* and Greek *pyr* from which originate the English "pyre," "pyro-," and "fire"; Hebrew *yayin* (wine), Greek *oinos,* Latin vinum, Arabic *waynun;* Hebrew *sheba,* Sanskrit *saptan,* Latin *septem,* English "seven." A medieval Jewish scholar collected over two thousand Hebrew words, which, in his opinion, were the basis of a similar number of words in Latin, Greek and Italian.[7] Such attempts are now largely discredited. If there is a relationship between the two language families, and there may be, the available evidence is inadequate and inconclusive. Mutual borrowing and mere accident may account for these relationships.

The division of languages is, according to biblical tradition, a curse or punishment inflicted upon mankind for the daring attempt of the people of Shinar to erect there "a tower, with its top in heaven" (Genesis 11). To this day the multiplicity of languages is viewed by some people as an affliction responsible for misunderstanding and dissension among individuals, groups and nations. If people spoke a common language, it is held, discords would disappear, wars would be eliminated, peace and good will would reign in the world. Unsuccessful attempts have accordingly been made to devise a universal language, or to urge the adoption of one of the most widespread languages as a common language.

That the adoption of a common language will serve as an effective instrumentality of peace is highly questionable. History can record many wars among peoples employing the same language. But it is a matter of grave doubt whether the adoption of a common language is feasible. Even if the peoples of the world would consent to adopt such a language, it would in the course of time split up into various, mutually alien languages and dialects. We may note, as an illustration, the tendency of American English to deviate in its development, both in idiom and vocabulary, from British English. Even in the same country the people of certain generations find it difficult or impossible to understand the language of their ancestors several generations back.

It may, incidentally, be seriously questioned whether the adoption of a common language would be desirable from a cultural point of view, even if it were possible. A common language would impose, to a considerable degree, common cultural and literary patterns. Witness the influence of English culture and literature on early American life and literature. Such a language would certainly result in the impoverishment of world culture and civilization.

The Trend in Language towards Diversity

Language (*Sprache* in German, *lashon* or *safah* in Hebrew), as indicated by its etymology, is basically a speech experience. It is transmitted by word of mouth from parents to children. We speak and pronounce words as we hear them spoken and pronounced by our elders, who in turn learned them from generations preceding them.

It seems quite obvious to us that we speak exactly as do our parents and elders, and they believe they do the like with reference to the generation which preceded them. Yet, over a period of several generations there have been evident linguistic changes and modifications. The language of Shakespeare is no longer the English we speak; while the fourteenth century English of Chaucer, and far more so the English of Alfred the Great of the ninth century, are to us virtually foreign tongues. When, for example, was the Latin *senior* reduced to the French *sire* and the English "sir"? When did the Anglo-Saxon *deofol* (Latin *diabolus*) evolve into the modern English "devil"?

How did these radical changes in form and pronunciation occur? When did they inject themselves into the language? Each generation of speakers would certainly disclaim responsibility.

Evidently the process of language transmission is imperfect. Both our hearing and our capacity for articulating or imitating the sounds which we hear are imperfect and inexact. Hence language is subject to modification and change. Both growth and decay are characteristics of language development, as they are of biological development. Some phonetic elements gradually disintegrate and disappear, while new ones sprout and emerge. Occasionally, the variations are so great as to produce an entirely new offshoot, a new dialect or a new member of the language family.

Two main factors generally operate as controls in the process of linguistic change: (1) isolation and (2) possession of written records. A people occupying a circumscribed territory and relatively unexposed to contacts with other races or peoples is more likely to preserve the original forms of its speech than a people bent on expansion, migration or collision with other races and peoples. Similarly a common literature often exercises a strong conservative influence on the language and shields it from the intrusion of alien elements and from radical phonetic and dialectical divergencies. For this reason, the changes in English since Shakespeare's time are not as pronounced as those during the interval between his period and that of Chaucer, and they are especially less significant than the changes during the five centuries preceding Chaucer, when England was assimilating the Normans.[8]

Reason for Relative Unity in the Hebrew Language

The literary control on linguistic change is particularly marked when, as in the case of the Hebrew language, the common literature is integrated with the religious traditions and experiences of the people. The Hebrew people were thrown into contact and collision with other people. Its vocabulary was considerably enriched by the admission of numerous foreign words borrowed from the many peoples among whom they dwelt. Yet the original linguistic pattern of Hebrew remained more or less intact. Thus we speak of biblical Hebrew as a unitary phase of the language, distinguished by typical characteristics of grammar and style. Yet, the interval between the earliest biblical documents, such as the Song of Moses or the

Song of Deborah, on the one hand, and the books of Koheleth and Esther, on the other, is as long as the interval separating the period of Alfred the Great from our own day. Furthermore, the twenty-two centuries subsequent to the biblical period failed to impair the pristine pattern of the language. The result is that modern Hebrew writers may choose to employ biblical Hebrew as the medium of their literary expression, without the need of apology and without fearing that their writings will be incomprehensible or even regarded as unduly archaic.

What is the explanation, in the case of Hebrew, of this unique linguistic phenomenon? How did the Hebrew language escape the transmuting effects of time which are in evidence in other languages?

To be sure, the fact that the ancient biblical texts lacked a fixed system of vocalization and were very scantily supplied with vowel-signs is in large measure responsible for the seeming phonetic uniformity of the Hebrew language. But it cannot be doubted that the Bible and the esteem with which it has been cherished throughout the centuries, counteracted and prevented fundamental changes in the structure of the language. Unlike Latin, which has been the language of the Catholic church, that is, of the clergy, without becoming the language of the faithful or of the multitude, the study of biblical Hebrew has been pursued throughout the generations by young and old with more or less zeal and assiduity. A great many new word-coinages, word-forms and idioms have indeed been added to the language since the days of the Bible. Yet the original organic pattern of the language remains intact. To this day children in elementary grades are trained and grounded in the intricacies of biblical Hebrew, while in the writings of practically every Hebrew author one may find a goodly number of word-structures, phrases, and turns of expression typical of the Bible. As a matter of fact, modern Hebrew sometimes shows preference for biblical usages over mishnaic or medieval usages. The biblical phrases and expressions of thirty-five centuries ago pulsate with vitality and vigor almost on a par with the language spoken in Israel today.

CHAPTER TWO
HOW THE HEBREW LANGUAGE BEGAN
Aramaic Background of Hebrew

Some forty centuries ago, during the first half of the second millennium B.C.E., a family or clan led by a chieftain named Terah, emigrated—so the biblical tradition has it—from Ur-Kasdim, a city of immemorial antiquity in Babylonia, to Haran in northwestern Mesopotamia, with the intention of proceeding from there "into the land of Canaan." For unspecified reasons Terah and his clansmen settled in Haran and apparently abandoned the idea of journeying on.

It must have been a long time after settling in Haran that one of the sons of Terah, named Abram (later renamed Abraham), after his father's death, received a call from God saying: "Get thee out of thy country . . . unto the land that I will show thee." Whereupon Abram, heeding the call, resumed the journey into Canaan, taking with him "Sarai his wife, and Lot his brother's son, and all their substance that they had gathered, and the souls that they had gotten in Haran . . . and into the land of Canaan they came."

This clan, headed by Abram, was by no means a nomadic or bedouin band. It was made up of settled or semi-settled herdsmen, who migrated with their wives and children and with their servants, cattle and other belongings. Abram must, accordingly, have achieved in Haran considerable status and authority. Jewish tradition explains his departure from there by attributing to him a revulsion from the idolatrous practices prevalent in his native land and by the "call" to go forth and establish a new and "great nation" in the "land of Canaan." It was to be a rather peaceful venture.

Yet, we find Abram capable of mustering fighting forces among his clansmen and allies adequate to attack and defeat the armies of four victorious kings, and thus retrieve his nephew Lot and all the booty that had been captured from five defeated kings headed by those of Sodom and Gomorrah (Genesis 14). Furthermore, Abimelekh, the Philistine king of Gerar, was eager to conclude with him a treaty of peace; the native Amorites, Mamre, Eshkol and Aner, were his confederates; while the Hittites accorded him honor and referred to him as "a mighty prince" (*ibid.,* 23. 6).

In the traditions of the Babylonians, Greeks, Romans, and other peoples, Abram would undoubtedly have been described as a mighty chieftain leading a victorious invasion. His heroic exploits and glorious feats of conquest would have constituted the theme of epic sagas and poems. But the Torah, as the etymology of the term implies, is primarily designed to teach moral and religious lessons, not to tell stories or report historical events. Hence, all these warlike exploits in the life of the "fathers" of the Jewish people are glossed over and mentioned only incidentally.

During a period of famine, Abram and his clansmen traveled to Egypt, but only for a brief sojourn. As soon as conditions improved they returned to Canaan, where they were to make their permanent home. They were part of a wave of migration that gravitated from the north and the east during the first half of the second millennium B.C.E. toward the grasslands of the more fertile South, with the object of conquest and occupation. This desire to seek "fresh woods and pastures new" may have been further stimulated by the pressure exerted by the growing power of the Elamites and the Babylonians in the East and that of the Horites, Amorites and Hittites in the North and West. Moreover, Syria and Palestine constituted a sort of bridge which joined the great civilizations of Mesopotamia and Egypt. Traders and herdsmen were constantly passing through these countries, and the provinces changed hands frequently during that period.

These migrants, or, as they may be called, Abramides, brought with them their own mother-tongue which they had acquired in Haran and which was closely akin to the language employed by the natives of Canaan, differing from it in forms of pronunciation and dialect in much the same way as Dutch differs from German, or perhaps even less. The Semitic languages at that time were in all likelihood very closely related to one another in grammar and pronunciation. The language of Abram was presumably the parent of Aramaic, in which were written some chapters of Daniel and Ezra, one verse in Jeremiah (10. 11) and especially parts of the Talmud and midrashim.

The Canaanite Origin of Hebrew

"And the Canaanite was then in the land" (Genesis 12. 6). According to the biblical account (*ibid.,* 10.15-18), the descendants of Canaan included the Zidonites, the Hittites, the Jebusites, the Amorites and others. "Canaanite" is therefore to be regarded as a geographic rather than a national term; it connotes the people who inhabited Canaan, who were mostly Amorites, generally of Semitic origin. Some of them were close kinsmen of the immigrants from the east and the north. They had come to Canaan several centuries previously, in a similar migratory wave, and had settled there, leaving a marked imprint on the civilization of the country. It is maintained by some archaeologists that the civilization of Canaan before the arrival of Abram was clearly Semitic, even Hebraic; that is, introduced there by the descendants of Eber, of whom the Abramides were a branch. Thus we find Joseph telling the chief butler of Pharaoh that he was "stolen away out of the land of the Hebrews" (Genesis 40.15), and this was long before the

Israelites settled in Canaan according to the biblical tradition.

Accordingly, the "Canaanite" language must have sounded not entirely foreign to Abram and his tribesmen, and especially to their descendants. It was readily adopted, modified and developed by them into what became known later as the Hebrew language. As is self-evident, this subsequent language could scarcely avoid bearing some traces, or linguistic deposits, of the original, native tongue of the new immigrants.

It is a common historical phenomenon that when a country with a high level of civilization is conquered by a people of an inferior civilization, the victors tend to yield to the influence of the superior indigenous civilization, instead of imposing their own civilization on the vanquished. The Norman invasion of England in 1066 is a case in point. The victorious French-speaking Normans submitted to the cultural cohesiveness and preponderance of the Anglo-Saxons and adopted the language of the vanquished.

Although at the date of the conquest the Normans were regarded as one of the most advanced and progressive peoples of Europe, both their language and civilization were young and uncultivated. Indeed, they had adopted their language from the French only a little over a century prior to their invasion of England, and they apparently had no deep cultural roots or any ardent attachment to the French language. As a matter of fact the language employed by them was not regarded by their contemporaries as "good" French.

Nevertheless, a vast number of French and Latin words were introduced in the course of time into the Anglo-Saxon language by the Norman conquerors. These words were assimilated with the grammatical and syntactical pattern of the Anglo-Saxon language. As a matter of fact, it was only after 1300 that English began admitting French words quite liberally. "The English of 1200 is almost as free from French words as the English of 1050" (Henry Sweet).

Similarly, in France and Spain, only very slight traces may be found of the German race which conquered them during the early Middle Ages. The German victors readily gave up the use of their mother-tongue in these countries. In like manner, the Mongols who conquered India in the sixteenth century, adopted the Hindustani dialect while remaining loyal to their Moslem faith.

The history of the Hebrew language presents an exact parallel. The Canaanite civilization during the period of the Abramide invasion was undoubtedly on a very high plane, as is attested by recent archaeological discoveries as well as by biblical evidence. Thus we are told that during the period of the Exodus, the Hebrews found there "fortified cities, with high walls, gates and bars; beside the unwalled towns a great many" (Deuteronomy 3.5). It is, therefore, reasonable to assume that the indigenous masses of the vanquished persisted in using their native tongue, which the conquering masters had to learn.

In the case of the Hebrews, the adoption of the Canaanite civilization and language was quite a simple process, since both the civilization and the language of Canaan were largely the creations of their own kinsmen, of the earlier migratory waves. Some of these kinsmen may have been of great assistance to the invading Abramides, especially to the later Israelites. They may have played there the role of a "fifth column." Thus we find the spies of the "house of Joseph" guided and aided by an inhabitant of Beth-El to find the entrance to that city, through which the Josephites entered and captured it (Judges 1.24-25). One may venture the conjecture that such help by the kinsmen of the Abramides, who had previously settled in Canaan and had more or less been assimilated with the native population, was not at all unusual. This help may have considerably facilitated the conquest of Canaan by the Israelites.

It is, indeed, significant that the earliest literary records of the Hebrews, such as the Song of Moses, after the passage through the Sea of Reeds (the Red Sea), as well as the Song of Deborah, dating back probably to the thirteenth and eleventh centuries B.C.E., respectively, are written in pure Hebrew, such as is characteristic of the language of the later prophets, a language relatively free from traces of Aramaic.[1]

It may be safely assumed, however, that these are not the first attempts of the Hebrews at literary self-expression on Canaanite soil. Many efforts by the Hebrews experimenting with this newly-learned language as a literary vehicle must have preceded the earliest available records; otherwise the Hebrew could hardly have been employed with such consummate skill. Unfortunately these early efforts are thus far still hidden in obscurity. However, valuable records antedating the biblical materials, written in a language akin to Hebrew, were recently discovered, such as the Ugaritic poems, which will be discussed in a later chapter.

Other Linguistic Influences on Hebrew

Aramaic is not the only language traces of which are found in early Hebrew. It should, of course, occasion no surprise to find that Egypt had an influence on ancient Hebrew. The sojourn of the early Hebrews in Egypt is now accepted by archaelogists as an established fact, although it is generally maintained that the greater part of the Hebrews had remained in Palestine and never entered Egypt at all.

All through the second millennium B.C.E. a close interrelationship existed between Egypt and Palestine. For a period of over a century and a half (c. 1720 to c. 1550) Egypt was ruled by Semitic tribes known later under the name of Hyksos, "rulers of foreign countries," who must have employed a Semitic dialect very much akin to Hebrew. Among the names recorded by them are to be found such good Hebraic names as *Hur,* as well as *Ya'akob-Har*—an exact equivalent of the Hebrew name Ya'akob (Jacob), which is an abbreviation of Ya'akob-el (may God guard). As a matter of fact, an Amorite name *Yakub-il(um)* was found in business documents in Babylonia, composed during the early part of the millennium. The same word is also recorded in an Egyptian document of the fifteenth century B.C.E. as the name of a place in Canaan. The word *har* (mountain) is a divine name, like the biblical *tzur* (rock or mountain), which is employed with reference to God in such instances as *tzur yisrael* (the Rock of Israel; 2 Samuel 23.3); it therefore corresponds to the Hebrew *el*.

When the Hyksos were later defeated and driven back into Asia, the Egyptians re-established their rule over Palestine, and mutual relationships between the peoples on both sides of the border were maintained. There can be little doubt that the superior Egyptian civilization exercised a tremendous influence on the religion, the language and the literature of the Hebrews.

Indeed, we find in the Bible a considerable number of Egyptian words, which were eventually incorporated in the Hebrew language as an integral part of its vocabulary.[2] Such Egyptian words as *ahu* (reeds), *gome'* (bulrushes), *keset* (trained person), *hartummim* (magicians), *suf* (reeds), *tebah* (writing-case), *shesh* (fine linen), *ye'or* (river) are now regarded as genuine Hebrew vocables. Similarly, some passages in the Pentateuch, especially in the Joseph story or in the book of Exodus, which are extremely difficult to explain, are readily explainable in the light of the Egyptian language. Thus, for example, in asking Joseph to become the governor over Egypt, Pharaoh tells Joseph *"we-al pikha yishshak kol ami"* (Genesis 41. 40), in which phrase the word *yishshak* from the Hebrew stem *nashak* (to kiss) makes no sense whatsoever. In Egyptian, however, this stem means "to eat," and the sense of the passage at once becomes perfectly clear and obvious, "according to thy word all my people shall eat," since Joseph was appointed in charge of the granaries in Egypt. Numerous other such examples can be adduced.[3] A number of familiar Hebrew names, such as Moses, Miriam, Phineas and, probably Aaron, are likewise of Egyptian origin.

Another center of civilization in the Near East, during the dawn of Jewish history, when the Hebrew language was struggling to be born, was Babylonia, situated in the Mesopotamian Valley and watered by the Tigris and the Euphrates rivers. The language spoken there is the oldest known member of the eastern group of Semitic languages. It is now generally designated as Assyro-Babylonian, since both the Assyrian and Babylonian languages shared common characteristics, with only minor dialectical differences.

This language was the international diplomatic language of the Near East during the patriarchal period and for several centuries subsequent to it. It has yielded more written records about the ancient period of that region than any other language. It was in this language that the famous code of Hammurabi (during the first quarter of the second millennium B.C.E.) was written. It was in the same language that the Canaanite princes of the fourteenth century addressed pleading letters to the Egyptian Pharaoh, the religious reformer Akhenaton, who established his new capitol in Tell-el-Amarna. In these letters the princes appealed for help against the invading Hapiru, who were overrunning the country and jeopardizing the Egyptian supremacy there.

The early Hebrews must have come in contact with this language, and some of them may have been conversant with it. Indeed, a great many Assyro-Babylonian words have a familiar Hebrew ring. In the following words: *ummanu, anaku, shipru, alaku, erebu, alpu, ayabu, urru, kirbu, ishten, eshrit, ekallu, shaknu, sharru,* it is not at all difficult for a Hebraist to identify the respective Hebrew equivalents: *omman* (artist, artisan), *anokhi* (I), *sefer* (book), *halakh* (went), *arbeh* (locust), *eleph* (cattle), *oyeh* (enemy), *or* (light), *kereb* (inward part, bowels), *ashte esreh* (eleven), *heikhal* (palace), *sokhen, segen,* or *sagan* governor (ruler) and *sar* (chief, captain).

It may be of interest to note that the name Tel Aviv given to the most important new city of Israel is traced back by some scholars to Assyro-Babylonian. This name is found in Ezekiel 3.15, by which the Prophet designates a certain place in Babylonia. The origin of this name is, according to some modern scholars, Til Abubi (the Mound of the Flood). In translating Dr. Herzl's famous book *Altneuland* into Hebrew, Nahum Sokolow chose the name Tel Aviv as the title of the book, because this name conveyed most appropriately the meaning of the German title: the word *tel* signifying a mound or heap of ruins and thus corresponding to the German *alt* (old), while the word *aviv* connotes spring and renewal which is implied by the German *neu* (new).

The similarities between Hebrew and Assyro-Babylonian or Akkadian[4] are not limited to vocabulary; they are also evident in grammatical structure. The Akkadian Infinitive *kashādu* (seize) resembles very closely the Hebrew Infinitive type *pa'ol*, since the long *a* in the second syllable of *kashādu* is the regular equivalent of the Hebrew long *o* in *pa'ol*. The prohibitive phrase *la tazkur* is clearly reminiscent of the equivalent Hebrew *lo tizkor* (do not remember). So is the Hebrew *yizkor* (will remember, was remembering, remembers), from the stem *zkr*, very much like the Akkadian *izkur* (remembered). Similarly, there are striking resemblances between the two languages in some idiomatic expressions. Thus, for example, the biblical idioms *be-shannoto et ta'amo* (Psalms 34. 1, when he changed his demeanor, that is, feigned madness), *ka-mayim la-yam mekhassim* (Isaiah 11. 9, as the waters cover the sea, that is, in large amounts), and *atah al safam* (Ezekiel 24. 17, covered the lip, as a sign of mourning) have their counterparts in the Akkadian idioms, respectively, *tema shunnu, kima gipish tamtim* (literally, like the onrush of the sea) and *katma shapte*. There must certainly have been some mutual influence between these two languages.

Simultaneously with the Hebrews another people appeared on the scene in the history of Canaan. These were the Philistines, who are referred to in Egyptian records as the Sea People. They apparently hailed from the Aegean and Minoan spheres, and were probably mainly Cretans. They invaded Canaan in migratory waves from about the middle of the second millennium down to the twelfth century B.C.E. and settled in the southwestern part of the country, which is designated in the Bible as the Land of the Philistines (Exodus 13. 17) or Pleshet (Philistia, *ibid.*, 15. 14). Their significant role in the history of

Canaan is marked by the fact that the name of the area they occupied was eventually extended to cover the whole country, which came to be known as Palestine.

The early contacts of the Philistines with the Hebrew settlers were apparently friendly,[5] but after having been reenforced by fresh waves of invaders from their native shores around the turn of the eleventh century, the Philistines turned hostile and belligerent in their relations with the Israelites. Bitter wars were fought between the two peoples until the Philistines were finally conquered by David.

The material civilization of the Philistines was superior to that of the early Hebrew settlers. The Philistines were recognized masters of the arts and crafts, including metallurgy. In fact, during the wars between the Hebrews and the Philistines in the early days of King Saul, "there was no smith found through all the land of Israel . . . and all the Israelites went down to the Philistines, to sharpen every man his plowshare, and his coulter, and his axe, and his mattock." (1 Samuel 13.19-20). They must have exerted a considerable influence on the more "primitive" Hebrew settlers and, although their language was non-Semitic, it left traces on the Hebrew language. Indeed, the biblical term *seren,* by which the rulers of their city states were designated, has been generally identified with the Greek city ruler *tyrannos,* from which word is derived the English "tyrant," while the Philistine word *koba'* (originally, "helmet") is the accepted word in modern Hebrew for "hat." Very likely the name of the river Jordan likewise stems from the Philistine or Cretan language.[6] Incidentally, *seren* has been adopted recently by the Israeli army as the regular term for "captain."

Yet, despite all these foreign admixtures, the organic distinctiveness of the Hebrew language remained intact. The alien elements were assimilated and incorporated into the language and its grammatical structure. Even Aramaic, which was most closely akin to Hebrew, and with the tint of which Hebrew was most strikingly colored, eventually became an unintelligible foreign tongue to the Hebrew masses. When Rabshakeh, the Assyrian general, who laid siege to Jerusalem in the days of Isaiah, addressed himself in Hebrew to the royal officers and asked for surrender, the latter pleaded with him to speak Aramaic, so that the conversation might remain private and confidential. Rabshakeh, however, retorted that he preferred to employ Hebrew, not Aramaic, in order to have his message understood by all the residents of the beleaguered city (2 Kings 18.17-35).

Origin of the Name

To go back to the invading Abramides, how did they come to be known as Hebrews? How did this name (*ibri*), by which Abraham and his descendants are designated in the Bible, originate?

The "foreign invaders," we may presume, were not always regarded with favor by the settled native population. In fact, as was mentioned above, toward the fourteenth century B.C.E., the princes, or governors, of Canaan sent letters of appeal to the rulers of Egypt complaining against these "wanderers," who were pressing into Syria and Palestine from the northeast and the east.[7] They refer to the invaders as "Habiru" or "Apiru," which term may be identifiable with the Hebrew *obrim* (wayfarers, nomads). The traditional account, according to which Abraham came from Babylonia by way of Haran, through Hittite and Amorite territory, into Palestine, seems to coincide with that given in this correspondence relative to the migrations of the Habiru tribes. The Canaanite plea for help against the invaders was apparently ignored by the Egyptian rulers; and the Abramides pushed on, pitched their tents, built altars and "journeyed, going still toward the south"—in fulfillment of God's promise to make them a great nation and to give this land "for a heritage"—gradually adopting the new country and its language.

There may have been a slur implied in the term "Habiru"

(nomads) which was not entirely pleasing to the ears of the conquering tribes, as they began to regard themselves as permanent settlers or citizens. They fought for this land and conquered it after many struggles and sacrifices. Had not God given them this land, according to their tradition, "for an everlasting possession," in keeping with the covenant established between Him and their ancestors? They struck deep roots in this land. They learned to love it and to regard it as their own. Why then should they be regarded as transients or nomads? They may therefore have modified the term by tacit popular consensus, changing it to a form with a more favorable connotation; namely, *ibrim,* presumably derived from *me-eber ha-nahar,* that is, people coming from the other side of the Jordan or Euphrates.[8] Thus, in the Septuagint, the early Greek version of the Bible, the expression *Abraham ha-ibri* (Genesis 14. 13) is rendered in the sense "he who crossed over."

Distinction between "Hebrew" and "Israel"

It is to be noted, however, that the name *ibri* is employed in the Bible only in a restricted sense. The name preferred there is *benei Yisrael* (the children of Israel, or Israelites), which was apparently a national name of honor, having religious and national connotations (see Genesis 32.29). The name *ibri* was generally employed by foreigners to identify an Israelite. Hence this name is used by the wife of Potifar (*ibid.,* 39.17) and by the chief butler (*ibid.,* 41.12) in reference to Joseph; or when the Israelites speak of themselves in contrast to foreigners, as when Joseph tells the chief butler that he "was stolen away from the land of the ibrim." For the same reason the name *ibri* is also used to signify the distinction between an Israelite and a non-Israelite, as in the case of seating the brothers of Joseph apart from the Egyptians, "because the Egyptians might not eat bread with the ibrim" (*ibid.,* 43.32); or when Jonah tells the mariners on the boat bound for Tarshish: "I am a Hebrew, and

I fear the Lord, the God of heaven" (Jonah 1.9). Pharaoh is unable to identify the God of Israel mentioned by Moses, where-upon Moses proceeds to explain that he is referring to the God of the Hebrews (Exodus 5.1, 3), a more familiar epithet.

Probably "Hebrew" is an old and generic name which includes other peoples besides the Israelites, such as the Ammonites, Moabites, Midianites, Edomites, and others. The Israelites were an offshoot, who dissociated themselves from the main stock and embarked, as a distinctive group, upon a national career and religious ideology of their own. Indeed, we find "Hebrews" allied with the Philistines in their war against the Israelites (1 Samuel 14. 21).

One may adduce in this connection the analogy of the designation for the Arab tribes or peoples. In ancient non-Arabic sources all Arabic tribes are referred to as Arabs. In their own literature, however, Arabs prefer to identify themselves by the particular tribe to which they belong. The same is true of modern Arabs. Among themselves they prefer to be known as Egyptians, Syrians, Irakis, etc.; although before the outside world they proclaim themselves as Arabs. Similarly, the bedouins are also known as Arabs, but only in relation to the outside world. Among themselves they prefer to be designated by the particular pedigree or tribe to which they belong.

This would explain why the Hebrew language is always designated in the Bible as *Sefat Canaan* (Isaiah 19. 18), "the language of Canaan," or *Yehudit* (2 Kings 18. 26; Isaiah 36. 11, 13; Nehemiah 13.24), "the language of Yehudah," the dominant tribe in the southern kingdom. Apparently, as long as the language was a living vernacular, and its dominance was not challenged by any competitive language, no sensitivity about its national significance existed. The language was taken for granted as is any modern vernacular in its national and natural milieu. Furthermore, the Jewish people or the Israelites were not the only ones who employed the Hebrew language; it was spoken and used for written communication also by the Moabites, Edomites, and other "Hebrew" peoples. Hence, the language was given a geographic rather than a national designation. It was referred to as the language spoken in Canaan or in Judea.

Hebrew Assumes a More Distinctive Connotation

During the Second Commonwealth, however, after the "Hebraic" peoples, outside of Israel, were wiped out or assimilated by the colossus of Hellenism, the term *ibrit*, "Hebrew" or the "Hebrew language," was employed by Jewish writers, as well as by the Greeks and the Romans, in reference to the language of the Scriptures and to that employed by the Jews at the time, the so-called mishnaic Hebrew. At the same time the Jewish people were referred to as Hebrews, although in talmudic literature the appellation *Yisrael* (Israelite) or *Yehudi* (Judean) were generally in vogue; the term *ibri* was rarely employed as a national designation.

The first use of the term Hebrew in reference to the Hebrew language is found in The Book of Jubilees, which probably dates back to about the third century B.C.E., if not earlier.[9] This term is also found in connection with the Greek translation of Ben Sira's Ecclesiasticus, in the prologue, which was composed by the grandson of the author around 130 B.C.E., as well as in the Letter of Aristeas and IV Maccabees. It is, however, to be noted that the use of the term by the writers of that period is not always clear. The term *ibrit*, or Hebrew, is employed occasionally in the Talmud,[10] as well as by Josephus[11] and the apostles,[12] in reference to Aramaic or the Aramaic dialect used by the Jews. Philo, on the other hand, designates the language of the Pentateuch as the language of the Chaldeans.[13] The confusion probably stems from the fact that the language was identified with the people employing it. Since a large number of Jews employed an Aramaic dialect during the second commonwealth, this dialect was referred to as Hebrew;[14] while Philo, who apparently did not know Hebrew and may have never read the Bible either in Hebrew or in Aramaic, mistakenly identified the Hebrew language of the Pentateuch with the Aramaic dialect employed by the Jews during his time, especially in Alexandria and Babylonia.[15]

Another Name for the Hebrew Language

The term most widely used in rabbinic literature in reference to Hebrew is *leshon kodesh,* that is, the language of the Scriptures, of "the holy Books." The Aramaic equivalent *lishshan kudsha* or *lishshan bet kudsha* (the language of the Temple) was also in vogue. These terms were calculated to emphasize the distinction between Hebrew and the Aramaic language, which began gaining vogue as the spoken tongue and was employed for secular purposes. The term *leshon kodesh,* moreover, was not confined to the language of the Scriptures; it was also used in reference to prayers, blessings and pronouncements written in mishnaic Hebrew.

In medieval Hebrew literature and especially in modern times the term *ibrit* in reference to the Hebrew language is predominant, although the term *leshon kodesh* is not entirely unused. Since the Hebrew language is now used extensively for secular purposes, especially in Israel, the term *ibrit* is more appropriate and has become generally accepted.

The Character of Classical Hebrew

The classical Hebrew of biblical literature, although its use extended over a period of more than a thousand years, has a unique stylistic and grammatical pattern. It is solemn, noble, and majestic; it has virility and vigor; it is succinct, but rich in imagery and picturesqueness. The rabbis, with true pedagogic insight, deemed it necessary to fill the gaps of the biblical narrative with aggadic tales and interpretations. Similarly, Thomas Mann, drawing from rabbinic and archaeological sources, was able to extend twenty verses in Genesis (chap. 39. 1-20) into a two-volume novel of 664 pages (*Joseph in Egypt*). The biblical artists paint, as it were, on a small canvas with a fine brush and with consummate skill and artistry, as well as with a burning passion. Through their keen and vivid senses we hear and see all nature astir, dynamic and articulate. When a house is built by evil and iniquity, "the stone shall cry out of

the wall, and the beam out of the timber shall answer it"
(Habakkuk 2.11). "The heavens declare the glory of God"
(Psalms 19.2). "The floods clap their hands and the mountains sing for joy together" (*ibid.*, 98.8). "The field and all
that is therein exult" (*ibid.*, 96.12), "while the morning stars
sing together" (Job 38.7).

Living word-pictures and vivid, graphic descriptions, rather
than wordy accounts and preachments, are employed in biblical
Hebrew to convey ideas and exhortations. When God was angry
"smoke arose in his nostrils" (Psalms 18.9). When a person
is frightened, he is pictured as "poured out like water, all my
bones are out of joint; my heart is become like wax; it is melted
in my inmost parts" (*ibid.*, 22.15). When he is sad "his
countenance falls" (Genesis 4.5). When two people love each
other "the soul of one is bound up with the soul of the other"
(Genesis 44.30). When the sun rises it is "like a bridegroom
coming out of his chamber, rejoicing like a strong man to run
his course" (Psalms 19. 6). The kings of Israel and Syria who
threatened to attack Judea are ridiculed as "these two tails of
smoking firebrands" (Isaiah 7.4), implying that their vitality
and strength are sapped; they are capable of emitting smoke,
but they possess no fire. The prophet deplores the fact that the
once beloved people of Israel whom God "had planted . . .
a noble vine . . . turned into a degenerate plant," and he is
outraged by their conduct which is like that of "a swift young
camel traversing her ways; a wild ass used to the wilderness,
that snuffeth up the wind in her desire; her lust, who can hinder
it?" (Jeremiah 2.21, 23, 24). And when the Lord emerges
ready for retribution "mountains shall be molten under him,
and the valleys shall be cleft, as wax before the fire, as waters
that are poured down a steep place" (Micah 1. 4). But on the
day of redemption "the mountains shall drop down sweet wine,
and the hills shall flow with milk" (Joel 4.18).

Even some of the prosaic parts of the Bible possess a distinct
poetic metre and rhythm. One need only recall the majestic
prose of the first chapter of Genesis, the Creation poem; or the
touching reply of Ruth to Naomi's pleas that she return to

Moab. Even in the translation much of the elegance of the original rhythmic swing is retained: . . . "for whither thou goest, I will go; and where thou lodgest, I will lodge; thy people shall be my people, and thy God my God . . ."

To quote the famous historian and orientalist, Ernest Renan, "A quiver full of steel arrows, a cable with strong coils, a trumpet of brass crashing through the air with two or three sharp notes—such is the Hebrew language . . . The letters of its books are not many, but they are to be letters of fire. A language of this sort is not destined to say much, but what it does say is beaten out upon an anvil. It is employed to pour floods of anger and cries of rage against the abuses of the world, calling the four winds of heaven to the assault of the citadels of evil. Like the jubilee horn of the sanctuary it will be put to no profane use; but it will sound the notes of the holy war against injustice and the call of great assemblies; it will have accents of rejoicing, and accents of terror; it will become the trumpet of judgment."

The biblical style was apparently a specialized literary *genre,* which was studied and cultivated by the artists and writers of that period. The early prophets and poets of that Golden Era of Hebrew literary creativity must have founded a classical tradition which served as a model for subsequent generations of prophets and writers. This literary *genre* may have been studied and fostered in the schools of the "sons of the prophets" (see 1 Samuel 19.20; 2 Kings 4.1, 38; etc.). The fledgling prophets may have been drilled in these classical models and trained to cast their ideas and feelings into the established stylistic molds. This may be what Isaiah referred to when he declared "The Lord God hath given me the tongue of them that are taught . . ." (Isaiah 50. 4).[16]

It may, however, be safely assumed that the classical models of the biblical language are not typical of the daily conversational language employed by "the butcher, the baker, and the candlestick maker." Undoubtedly, the conversational language was simpler, more flexible, and lacking the artistry characteristic of the biblical style. It had more in common with the so-called mishnaic or post-biblical Hebrew. It made up in simplicity, flexibility, and dynamic qualities for what it lacked in grandeur and elegance.

In corroboration of this assumption one may cite the analogy of the linguistic division in the old Indian drama, where "there were two distinct forms of language, sanscrit (*samscrta,* elegant language), spoken by the gods, kings, princes, brahmins, etc., down to dancing-masters, and prakrit (*pracrta,* natural or simple language), spoken by men in inferior positions, such as shop-keepers, officers of justice, policemen, bath-masters, fishermen, and by nearly all women" (Jespersen, O., *Mankind, Nation and Individual,* p. 141).

There was apparently a tendency among the ancients toward stratification in language as there was in dress, manners, and the like. No such linguistic differentiation is conceivable in modern times. The modern means of intercommunication, such as the radio and the press, militate against such differentiation. Virtually everybody is exposed and affected more or less by the talk of people from every class of society, although some of these linguistic distinctions still persist in some measure even in modern days (*ibid.,* 145).

To conclude, there seems to have existed, side by side, in pre-exilic Palestine two distinct linguistic traditions, the literary or classical and the popular-conversational. The first tradition followed generally the Canaanitic or Ugaritic literary models, which date back to the pre-biblical days. In its poetic style, its parallelisms, vocabulary, metaphors, and locutions, the Bible frequently evinces a striking resemblance to these ancient documents. The second tradition had its roots, apparently, in the vernacular, which the early Hebrew ancestors had brought with them from their native homeland in Mesopotamia, namely, Aramaic. These two linguistic traditions admitted, on occasion, of free intercrossing and mutual influence, as will be pointed out in Chapter IX of this volume. It is nonetheless quite probable, as will be indicated later, that the Canaanitic influence was prevalent in literary Hebrew, while the Aramaic influence was preponderant in the vulgar or conversational Hebrew.

CHAPTER THREE
THE EARLY NON-BIBLICAL SOURCES OF
HEBREW

Reason for the "Uniformity" of the
Hebrew Language

The traditional Jewish attitude toward the Bible, as stressed in the foregoing discussion, has been a very conservative influence on the Hebrew language and has prevented radical transformation of its structural character. Yet the uniformity of the language is less real than appears on the surface. There can be no doubt that Hebrew has undergone considerable changes in pronunciation and word-formation since its inception, especially during its pre-literary career, or before the biblical writings gained currency and began to be regarded with reverence.

There was, clearly, a vast difference between the Hebrew used by Moses and Deborah and that employed by the author of Kohelet. Moses would have had some difficulty in understanding the Hebrew spoken by Kohelet or by the later Psalmists, let alone the Hebrew of Rabbi Judah the Prince 1500 years after him, or Judah Halevi in the Middle Ages, or of Bialik of our own day. Furthermore, the people in the Northern Kingdom must certainly have employed a different dialect from the people in the Southern Kingdom. Indeed, the Ephraimites were identifiable by their distinctive pronunciation even from their close kinsmen and neighbors, the Gileadites (Judges 12.6). According to Herodotus, the ancient Greek historian, five different Ionian languages were spoken in Asia Minor. A similar situation may have obtained among the Hebrews. Yet the vocalization of the Hebrew of Kohelet, or of any modern Hebrew text, is based on the same principles as the vocalization of the Song of Moses or of the Song of Deborah. There were doubtless considerable changes in the Hebrew vocabulary in those widely separated periods, since over such a long stretch of time many new words were admitted and many old words discarded; but the grammatical divergencies remained comparatively small.

What is responsible for this apparent "uniformity" in the Hebrew language?

The ancient Hebrew texts of the Bible were transmitted in a consonantal form of writing. There were no signs, or very scanty and inadequate signs, to indicate vowel-sounds. Consequently, when the masoretes of the seventh and eighth centuries C.E. (see Chapter VII) undertook to fix the Hebrew vocalization, they treated alike all the texts, regardless of their respective antiquity, in consonance with the traditional pronunciation which had become more or less standardized in Palestine during the talmudic age. They therefore vocalized the texts of the early biblical period in accordance with the same vocalic principles as those of the late biblical periods. The system was thereupon adopted as the norm for Hebrew texts and has remained the basis for Hebrew grammar down to modern times. It may consequently be stated that our masoretic vocalization records the pronunciation of Hebrew in vogue in Palestine during the late talmudic period, but not necessarily the exact pronunciation of the earlier periods.

To illustrate: if we were to take a selection from the writings of Chaucer and if we were to modify its orthography by retaining the consonants but changing the vowels in accordance with the modern spelling, the Chaucerian English would then differ very little from modern English. Here is an example:

Chaucerian Orthography	*Modern Orthography*
Whan that Aprille with his shoures sote	When that April with his showers sweet
The droghte of Marche hath perced to the rote,	The drought of March has pierced to the root,
And bathed every veyne in swich licour,	And bathed every vein in such liquor,
Of which vertu engendered is the flour;	Of which virtue engendered is the flower;
When Zephirus eek with his swete breeth	When Zephyr eke with his sweet breath
Inspired hath in every holt and heeth	Inspired has in every holt and heath
The tendre croppes, and the yonge sonne	The tender crops, and the young sun
Hath in Ram his halfe course y-ronne	Has in Ram his half course run
And smale fowles maken melodye,	And small fowls make melody,
That slepen al the night with open ye,	That sleep all night with open eye,

The interval separating the English of our own day from Chaucerian English is a period of less than six hundred years. Yet the differences in pronunciation, apart from those in orthography, are considerable, especially if we bear in mind the fact that many vowels and consonants now mute but left in spelling for etymological reasons were sounded in Chaucer's days. Since the masoretes, the recorders of the traditional Bible text, actually recorded the pronunciation of biblical Hebrew in vogue in their own days, around the eighth century C.E., one can readily realize how different the recorded pronunciation must have been from that of Moses or the Patriarchs who lived over two thousand years before the masoretic period. It can also be readily realized how unreliable our vowel-system is as a basis for determining the pronunciation of Hebrew during the days of the early "Hebraists."

Early Hebrew Pronunciation as Recorded in the Amarna Letters

What was the pronunciation of the Hebrew that our Patriarchs heard when they migrated into Canaan? How was the Hebrew pronounced and inflected during the times of Moses and the Judges?

Fortunately, we are now in possession of some ancient documents which help us penetrate the veil of masoretic tradition and guide us in reconstructing with some degree of accuracy the pronunciation and grammatical forms of Hebrew during these early stages in the history of the language.

In the autumn of 1887 an Egyptian woman accidentally stumbled upon some clay tablets in the soil of Tell-el-Amarna, situated some 200 miles south of Cairo on the east bank of the Nile. She sold her rights to her find for ten piasters. This discovery led to the unearthing of some 400 clay tablets, inscribed in the Assyro-Babylonian language and characters, which opened up an entirely unknown vista in the history of Palestine and the surrounding countries. The tablets were written about a century and a half prior to the Exodus and they tell of invasions of Palestine by a tribe or a people designated as Habiru or Hapiru.

The fourteenth century B.C.E. was a turbulent period in the history of Egypt. Akhenaton, the "heretic king," the father-in-law of Tutankhamen, the discovery of whose tomb by Howard Carter on November 4, 1922, caused a sensation, was then the ruler of Egypt. He was, according to the Egyptian records, a religious reformer who attempted to impose a monotheistic religion on the Egyptians whose gods were legion. He was compelled by the opposition of the priests of Thebes to abandon the capital, and he built a new one in the middle of Egypt, at what is now known as Tell-el-Amarna, where he also gathered his court. This was the period portrayed in the Bible as that preceding the invasion of Canaan by Joshua.

It was during that period that the chieftains and provincial kings of the country sent letters to the Pharaoh in Egypt, the supreme ruler of Canaan, appealing for help against the foreign invaders. But in his preoccupation with his religious problems, the Pharaoh apparently neglected the interests of his Palestinian vassals, and the letters went unheeded.

The importance of these letters rests, not only on the light they shed on an obscure period of Palestinian history, but also on their help in unravelling the mystery of the pronunciation and formation of Hebrew during the invasion of Canaan by Joshua and the Judges, or even earlier, during the migration of the Patriarchs. In the first place, these documents, although written in Assyro-Babylonian language, the international language of that time, contain also glosses (translation and explanations) in the Canaanite vernacular employed by the writers in their daily work. Secondly, the Assyro-Babylonian script used in these tablets possesses vowel-signs, thus affording us fairly authentic evidence on the pronunciation of the language.

Various facts relative to this stage of the Hebrew language emerge and deserve to be pointed out.

1. There are remarkable variations in the pronunciation of Hebrew among Jews in modern times. For example: the *a* sound in *shalom* or *barukh* is pronounced *a* (as in "far") by the Sephardic and Palestinian Jews, *o* (as the *a* in "fall") by the Jews of Lithuania, and *oo* (as in "food") by the Jews of Poland, Ukraine, and others. An analogous example of sound modification may be found in the case of the long *a* in such words as the German *Vater* (father) which the Lithuanian Jews pronounce *foter* and the Polish Jews *footer*.

It will, therefore, be of interest to note similar variations in pronunciation, as may be inferred from the Canaanitish glosses, in vogue in the ancient days of the *Habiru* invasion. According to the records, it seems that the early "Hebraists" or Canaanites, were incapable of pronouncing a long *a*, as that in *father*. This long Semitic *a*, which has been preserved in Arabic, was rounded like *oo*, as it is rendered in these glosses (although the same symbol in cuneiform represents also *o*).[1] Such Canaanitish pronunciations as *tzunu* (= *tzon*) "sheep," *sukinu* (= *sokhen*) "guardian," *humitu* (= *homah*) "wall," *abutinu* (= *abotenu*) "our ancestors," *rushunu* (= *roshenu*) "our head," may have sounded peculiar to our "Aramaic" ancestors, who had immigrated into Canaan. In all these cases the *u* sound in the initial syllable is the equivalent of the primitive Semitic long *a* (as in *father*). How this primitive vowel was sounded in the Aramaic dialect spoken by the Abramide immigrants cannot now be determined, since no contemporary records of this dialect and its phonetic pattern is available, but it was in all likelihood different from that employed in Canaan.

2. In modern English, as in Hebrew, the relation of words in a sentence is indicated by a fixed order. In the sentence "a dog bit a cat" the sense is clearly distinguished from that in "a cat bit a dog." The difference is determined merely by the order. But in the Latin sentence *Deus creavit coelum et terram* (God created the heaven and the earth), the word order may be changed without affecting the meaning at all. The relation of words is indicated by means of inflections, or case-endings attached to the nouns (*coelum* and *terram*, derived from the absolute forms *coelo* and *terra*). The Indo-European languages, as well as the Semitic, at one time possessed case-endings. In the course of time these case-endings were dropped in some languages, but were retained in others. In modern English the case-endings have disappeared,[2] while in German they have been preserved.

In the Semitic languages the case-endings were as follows: nominative—*u*, accusative—*a*, genitive—*i*; which may be traced to earlier forms *um*, *am*, and *im*. Classical Arabic still retains these case-endings, but in Hebrew and in modern Arabic there are few traces left of them.[3] Proper names, because of their stereotyped character, preserve these case-endings, for example, Shemuel (for *shem-El* "the name of God"), Malki-tzedek (for *melekh-tzedek,* "the king of justice"). In the same category belong also the familiar names of Hannibal, the famous Carthaginian general, and Haile Selassie, the king of Abyssinia. Since the Phoenician language spoken in Carthage was very closely related to Hebrew, the name Hannibal (for *han-Baal,* "the grace of Baal") has a familiar ring in Hebrew and would correspond in meaning to the Hebrew Hananyah or Hananel. Similarly the name of the king of Abyssinia, Haile Selassi, should be recognized by every student of Hebrew as the equivalent of the Hebrew *heil ha-sheloshah* (the power of the Trinity). In both these names, Hannibal and Haile Selassie, the case-endings are in evidence.

In the Canaanitish Hebrew glosses, the Semitic case-endings are still consistently preserved. Thus we find there such forms as *batnu* (belly), *hullu* (yoke), *kilubi* (cage), *gitti rimmunima* (pomegranate press); which are equivalents, respectively, of the Hebrew forms *beten, 'ol, kelub,* and *gat rimmonim.*

3. There seems to be a tendency in some languages to drop off final vowels in unaccented syllables, as, for example, the final *e* in *hope* (Middle English *hopen* = German *hoffen*). In Hebrew, likewise, this tendency appears to be operative. But when our Patriarchs and ancestors invaded and settled in the land of Canaan, they still heard and probably used these final unaccented syllables in pronunciation, in nouns as well as in verbs, as is evidenced by the spelling in the Amarna tablets of such verbal forms as *yazkuru* (Hebrew *yizkor*), "he will remember" or "he remembers," *tanshuku* (Hebrew *tishshokh*) "he bites."[4]

4. The Hebrew letter *ayin* is rendered in these glosses generally by *h,* and it must have been approximately so pronounced, for example, *haparu* (dust), *hullu* (yoke), *zuruhu* (arm); which are the equivalents, respectively, of the Hebrew *'aphar, 'ol,* and *zero'a.*

5. The possessive suffix, first person dual, in Hebrew is *ai,* for example, *yad* (hand), *yadai* (my hands). But in the

Canaanitish glosses this suffix is *ya,* hence *hinaya* (my eyes) for the Hebrew *'einai.*

The Ugaritic Poems

One of the most remarkable discoveries in the realm of the literature of antiquity is that of the Ugaritic poems. These poems have significant implications for the study of the Bible and the Hebrew language, as well as for the history of religion and the development of the alphabet.

In the spring of 1928, an Arab peasant, while ploughing his field in the village of Ras Shamra, a sloping Arab hamlet on the Syrian coast opposite the most easterly cape of Cyprus, suddenly found his plough striking some stone slabs. Removing them, he discovered underneath an ancient tomb, covered with the debris of the ages.

Little did the simple peasant realize that he had hit upon the records of an ancient kingdom and civilization some thirty-five centuries old. Little did he dream that his chance discovery would push back and expand the frontiers of biblical history and civilization and shed much light on the historical background of the Hebrew language and religion.

When this discovery was brought to the attention of the French authorities in Beirut (Lebanon), plans were immediately launched to organize an archaeological expedition, under the auspices of Professor Charles Virolleaud, with a view to excavating the mound. The work began in the spring of 1929, but it was only about two years later that sufficient evidence came to light on the basis of which this mound could be identified as the site of the ancient kingdom that had borne the name *Ugarit,* which is also mentioned in the Amarna letters.

The excavations continued until 1939, when they were stopped because of the war. But by that time a large collection of inscribed clay tablets had been exhumed which attracted the attention of every student of antiquity.

A variety of matters are dealt with in these inscriptions. But of particular interest to us are the poems which contain specimens of pagan Semitic literature dating from the fifteenth century B.C.E., just about the period of the Hebrew invasion of Canaan, or shortly before the Exodus. They are written in a language akin to ancient Hebrew and in an alphabet hitherto unknown, consisting of thirty letters. In vocabulary, style and phraseology these poems exhibit characteristic features of biblical Hebrew, and their content is likewise reminiscent of some parts of the Bible. They were probably designed to be recited on certain solemn and festive occasions, such as seasonal festivals and cult ceremonies. One can find there mention of such sacrifices, familiar to students of the Bible, as *asham* (trespass offering), *shelem* (payment offering), *tenufah* (wave offering); as well as reference to *kohanim* (priests) and *kedeshim* (sacred acolytes). Like cuneiform, the writing was impressed with a stylus on soft clay tablets, but unlike cuneiform it consists of single signs and not of syllables. These signs have no connection with the cuneiform writing of Sumeria, Babylonia and Assyria.

Considerable light is shed by these poems on some obscure and indirect references in the Bible to the pagan worship of the Canaanites. Most of the gods and heroes mentioned are referred to in the Bible. The supreme god is called *El* (compare *El Elyon* in Genesis 14.18, 19, 20, 22: "the supreme El"), but the counselor of the gods is his wife, *Atirat* or *Ashirat* (Hebrew *Asherah*) and their son is Baal or Baal Al'iyān (the mighty).

The influence of Ugaritic on Hebrew is evident not only in vocabulary and religious concepts, but also in idiomatic expressions, in syntactical structure, and in poetic style and imagery. Thus David, in his dirge of the death of Saul and Jonathan, invokes a curse of drought on the locality where they were slain, employing the expression *al tal we-al matar* (2 Samuel 1.21). This is almost a verbatim equivalent of the Ugaritic, *bl tl bl rbb* (nor dew nor rain), included in a dirge recited on a similar occasion. So is Isaac's blessing *mi-tal ha-shamayim umi-shemannei ha-aretz* (Genesis 27.28) reminiscent of the Ugaritic *tl shmm shmn artz* (dew of heaven, fat of earth). Metaphors like the opening of the windows of heaven (Genesis 7.11), going down to the grave of a departed son (*ibid.*, 37.35), melting away the couch with tears (Psalms 6.7), the rider of the clouds in reference to God (*ibid.*, 68.5), death coming up into windows (Jeremiah 9.20); or such similies as biting like a serpent (Proverbs 23.32, etc.), goring like a wild-ox (Deuteronomy 33.17), panting like a hart after the water brooks (Psalms 42.2), and the like—all have their parallels in Ugaritic literature. Similarly common in this literature are such familiar biblical locutions as *wa-ya'an . . . wa-yomer* (and he answered . . . and said: Genesis 18. 27), *wa-yikkah . . . wa-yelekh* (and he took . . . and went: *ibid.*, 11.31), *wa-yissa kolo wa-yikra* (and he lifted his voice and called: Judges 9. 7), *wa-yissa einaw wa-yar'* (and he lifted his eyes and saw: Genesis 18.2).

The scheme of parallelism current in biblical poetry is also a characteristic feature in Ugaritic. According to this scheme each verse is composed of two halves, which are either similar in thought, contrasting or supplementary. Such a verse, for example, as "Thy kingdom is a kingdom for all ages and thy dominion endureth throughout the generations" (Psalms 145. 13) is almost an exact paraphrase of the Ugaritic "Thou wilt obtain thy kingdom eternal, thy reign throughout the generations."

There seems little doubt that the early Hebrews were directly exposed to the culture, beliefs and practices reflected in these mythological poems and that they were influenced by them. In some cases the influences were negative, that is, they evoked a revulsion. Here and there we find in the Bible reverberations of the protests against some of the practices and beliefs with which the Hebrews became infected. One of the glaring examples is the prohibition in Exodus 23.19, 34.26 and in Deuteronomy 14.21 "Thou shalt not seethe a kid in its mother's milk," which is the basis of some of our dietary laws. This is apparently a direct reference to the ritual mentioned in the Ugaritic poems prescribing such a practice ("a kid in milk, a lamb in butter") as an item in the magical technique for producing rain. Many other such examples could be cited. Indeed, an extensive literature has already appeared discussing the influence of pagan culture and religion portrayed in these poems on the practices and religious beliefs reflected in the Bible.

Other Extra-Biblical Documents

There are also extant literary non-biblical records contemporaneous with the period of Ahab and Joram (around the middle of the ninth century B.C.E.), perhaps also with the Solomonic period, and with periods of Isaiah and Jeremiah, respectively, which reveal the state of the language at these periods, before it was subject to standardization by the later scribes and masoretes. Some of these records are most significant.

1. The Mesha Stone was discovered in 1868 in the ruins of Dibon, in the neighborhood of the Dead Sea. It contains an inscription of thirty-four lines in which Mesha, the king of Moab, records his triumphs over the kings of Israel. There are quite a number of divergencies in the account given in this inscription and in that rendered in the Bible (2 Kings 1. 1 and 3. 4 ff.) of presumably the same military incident, unless these two accounts report two entirely different events.

Both accounts concur in that Mesha, the king of Moab, had been a tributary to Israel, paying to the king of Israel annually an enormous tribute of wool, and that he subsequently rebelled against Israel. But from this point on the two accounts diverge. According to the biblical account the revolt took place after the death of Ahab, during the reign of his son Joram. The Bible further narrates that "the Israelites rose up and smote the Moabites, so that they fled before them." It was only after the Moabite king, facing certain disaster, had offered his eldest son "for a burnt offering upon the wall" that "there came a great wrath upon Israel; and they departed from him and returned to their own land."

Quite a different story is related by the king of Moab as recorded on this stone. He confesses to the state of complete

Transcription of the Mesha Stone

From I. J. Gelb, *A Study of Writing* (University of Chicago Press), 1952, page 134.
(*For a picture of the Stone see illustrations between pages 244-5*)

subjugation to which Moab had been reduced in the days of
Omri, the father of Ahab, "because Kemosh (the god of Moab)
was angry with his land." But during the reign of Omri's son
and successor, Mesha maintains, the situation changed. He rebelled against the king of Israel and defeated him thoroughly
"and Israel perished with an everlasting destruction." He then
goes on to recite in great detail and with considerable swagger

his great exploits against Israel and his grandiose achievements in his own land.

In reconciliation of these two contradictory accounts one may offer the theory that Mesha is reporting an attempted revolt, which had apparently succeeded temporarily, before it was subdued by the punitive invasion of Ahab; or that Mesha started the revolt at the end of Ahab's reign and continued it during the reign of his successor Joram. In any event, such statements as that "Israel perished with an everlasting destruction" may be regarded as another typical oriental exaggeration.

What concerns us chiefly at this time, however, is the language and style of this inscription. The Moabitish dialect in which it is written is so closely akin to the language of the Bible, both in style and in grammatical construction, as to render it extremely valuable for an understanding of the development of the Hebrew language. It contains also vocabularies and grammatical forms, which although not found in the Bible, can be traced to Semitic origins and may have been in vogue in Hebrew during the biblical period, as will be pointed out below.

2. The Siloam Inscription was discovered in 1880 in the vicinity of Jerusalem. It gives an account, in six lines, of the manner in which the tunnel joining the pool of Siloam with the well of Miriam, was constructed. The pool of Siloam is situated at the extreme south of the eastern hill of Jerusalem, on the north of which the Temple had been located. The tunnel was driven through the rock presumably in the time of Hezekiah (around the turn of the seventh century B.C.E.) in order to bring water into the city (2 Kings 20. 20), "to the west side of the city of David" (2 Chronicles 32. 30). It may have been cut in preparation for the anticipated siege of Jerusalem by the Assyrians under Senacherib (around 701 B.C.E.).

A youth wading in the pool with a lighted candle in his hand observed on the lower part of the wall of the tunnel something that looked like characters engraved on the rock. A gypsum cast was obtained the following year (1881), and the inscription, although partly mutilated by the wearing away of the rock, was clearly deciphered. The language and the style resemble biblical Hebrew very closely. Although it, too, like the Mesha inscription, includes some words not found in the Bible and some archaic grammatical constructions, the sense of it is fairly simple, and it reads just like a passage from the Bible It relates vividly and graphically how the miners cut through the rock. "While the axes of one group were lifted opposite those of the other," the story proceeds, "and there were only three cubits to be pierced, it was possible for one to call to the other, for there was a fissure on the rock to the right . . . and on the day of its completion the miners, facing one another, struck axe facing axe, and the waters flowed from the spring to the pool for a distance of 1,200 cubits. The height of the rock above the workers was 100 cubits."

3. The Lachish Letters were found in 1935 at Tell-ed-Duweir, the site of the biblical fortress of Lachish, southwest of Jerusalem. These letters consist of twenty-one inscribed potsherds, or ostraca, written during the lifetime of the prophet Jeremiah, in the early part of the sixth century B.C.E. (probably 597 and 588 B.C.E.). They were sent by Hoshaiah, the commander of a small outpost close to Jerusalem, to Yaush, the military governor of Lachish and its vicinity, or just a person of high rank and influence with the king and his officers, for the purpose of conveying military as well as political information. We hear in reading these letters the last gasps of Judea's struggle for life against the Babylonian armies, as well as the reverberations of the tragic events described in the book of Jeremiah.

In one of these letters the writer mentions the name of a prophet, whom the king of Judea accused of demoralizing the people by words which "loosen the hands, weaken the hands of the country and the city" (cf. Jeremiah 38.4), and he pleads with Yaush to intercede on behalf of the prophet before the king and the officers. In another letter it is reported that Koniahu, the son of Elnathan, the commander of the army, has gone down to Egypt with some men.

The name of the prophet mentioned in these letters is unfortunately not decipherable. However, it has been suggested, with some plausibility, that this prophet is to be identified with Uriah of Kiriat Ye'arim, who, according to the story in Jeremiah 26.20-23, spoke against the government in the days of King Jehoiakim, and whom the king wanted to kill. Thereupon the prophet fled to Egypt. But he was brought back to Jerusalem by Elnathan, the son of Akhbor, the commander of the army, who had been dispatched to Egypt for this purpose, and the prophet was put to death. But the difference in the names of the commander of the army is a problem that still awaits solution.

In still another letter, the writer complains that he can no longer receive orders from Yaush in Lachish, for the fire-signals from Azekah, a sister fort about six miles northeast of Lachish, through which these orders were apparently relayed, are no longer visible.[5] This letter must have been written toward the end of the war, for Azekah and Lachish were the last two fort-cities captured before the capture of Jerusalem (cf. Jeremiah 34. 7). Apparently at the time of the writing of this letter Azekah was already in the enemy's hands and the signal station there was already not in operation.

These letters are written in true biblical style and they show evidence of a literary tradition. In reading them one is strongly reminded of the books of Kings and Jeremiah. They also contain some rare grammatical constructions and some new words, although the Hebrew origin of these is clear and unmistakable.

4. The Gezer Calendar was discovered in 1908 by Macalister, during his excavations at Gezer in Central Palestine. Its date is not entirely certain. It has been variously assigned to the third, sixth and eighth centuries B.C.E. But according to the latest authoritative views it is to be dated from the age of Solomon, around the last quarter of the tenth century B.C.E. It consists of eight lines, seven of which are legible. Some of the characters are of an archaic nature, resembling those in the ancient Canaanite texts of the Late Bronze Age. It must have served as an agricultural calendar, indicating the months of the year in

accordance with the rotation of the seasons; such as "the months of ingathering, the months of sowing, the months of late sowing, the month of hoeing up of flax," etc. It is the consensus of some modern scholars that this calendar was employed as an exercise tablet for a school-boy, by which he was aided in the memorization of the sequence in the immutable seasonal activities, somewhat in line with our familiar "Thirty days hath September . . ." Although a number of difficult linguistic and grammatical difficulties in this inscription still remain to be settled, we thus find in this inscription further evidence attesting the widespread use of writing and schooling among the Hebrews during the early period of the monarchy.

The Distinctive Hebraic Characteristics of These Documents

Some of the outstanding characteristics in these documents are significant for the study of the history of the Hebrew language.

1. Hebrew, like the other Semitic languages, is essentially a consonantal language, that is, the meaning inheres in the consonants, while the vowels serve to denote the shades or modifications of the basic meaning. To illustrate: the three consonants *l m d* (learn) could be read *lamad* (he learned), *lomed* (he learns), *lemed* (study), also *limmed* (he taught). The context was adequate as a clue for determining the exact meaning, and no need was felt in the early history of the language for special signs to denote vowel-sounds.

The orthography in our early non-biblical documents reveals clear evidence of the consonantal status of the Hebrew alphabet. The vowel letters *aleph* (א), *he* (ה), *waw* (ו), and *yod* (י), which occur frequently in our biblical texts and regularly in post-biblical Hebrew as indications of vowel-sounds, are completely lacking in these documents, especially in the middle of the words. Thus we find in the Ugaritic poems such defective spelling as *khnm* (= Hebrew *kohanim*) "priests." So also in the Mesha inscription *hsh'ni* (= *hoshi'ani*) "he delivered me," in the Siloam inscription *kl* (= *kol*) "voice," and the Lachish letters *tbm* (= *tobim*) "good."[6] This is as if the word "power" would be written "pr," since these are the only two consonants in the word, which could also represent such words as "pair," "poor," "pure," "peer," "pare," "pore," "pier," "par," "pyre." These vowel letters were omitted even in cases where they were presumably to serve as consonants, as, for instance, in *yn* (for *yayin*) "wine" and *shmm* (for *shamayim*) "heavens" in the Ugaritic poems; as well as *m'tn* (for *ma'tayim*) "two hundred," *tzhrm* (for *tzohorayim*) "noon" in the Mesha inscription; also *Ktz* (for *Kayitz*) "summer-fruit" in the Gezer Calendar. These words were apparently pronounced at that period as *yayn, shamaym, ma'tayn, tzohoraym*. An analogous example still extant in our text of the Bible is *Yerushalm* (Jerusalem) which we read as though it were written *Yerushalayim*.

2. The indication of the feminine in the Semitic languages, in nouns and in verbs, is a *t* suffix, thus *kataba* (he wrote), *katabat* (she wrote); as is still the case in Arabic. This *t*-ending gradually disappeared in Hebrew, after going through the following stages: *katabat, katabath, katabah* (with consonantal sounding of the *h*), *kataba(h)*, and finally *katba(h)*. The final *h* in the last two instances merely indicates the existence of the preceding vowel and is not sounded. This process of gradual elimination of the final *t*-sound is a common phenomenon also in other Semitic languages, and even in Indo-European languages.[7]

Our inscriptions and documents normally employ the older forms, such as *ha-bamat* "the height," also *me'at* (100) (Mesha); *hayat* (Siloam) "she was," but also *nikbah* "tunnel" (*ibid.*). In the cases where the *t*-ending was replaced by *he* in these documents, this *he* still retained in all likelihood, its consonantal value; it was sounded like *h* and had not yet passed into the vocalic stage, where it merely indicated the existence of the preceding vowel. Remnants of the older forms are still found in the Bible, for example, *'azlat* in Deuteronomy 32. 26, "it (she) has gone"; *huva't* in Genesis 33. 11, "she was brought"; *'ezrat* in Psalms 60. 13, "help." The normal biblical equivalents of these forms, which are preserved in modern Hebrew, would be *'azlah, huv'ah, 'ezrah,* in all of which the final *he* has no consonantal sound at all and serves only as a vowel-letter. In the inflexions, however, the feminine *t* is retained in both nouns and verbs, for example, *'ezrati* (my help), *shemaratni* (she watched me), and so in the others.

3. The plural ending *in* is employed in the Mesha inscription consistently, as in Aramaic and Arabic, and not as in Hebrew, where the normal masculine ending is *im*. In Ugaritic, however, the *m*-ending is consistently used.

These ancient documents are of inestimable value to the student of ancient civilization and, particularly, to all those concerned with the history of the Hebrew people, its language and literature. Many problems and difficulties of Hebrew grammar, syntax and vocabulary, as well as of biblical practice, belief and law, are illuminated by a study of these documents. No student of the Bible or of Hebrew can afford to ignore them.[8]

There are also some important inscriptions in the Phoenician language, a sister dialect of Hebrew, dating from approximately the twelfth and fourth centuries B.C.E., respectively, in which are displayed some characteristics of the ancient Hebrew texts and documents, both with regard to syntax and orthography, as well as of grammar. The use of vowel-letters is even more restricted in these documents than in the Moabite and Hebraic inscriptions. We find in them such spellings as *'nk* (for the Hebrew *'anokhi*) "I," *shm'* (Hebrew *sham'ah*) "she heard," *p'l* (Hebrew *pa'alah*) "she did," *z* (Hebrew *zeh*) "this," *k* (Hebrew *ki*) "because" or "that," and the like. The Punic dialect spoken in Carthage in North Africa was an offshoot of this language, and it lived on for several centuries into the Christian Era.

Conclusions

These extra-biblical sources have shed much light on the history and religion of the biblical period, as well as on the orthography and grammar of biblical Hebrew. They have also brought to light some new words and expressions, which were apparently in vogue during the biblical period but do not appear in the Bible. This Book, it should be recalled, is only a remnant of a vast literature produced during that period, which in the course of time sank into oblivion and disappeared. Undoubtedly, the Hebrew vocabulary of that time was much richer than that which occurs in the biblical records. Little wonder then that heretofore unknown words and expressions make their appearance in the newly discovered non-biblical records.

Among such newly discovered words and expressions, some of which have been brought back to life and restored to use in modern times, the following deserve mention: *ashuah* or *asuah* (probably, as found later in Ben Sira, *ashiah*, 50. 3, "reservoir" or "pool," also *shiah*, Mishnah B.K. v, 5), *riat* (biblical *ro'i*, Nahum 3.6, or *rd'awah*, "spectacle"), and *mibko'a ha-shahrit* (from the break of dawn, reminiscent of the biblical *me-alot ha-shahar*, but see Isaiah 58.8)—all in the Mesha stone; *nikbah* (tunnel) and *zadah* (fissure) in the Siloam transcription; *bet ha-refed* (the sleeping-house, the lodging), *masu'ot* (fire signals, found in mishnaic Hebrew), *tesibbah* (patrol, inspection tour)—in the Lachish letters; *etzed* (hoeing up, see *ma'atzad* "axe" Isaiah 44. 12); and *zamir* (pruning season) in the Gezer inscription. The expression *et ha-zamir* (Song of Songs 2. 11) generally rendered by "the time of singing," should accordingly be interpreted to refer rather to the season of pruning and cleaning of the vines, which generally comes in the spring.

Of particular interest is the verb *halaf*, employed in the Mesha inscription in the sense of succeed (follow after), a term of which neither biblical nor later Hebrew offers an equivalent. This verb does occur in biblical Hebrew, but in an entirely different sense, namely, that of pass or exchange. Modern Hebrew has thus gained an important term, in place of the rather cumbersome expressions, generally employed, *ba aharei* (came after), or *mille makom* (filled the place). Incidentally, the stem *halaf*, in the sense used in the Mesha inscription, is the basis of the title *calif* (Arabic *halifa*) given to the successor of Mohammed as the head of the Moslem State and Defender of the Faith.

Similarly interesting is the expression *atta ka-yom,* which recurs quite frequently in the Lachish letters in the sense of "even now," or "immediately, on this very day." It has been regarded by scholars as an unusual expression, not found in the Bible. This usage might, however, shed light on some difficult passages in the Bible, for which no plausible interpretation has thus far been suggested; namely, *mikhrah ka-yom* (Genesis 25.31) and *hishab'ah li ka-yom* (*ibid.,* 33), which the J.P.S. version renders "sell me first" and "swear to me first" respectively, a translation which does not fit the Hebrew original words. Even more strikingly analogous is the passage *attah ki ha-yom* (1 Samuel 9.12) which can be readily emended to read *attah ke-ha-yom,* the equivalent of *attah ka-yom.*[9] The usage of the expression *attah ka-yom* in the Lachish letters makes perfect sense in all these instances.[10]

To conclude: these ancient documents resemble the Hebrew text of the Bible to a remarkable degree, both in syntax and in grammatical form. But this resemblance relates only to the written language. We are still left in the dark as to the pronunciation of the writers of these documents, because of their failure to employ vowel signs. It is well-nigh impossible to determine, for example, the difference between the pronunciation of Mesha and that of the authors of the Lachish letters, because of the resemblance in the orthography of these documents, for an interval of some four centuries must certainly have produced a considerable difference in pronunciation. It is just as impossible, if not more so, to reconstruct the different pronunciations of the writers of the biblical texts, which range over a period of about a millennium, because of the stamp of uniformity imposed upon them by the masoretes. Yet, it is very clear, as demonstrated by these ancient extra-biblical records, that the consonantal text of the Bible has, relatively speaking, not been tampered with, and is preserved substantially in its original form.

PART TWO
How the Written Language Took Form

CHAPTER FOUR
HOW THE HEBREW ALPHABET
ORIGINATED

The Origin of Language

What is the origin of language? What motivated people to express themselves in verbal forms? Why are there so many different languages in the world?

All these questions have occupied the minds of thinking people since time immemorial. The problem of the origin of language was an especially favorite topic of discussion among philosophers and thinkers since the days of the early Greeks.

In recent times, however, the tendency among linguistic students is to shun discussion on this subject. They regard such discussions as futile, since we do not at this time possess adequate data which may offer any significant clues or "leads" relative to this subject. Even the most primitive languages spoken today have behind them an evolutionary history of thousands of years, and no effort to enter into the workings of the minds of those early coiners of human speech can prove successful. The loom of primitive speech remains so far an insoluble mystery. *La Société de Linguistique de Paris* refuses to permit even the reading of any papers on this topic.

One thing seems certain, however, namely, that the motivation for speech is twofold: (1) a desire for self-expression and

73

(2) an urge to communicate wishes and ideas to others. "It is not at all improbable that human gestures, dance and song have developed out of the same complex of behavior that yielded language; and although language has, throughout historic time, been our chief means of communication, the comparison of all four activities may be suggestive."[1] All these four activities are motivated by a desire for self-expression and communication.

The Origin of Writing

This is particularly true of the invention of writing. Primitive people, like children, love to paint, to scratch, to carve and to draw. They like to engage in such activities for amusement and because of the opportunity for physical activity, manipulation and self-expression. Occasionally the pictures drawn or carved serve as reminders or messages. American Indians were especially adept in conveying messages by means of picture writing. Since they had to communicate with people whose language they did not understand, or to whom their own language was unintelligible, they had to resort to all sorts of intricate devices to make their ideas clear; and their resourcefulness in this regard stood them in good stead. Thus an Ojibwa Indian is said to have "owned a long strip of birch-bark with a series of pictures, which he used to remind himself of the succession of verses in a sacred song. The third picture, for instance, represents a fox, because the third verse of the song says something about a fox, and the sixth picture represents an owl, because the sixth verse says 'It is an ill omen.' "[2]

The term *language*, as indicated by its etymology in English and in other languages (German *Sprache*, Hebrew *Lashon*, etc.) was originally restricted to human articulate speech. Long ages of language usage preceded our available written records, for writing is a comparatively recent invention. Long before people acquired the ability to express themselves and to communicate their ideas and wishes graphically in a more or less intelligible manner, spoken language had acquired a relatively large vocabulary and a considerable variety of sounds had been extensively employed. It was, therefore, no easy task to devise a system whereby speech could be more or less adequately recorded in writing. It took many more ages of experimentation before men arrived at a system, such as our alphabet, where each letter is associated, in some degree of accuracy, with a specific sound.

The Stages in the Development of Modern Systems of Writing

On the basis of available records the development of writing can be traced through five stages.

1. In the pictographic or ideographic stage, represented chiefly by the "hieroglyphic" writing of ancient Egypt and by

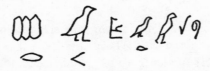

Hieroglyphic Inscriptions found in Sinai
From G. R. Driver, *Semitic Writing* (British Academy, London), 1954, page 94.

the Indian pictograms, writing consisted of picture drawing. Objects and ideas, even complex objective and ideational situations, were directly represented by pictures. Most of the symbols are realistic pictures actually denoting the name of the object which they represent. In the course of time, these pictures became conventionalized, and their resemblance to the thing signified became more remote, until it was almost completely obliterated. Their merest suggestion or trace sufficed to elicit the desired response. Thus "ill omen" might be indicated by an owl; "justice" by an ostrich feather, probably because it was employed by the judge; the idea of "bad" by an abnormality; "peace" and "friendship" by hands clasped together; "night" by a circle with a star in the middle; and the like. Some of the older Chinese symbols, as well as some of the cuneiform (wedge-shaped) characters still betray a resemblance to the picture of the meaning symbolized by the word.

In order to render such a system of writing useful as a means of intercommunication, the matter of the choice and shaping of the symbols had to be settled by common consent. How was this consent achieved? This was not so difficult in the primitive period as it now appears. It should be remembered that the number of writers in those days was not very large, and the agreement on the shaping and selection of conventional signs could be obtained without much difficulty. Indeed, lists of signs have been unearthed among the finds of the early Sumerians, dating back to about the middle of the fourth millennium B.C.E., where the progress from the original pictograms to the conventional forms can, in many cases, be clearly traced, thereby indicating how agreements on conventional signs may have been settled.

These pictures or signs, during this stage, bore no relationship to linguistic forms. They merely suggested "ideas"; namely, features of the practical world, rather than features of the writer's language, much in the same manner as do traffic signs, the barber's pole, or pictorials and cartoons. The ideas conveyed could be expressed in different ways and even in different languages. It is not at all impossible to tell a story effectively by means of pictures, with only slight use of titles, as has been demonstrated by some writers of children's story books, also by Lynd Ward (*God's Man,* a Novel in Woodcuts, New York, 1929; and in several other books). Such stories could be read even by those who do not understand the writer's language.

2. This was followed, after a long interval, by the word-writing or logographic stage, during which the symbols or signs came to be associated with definite linguistic forms and with specific words. The sign of a picturable word served to represent all other words that were phonetically similar or homonymous, as, for example, "son" and "sun." Furthermore, a picture of a sun can also stand for "bright," "white" or "day."

A pictogram, or sign, associated with a certain word in one language may be borrowed by another language and, consequently, given a different phonetic value, although representing the same concept. When, for example, the Persians began fashioning their script after the model of the Aramaic phonetic system, they used the signs representing Aramaic words and read them as though they stood for the corresponding Persian words. The sign for the Aramaic word *malka* (king) was employed by the early Persians and read, like the Persian equivalent, *shah*. A parallel may be found in English, where the abbreviated form of the Latin *videlicet* is written *viz.*, but pronounced "namely."

The use of our numerals may serve as a further illustration of this stage. Each of the numeral symbols is associated with a specific linguistic form, although the phonetic value of this

Hittite Hieroglyphic Writing

From I. J. Gelb, *A Study of Writing* (University of Chicago Press), 1952, page 82.

form varies in the different languages. Thus the symbol *2* is read "two" in English, *zwei* in German, *deux* in French, *dva* in Russian, *shetayim* in Hebrew.

3. In the phonogramic or syllabic stage, successions of pic-

tures or signs were employed to represent a word of two or more syllables, somewhat like the picture syllables in a rebus. For example, in order to indicate the word "catalogue" one could employ a picture of a cat on a log. Similarly the picture of a man and a date-tree (𝍢) could signify the word "mandate." So in Egyptian, a figure in a seat (*hes*), with a character for eye (*iri*), represented *Hesiri,* the Egyptian name of the god Osiris. In some languages, such as Chinese and Japanese, the writing system has not advanced beyond the logographic or syllabic stage; and several hundred characters have to be mastered by the readers of these languages.

4. Gradually the uniconsonantal stage, a further stage in the direction of the alphabetic system, evolved by the principle of acrophony, namely, by using the picture or sign of a picturable word to represent the initial syllable and eventually the initial sound of the word. The Egyptian hieroglyph or symbol *nefer* (the vowels are uncertain, since Egyptian writing records no vowels) which means "good," came to represent the phonetic value of *ne* (or *n* with some other vowel), or just the consonant *n* by itself. We may see this principle operative in our Hebrew alphabetic system. Thus, for example, in the word *adam* (Adam or man), in its equivalent form in "old Hebrew" script (𐤌𐤃𐤀), one may see the succession of "pictures," from right to left, of an ox (Hebrew *eleph,* represented by the picture of the ox's head), of a door in a tent (Hebrew *delet*), and of *water* (Hebrew *mayim,* represented by the waves), the initial sounds of these three "picture words" yielding the word *adam.*

5. The alphabet stage was the final development. Hebrew, as has already been indicated above, like all Semitic languages, is a consonantal language; that is, the basal meaning is inherent in the consonants; the vowel changes generally serve to signify grammatical modifications of the basal meaning. In the Indo-European languages vowels play a major role; any vowel change may lend the word an entirely different meaning. For example, the English words "bat," "bait," "bet," "bate,"

"but," "boat," "beat," "boot," "about"—all have a common consonantal basis *bt,* but they have nothing in common either in etymology or in meaning. In Hebrew, on the other hand, the consonantal stem *kdsh* yields a large number of words varying in vowels, in prefixes and in suffixes and internal changes, in all of which words the basal meaning *holy* always inheres. Thus, the consonants *hkdsh* may be read *ha-kodesh, ha-kadosh, ha-kiddush, hikdish, hekdesh, hokdash, hikkadesh,* all of which are nominal and verbal derivations of the same basal stem and connote the same basic idea—holiness. Words containing these consonants and differing essentially in meaning are rarely possible. Furthermore, in the Semitic languages all syllables begin with a consonant. A word like the English "owe," composed exclusively of vowels, would be inconceivable in these languages; it could not be represented by a purely consonantal alphabet.

Hence, in Hebrew, as in the other Semitic languages, the need for vowel indications was not felt until later in the history of the language (see the next chapter). But when the ancient Greeks took over the Semitic alphabet from the Phoenician traders about 800-900 B.C.E. they found it necessary to devise signs indicating vowel values. They, accordingly, employed for this purpose those symbols which represented consonants alien to them; that is, the phonetic equivalents of which were lacking in their language, and for the pronunciation of which their vocal patterns were not adapted; namely: *alef* (א = old Hebrew ⟨) for *A, he* (ה = old Hebrew ⟨) for *E* (both long and short), *het* (ח = old Hebrew ⟨) for *E* (long), and *ayin* (ע = old Hebrew **O**) for *O.* Since the *waw* and the *yod* were employed already in early Semitic documents to some extent in the capacity of vowel letters, they must have been taken over directly by the Greek borrowers of the Semitic syllabary, thus employing the *waw* (ו = old Hebrew ⟨) for *u* or *y* (in ancient Greek the *u* sound resembled the French *u*) and the *yod* (י = old Hebrew ⟨) for *i.* The Greek historian Herodotus attributed the origin of the alphabet to a

Phoenician, named Kadmos (Hebrew *kadmi,* "the *Easterner*"), who brought it to Greece, while Plato regarded the Egyptian Thoth (name of an Egyptian god) as the inventor of the alphabet.

The Greeks took over the forms, as well as the names of the letters (for example, *Alpha, Beta,* etc.)[3] and they introduced a few minor variations to suit the particular needs of their language. The modifications in the form of the letters were due in the main to the change in the direction of writing, since the Greeks, unlike the Hebrews, wrote from left to right as well as from right to left. Hence some of the letters had to be turned around. Further slight modifications in the alphabet were introduced by the Romans, one of which was to differentiate the *gimel* (ג = old Hebrew ⅄) into *C* and *G,* giving the former the place of the gimel in the order of the Hebrew alphabet, while the latter was inserted in place of the Greek *zeta* (Hebrew *zayin*), for which ancient Latin had no equivalent sound. Our English alphabet is derived from the Greek via the Latin alphabet.

The Origin of the "Hebrew" Script

The ancient Hebrew documents dating from the tenth and following centuries B.C.E. were written in the script designated in the Talmud as *ketab Ibri,* "Hebrew script." This script was a Hebrew adaptation of the alphabet employed in Canaan during the middle of the second millennium B.C.E. The oldest Semitic inscriptions in this form of writing, at the present time, are dated as early as 1100 B.C.E., and perhaps earlier. An ostracon(sherd inscribed in ink) in old Hebrew characters was found by E. Grant in Bet Shemesh in 1930, dating back, according to Albright,[4] to the fourteenth century B.C.E. The "Hebrew" alphabet gradually superseded the more intricate cuneiform writing used in the Amarna letters, as well as the simpler cuneiform consonantal script employed in the Ugaritic poems.

The square script now employed in printed Hebrew and

שמע ישראל יהוה אלהינו יהוה אחד ואהבת את
יהוה אלהיך בכל לבבך ובכל נפשך ובכל מאדך והיו
הדברים האלה אשר אנכי מצוך היום על לבבך ושננתם
לבניך ודברת בם בשבתך בביתך ובלכתך בדרך
ובשכבך ובקומך וקשרתם לאות על ידך והיו לטטפת
בין עיניך וכתבתם על מזוזת ביתך ובשעריך
והיה אם שמע תשמעו אל מצותי אשר
אנכי מצוה אתכם היום לאהבה את יהוה אלהיכם ולעבדו
בכל לבבכם ובכל נפשכם ונתתי מטר ארצכם בעתו
יורה ומלקוש ואספת דגנך ותירשך ויצהרך ונתתי
עשב בשדך לבהמתך ואכלת ושבעת השמרו לכם
פן יפתה לבבכם וסרתם ועבדתם אלהים אחרים
והשתחויתם להם ולרה אף יהוה בכם ועצר את
השמים ולא יהיה מטר והאדמה לא תתן את יבולה
ואבדתם מהרה מעל הארץ הטבה אשר יהוה נתן לכם
ושמתם את דברי אלה על לבבכם ועל נפשכם וקשרתם
אתם לאות על ידכם והיו לטוטפת בין עיניכם ולמדתם
אתם את בניכם לדבר בם בשבתך בביתך ובלכתך
בדרך ובשכבך ובקומך וכתבתם על מזוזות ביתך
ובשעריך למען ירבו ימיכם וימי בניכם על האדמה
אשר נשבע יהוה לאבתיכם לתת להם כימי השמים
על הארץ

The Contents of a Mezuzah

An example of hand-written Hebrew

in the writing of the texts of the Torah, *tefillin* (phylacteries) and *mezuzot* (encased parchment-inscribed biblical quotations placed on the doorposts in the homes of observant Jews) has been in vogue among Jews only since the time of Ezra and Nehemiah (c. 430 B.C.E.). Previously the *ketab Ibri* mentioned above had been in vogue, a script which resembled closely the Phoenician script. According to an ancient Jewish tradition Ezra brought the square script to Palestine from Babylon. It is called in the Talmud *Ashurit*[5] or *ketab Ashuri,* "Assyrian," rather "Syrian" or "Aramaic" script. The name *Ashur* (Assyria) is used here loosely, to include the countries in the Mediterranean inhabited by Arameans. It is also possible that this script was so designated because it had been in vogue in business documents among the Assyrians and Babylonians since the eighth century B.C.E.

The origin of the original "Hebrew" script is shrouded in obscurity. It is certainly the outcome of a long evolutionary process, the beginnings of which are hidden in the dim past. But the evidence seems to be preponderantly in favor of regarding it as derived from the Egyptian.

During the fourth millennium B.C.E., both the Egyptians and the Sumerians began experimenting with pictographic, ideographic and syllabic writing. But while the Sumerian syllabary emphasized vowel-indications as much as consonantal signs, the Egyptians invented a script where no signs for specific vowels were included. This script consisted of twenty-four consonants, which the reader was left to supply with the appropriate vowels in accordance with the needs of the context. It thus had the potentialities of a full-fledged alphabet. But the Egyptians, for some obscure reason, failed to take advantage of their pseudo-alphabet and they restricted its use to such purposes as the spelling out of foreign words, and especially proper names. For all other purposes they continued to use their cumbersome ideographic and syllabic system of writing, thereby retarding the progress of writing by many centuries.

The "Hebrew" alphabet may have been derived from or

influenced by this Egyptian syllabary, but the relationship between these two writing systems is hard to trace. A considerable
passing of time must be assumed during which the link between
these two systems evolved and took shape. But where is that
link? That is the question.

Inscriptions from the Sinaitic Peninsula
From G. R. Driver, *Semitic Writing* (British Academy, London), 1954, page 94.

Some scholars think that this "missing link" is to be found
in the numerous inscriptions discovered in recent years in the
ancient copper mines of the Sinai peninsula, dating back to
about the middle of the first half of the second millennium
B.C.E. These mines were under Egyptian control, and the
miners were Semitic nomads. The inscriptions are written in an
alphabet consisting of over thirty signs, some of which bear a
close resemblance to certain characters of the "Hebrew" alphabet as well as to various forms of Egyptian hieroglyphs.

It seems like a plausible hypothesis. But the interpretation
of these inscriptions is still largely a matter of speculation, and
future discoveries and interpretations may upset the whole
hypothesis. Indeed, what is more likely, the two systems may
be mutually independent inventions, although they may have
influenced each other in their process of development. One
must bear in mind the fact that the Egyptians were not the only

ones who experimented with an alphabetic system of writing, as may be inferred from the discovery of the Ugaritic poems[6] and from a group of inscriptions of a much earlier period (about 2100-1700 B.C.E.) discovered in Gebal, whose Greek name was Byblos, a Phoenician town on the coast not far to the north of Beirut.

But whatever the derivation of the alphabet, credit must be accorded to the Western Semites (Phoenicians, Arameans and Hebrews) who recognized its practical value and perfected it. The commercial contacts of the Phoenicians with the Greeks from the eleventh to the fourth century B.C.E. gave them the opportunity to disseminate this alphabet among the Greeks. Through them, in turn, it was adopted, with slight modifications, in all European languages, thus securing "a permanence assured to no other invention of the human race."[7]

The Evolution of the Square and Cursive Hebrew Scripts

The old "Hebrew script" must have been used in the manuscripts of the biblical texts at least as late as the fourth century B.C.E., since the Samaritans, who seceded toward the end of that century, took it over in their Pentateuch and have used it with certain embellishments of their own ever since. However, during the Persian world empire, when the Aramaic language came into fashion as the international language among the Jews, as well as among the other peoples of that empire, the Aramaic script, likewise, gained prominence. Hence, it is conceivable that Ezra and his disciples, in their eagerness to popularize the biblical texts and the knowledge of Hebrew among the Jewish masses as well as to dissociate themselves from the Samaritans, deemed it advisable to transcribe these texts into the common Aramaic script. But for secular purposes the "Hebrew script" was apparently in vogue throughout the Second Commonwealth.

The oldest extant Hebrew document in the Aramaic script in Palestine is the so-called Nash papyrus (discovered in 1902), which dates back to about the beginning of the Christian Era.

But this script must have passed through several stages in its evolution from the Hebrew characters to the "square script" as represented in this early Hebrew document. As a matter of fact, inscriptions in the "transitional scripts" indicate the widespread use of the "Aramaic script" among the Jews several centuries prior to the beginning of the common era. Yet, the coins of the Hasmonean period, as well as those of the period of the first, and even of the second rebellion against the Romans, that is, as late as 135 C.E., all bear inscriptions in the old Hebrew alphabet. The persistent use of the old Hebrew characters for the purpose of coinage may have been intended as a nationalistic demonstration, or as a symbol of national independence, recalling "old glories." The tendency to use the old Hebrew script, especially on some series of postage stamps, is also in evidence in modern Israel for the same reason.

The "Syrian" or Aramaic script which is, as mentioned above, an Aramaic adaptation of the old Hebrew or Phoenician alphabet, passed through further developmental stages since the beginning of the Christian Era, until it attained its present square form. It is impossible to trace these stages, since there are few extant intermediate records between that biblical fragment and the biblical manuscripts of the 10th and 11th centuries of the Christian Era.[8] It is, however, apparent that the use of the square script can be traced as far back as the period of the Septuagint translations, or the reign of the second Ptolemy (285-247 B.C.E.). The Greek translators of the Septuagint must have employed texts written in the square script. Some of their translations which deviate from our masoretic text can be plausibly explained on the basis of confusion which is possible only in the case of letters in the square script. Thus *ibri anokhi* (Jonah 1.9) is rendered in the Septuagint in the sense of "I am the servant of the Lord," which postulates a reading of *ebed adonai* for *ibri*, the *resh* in *ibri* having been taken for *dalet* and the *yod* as an abbreviation of *adonai*. The confusion of *resh* and *dalet* is not as readily explainable in terms of the old Hebrew script as it is in those of the square script. Similarly, the rendering in the Septuagint of the expression *khebodi li-khlimah* (Psalms 4.3) would indicate that the translator read *kibdei leb* (heavy of heart), in which case he broke up the second word *li-khlimah* into two words, namely, *leb* (heart) and *lammah* (wherefore), thus reading a *b* in place of the *kh* found in our text. Such a confusion is likewise implausible except in the square script. In the old Hebrew script the *b* and the *k* (or *kh*) are entirely different in form.

Another, perhaps, even more cogent instance is the translation of *lephi ha-taph* (Genesis 47.12), where the word *ha-taph* is rendered by *soma* (body). This curious Greek translation of the Hebrew *taph* (children) can be explained only as due to the fact that the Hebrew letter ט (t) in *taph* in the translator's manuscript was broken at the base, thus misleading him to read it גו (goo) which consequently suggested the word *ha-gooph* (the body).[9] Such a possibility is conceivable only in a text written in the square script. Similarly, when Jesus is quoted as saying: "Not one iota (*yod*) shall pass away from the Torah" (Matthew 5.18), he could have referred only to the *yod* (iota) in the square script, since in the old Hebrew script the *yod* is no smaller than any of the other Hebrew letters. In the Nash manuscript the square script is already definitely established.

The term *ketibah meruba'at* or *ketab meruba'* (square script) has been applied to this script since the thirteenth century.[10] The reason for this term is obvious, since most of the letters in the Hebrew alphabet are more or less square in form, especially as compared with the alphabets of other languages.

The significant cursive scripts, worthy of mention because of their wide currency, are the Rashi script (so-called because Rashi's commentaries on the Bible and the Talmud are printed in it, but it must have been in vogue previous to Rashi's days) and the Yiddish, or neo-Hebraic current script. Both, of course, have evolved from the square script, in different localities and periods. The neo-Hebraic script is now used almost universally both in Hebrew and in Yiddish cursive writing. The

NUMBER	NAME	MEANING	OLD HEBREW	SQUARE	CURSIVE	RASHI	OLD GREEK	LATIN
1	ALEPH	ox						A
2	BET	house						B
3	GIMEL	camel						C
4	DALET	door						D
5	HE							E
6	VAV	hook, nail						F
7	ZAYIN	weapon						G
8	HET	window						H
9	TET							
10	YOD	hand						I
11	KAPH	palm, frond						K
12	LAMED	goad						L
13	MEM	water						M
14	NUN	fish						N
15	SAMEKH	fish? support						
16	AYIN	eye, well						O
17	PE	mouth						P
18	ZADE							
19	KOPH							Q
20	RESH	head						R
21	SHIN	tooth						S
22	TAV	sign, cross						T

From the Hebrew to the Latin Alphabets

Yiddish cursive script, as well as the Rashi script, has been in use since the Middle Ages. Although the cursive script is clearly traceable to the square script as its origin, it also possesses traces of the old Hebrew script. This is particularly evident in the case of the Aleph letter, which in the Yiddish cursive form is closer to the old Hebrew than is the same letter in the square script. A type of script, dating from the fifteenth and later centuries, was designated as *Weiber-Taitsh* (women's German), because of the fact that it was employed especially in Yiddish books intended for women, who were not versed in Hebrew texts. Documents in this script, in both printed and manuscript forms, are available. This represented an intermediary stage between the square and the modern Yiddish cursive script. A letter by the famous commentator of the Mishnah, Yom Tob Lipman Heller (1579-1654) is written in a script very closely resembling our modern script.

The Meaning and Use of These Letters

What is the origin of the names for these symbols? What is the meaning of these names? In only some cases can this be established with a fair degree of certainty; in others, the matter is, as yet, in dispute and in doubt. It is likewise still a moot question whether the signs were designed, on the principle of acrophony,[19] to represent the picture signified, as well as the initial sound of that word, for example, 𐤀 = picture of ox's head = א sound, the initial of *aleph* "ox"; or, conversely, whether the names were later invented and were suggested by the "pictures" of these symbols. Very likely, only some of the alphabet symbols were originally pictographs or ideographs, while others are amplifications or combinations of other simple signs. Thus, the sign 𐤇 (No. 8) may have evolved from that of 𐤄 (No. 5), in which case the additional stroke on the left merely served to indicate the intensive form of the *h* sound. In the same manner the 𐤈 (No. 9) may be a compound of 𐤏 (No. 16) and 𐤕 (No. 22), since the sound of ט is but an emphatic form of ת; while the sign 𐤎 (No. 15) for *s* was distinguished from 𝒯 (No. 7) by an additional stroke for the same purpose, since the *s* was the intensive of *z* in sound.[20]

In post-biblical Hebrew, the letters of the alphabet were employed as numerical signs. The units were denoted by ט — א; the tens by צ — י; 100-400 by ת — ק; the numbers from 500-900 by ת (400) with the addition of other hundred-symbols, for example, ת״ק = 500, ת״ש = 700, and so on. The thousands are sometimes denoted by the units with two dots placed above, for example, א̈ — 1,000, etc. This use of alphabetic symbols was already in vogue during the Maccabean period, as is evidenced by the coins of that period (135-6 B.C.E.); שא(אחת שנה), *first year;* (שנת ארבע(שד *fourth year,* etc. The practice became widespread, especially for the purpose of indicating numbers of verses and chapters in biblical texts. In biblical Hebrew, however, number values were expressed by special words and not by numerals.

The order of the sequence of the Hebrew alphabet can be traced back to the biblical period. In a number of chapters of the Bible the verses are arranged in the alphabetical order. Each verse, or verse group, begins with a letter of the alphabet, with occasional variations which may be due to textual corruptions or to some other reasons.[21]

It is not at all unlikely that the use of the alphabet as numerals is to be traced to this practice of arranging verses in an alphabetical order. However, the Greeks, as well as the Romans, likewise employed their alphabet as numerals. It is therefore probable that this practice was not original with the Hebrews. Evidence of the use of the alphabet as numerals by the Greeks dates back to the third century B.C.E.

The Varied Pronunciations of Some Letters

Although the alphabetic system has been widely accepted in Semitic and Indo-European languages as the one best adapted to graphic representation of any spoken language, it falls short of representing accurately every shade of human speech sound; it merely succeeds in recording these sounds approximately.

Thus the *n* and the *t* in the word *nature* have different sound values from those of the same two consonants in the words *king* and *table*. Similarly the vowel-letter *a* serves to indicate such widely different sounds as those in "far," "fat," "name" and "all." Conversely, consonants of kindred sound values may lose their respective nuances and become assimilated in sound to one another. Thus even during the talmudic period the throat-letters (*aleph, he, het, ayin*) had lost their respective phonetic distinctions in the pronunciation of the Jews of Babylonia and of certain provinces in Palestine. A Babylonian scholar named *Hiyya* was nicknamed in Palestine 'Iyya, because he pronounced the *het* like an *ayin*.[22] Similarly the Jews of certain provinces in Palestine were prohibited, according to the Talmud, from functioning in the capacity of official Synagogue readers or cantors, because they failed to make the phonetic distinction between *aleph* and *ayin* and between *he* and *het*.[23] Indeed, there is ample evidence available on the basis of which it is safe to conclude that these letters generally lost their consonantal value after the beginning of the Christian Era.

Twofold Letters

As can be seen from the alphabetic table, five of the twenty-two letters have twofold forms. The forms ץ,ף,ן,ם,ך, are used at the end of the word and are called finals. Of these ץ, ף, ן, ך are distinguished by shafts drawn straight downward, which, be it noted, represent the original shapes of the letters. The corresponding non-finals have developed through the connective stroke, or ligature, in the leftward direction, as a result of the tendency to cursiveness, just as we are accustomed to connect letters in the cursive script in English. In the case of the *m* there were probably in existence two forms, one of which was used in some localities, the other in other localities. Eventually one came to be employed as the final, the other as the non-final.

The dual forms of these letters are already found in the Nash papyrus, dating from about the beginning of the Christian era.

But during the period of the Septuagint (around 200 B.C.E.) this differentiation had not yet been clearly established, as is evidenced by various translations indicating readings which deviate from those in our text. These dual forms are already commented on in the Talmud,[24] and are designated by the medieval grammarians *'otiot kefulot* (double letters). All the twenty-two letters, as well as the five final forms, occur in one verse of the Bible, namely, Zephaniah 3. 8.

The six letters ב,ג,ד,כ,פ,ת have a twofold pronunciation. Originally, during the period of the First Temple, all these letters had a hard explosive pronunciation, namely, *b, g, d, k, p, t*. In the course of time, they were softened or spirantized when preceded by a long vowel. The process of spirantization was gradual. It must have begun soon after the Babylonian Exile, and it reached its full development during the early medieval period, probably under Aramaic influence. Traces of this process are already found in transliterations by Origen and Jerome. The letters *k, p, t* were the first to undergo this process. An analogous case is that of the *b* in the Teutonic stem *habai* (German *haben*) which evolved into *v* in the English "have." In our system of vocalization a dot inside the letter marks its explosive pronunciation. In modern usage the spirantized pronunciation of the *gimel* (gh) and the *dalet* (dh) has generally disappeared.[25]

Local Pronunciation

After a system of writing gains currency and becomes well established in a community, not only the spelling of the words, but also the grammatical forms become conventionalized for written records. Thus a "literary dialect" is adopted, in which variations and deviations from type are ignored. It is, therefore, impossible for us to reconstruct now, except approximately, the actual pronunciation of Hebrew in the various localities and periods of the respective writers. In modern times as many as nine main phonetic variations have been recorded. The most widespread of these are the so-called Ashkenazic (subdivided into: Lithuanian, Polish, Southern Russian, German and

Ukrainian) and Sephardic (now generally adopted in Israel). One of the characteristic distinctions between the Ashkenazic and Sephardic pronunciations of Hebrew is the sounding of the letter ת, when it has no dot in the middle. In the Ashkenazic pronunciation it is sounded as *s,* while the Sephardic Jews pronounce it *t.* It is apparent from the above that even sounds of letters, let alone the pronunciation of words, never cease to be affected by the local environment.

CHAPTER FIVE
HOW DID THE VOWEL-SYSTEM EVOLVE?

The Role of Vowels

A European language written without vowel-letters is inconceivable; it would be hardly decipherable. Let us attempt, for example, to identify the following familiar lines from a poem by a famous American poet.

ncpnmdntdrrwlpndrdwkndwr
vrmnqntndcrsvlmffrgttnlr

It would take a good deal of ingenuity to decipher them. Yet they are the first two lines of Poe's well-known poem, *The Raven.*

Once upon a midnight dreary, while I pondered, weak
    and weary,
Over many a quaint and curious volume of forgotten lore.

What makes these lines unrecognizable is the removal of the vowel letters and the separation spaces between the words.

Ancient Hebrew texts were generally written in just such a form without vocalic indications or vowel signs; and probably without any markings or divisions between words, or with only occasional division signs. This was not unusual in ancient times. In fact, most of the old Greek documents are written in continued series of letters, without any division of words. In some ancient inscriptions and manuscripts a point or a perpendicular line marks the division of words or clauses; in others, separations between words are not marked. Our masoretic text contains in some instances questionable divisions of words, which are challenged by the masoretic note *kere* ("to be read" differently). The Septuagint and Vulgate translations likewise presuppose in some cases a different word division from that in our masoretic text. The consistent separation of words as represented in our masoretic text is apparently a comparatively recent development.[1] Even in the Nash papyrus the separation is not always marked, although this text already contains the distinction between the medial and the final forms of the letters *k, m, n, p, tz.*

As long as the people employed the Hebrew language orally and were conversant with its written records and texts, the need of a vowel-system as an aid to reading was not seriously felt. Even the absence of signs for word divisions did not much hamper comprehension. As was pointed out in the preceding chapter, the basic meaning of a Hebrew word inheres in its consonants, not in the vowels. The vowel changes indicate mere variations of shadings and modifications in the basic meaning. In modern times, too, people well versed in Hebrew and its texts experience no need of vowels to facilitate their reading of the language; and Hebrew books, with the exception of biblical texts, children's books and poetry, are generally published without vowels. Indeed, the experienced and trained Hebrew reader may find the vowels distracting.

As the practice of reading and writing became more popular and widespread, and especially in the Diaspora where the people began to grow away from the Hebrew language and its literature, the need of vocalic aids in reading Hebrew was increasingly felt. As a matter of fact, since the practice of training children in the reading of the Torah can be traced to a very early period in the history of the Hebrew people, the use of vocalic aids in reading must have begun to germinate even during the biblical period. Thus the letters *aleph, he, waw* and *yod,* which were originally employed consistently as consonants, gradually began to lose their weak consonantal value in some instances and became silent. Eventually these silenced letters came to be utilized as vowel letters, on the analogy of Greek and other Indo-European languages. Indeed, in some Semitic languages, in Mandaic (an Aramaic dialect still spoken by a small gnostic sect in Iraq) and Neo-Punic (the language employed in Carthage during the Roman period), the *ayin* (Indo-European *o*) was also used as a vowel-letter to denote *i* or *e*. It is still used as an *e* vowel in Yiddish. All these letters, including the *ayin,* were already designated as vowel-letters by Jerome (fourth century C.E.).

Arguments Regarding the Age of the Hebrew Vowel Signs

Why didn't Hebrew pursue the same course and develop a vowel-system like that of the Greek and other European languages? Why did Hebrew tradition prefer to resort to the peculiar dot-system for the indication of vowels, a system which is troublesome from the pedagogic and economic viewpoints? How old is our present vowel-system? How deeply rooted is it in time-hallowed Jewish tradition? Why have all modern proposals and attempts to simplify this system met with resistance?

The question of the authority and antiquity of our vowel-system was a matter of controversy among early medieval, as well as among later, scholars—Jewish and Christian alike. Some maintained that the vowel-signs were communicated to Moses on Sinai. Others ascribed their establishment to Ezra and the Men of the Great Synagogue, while still others traced their origin to Adam.

The first instance on record of raising the question about the authority and antiquity of the vowel-system was a query addressed to Natronai II, the Gaon of Sura (859-69). He was asked whether it was lawful to vocalize the scrolls of the Pentateuch in use at the synagogue. His reply was clear and unequivocal. He maintained that the text of the Torah which was given to Moses on Sinai was without any vowel-signs and that these were not Sinaitic, but were invented by the sages as reading-signs and aids. Hence the Torah Scrolls must remain unvocalized, so as not to violate the law of *lo toseph*, "thou shall not add thereunto" (Deuteronomy 13. 1).[2] Nevertheless, Ben Asher, a Palestinian, about half a century later, was already attributing the invention of the vowel-signs and accents to the "scribes, prophets, and wise men, who constituted the Great Synagogue or Sanhedrin."[3] About a century later, the Karaite Yehudah Hadassi (1075-1160), in his book *Eshkol ha-Kopher,* ascribed the authorship of the vowel-signs to Moses on Sinai. But Ibn Ezra, a younger contemporary of Hadassi, challenged the antiquity of these signs and regarded their authorship as of Tiberian origin,[4] although on another occasion he appeared to trace them to a much earlier date.[5]

The first real attack on the early dating of the vowel-system was launched in the sixteenth century by Elias Levita (1469-1549), a masterful student of grammar and Masorah. In his book, *Masoret ha-Masoret,* Introduction III, he asserted that the establishment of the vowel-signs could not have antedated the period of the compilation of the Talmud (about 500 C.E.), although the proper reading and pronunciation had been communicated to Moses, and by him, through oral transmission, to subsequent generations of Israel. This thesis was set forth and fortified with an array of cogent arguments, based on references to the early grammarians and on the Aramaic names of the vowels and accents.

Levita's scientifically buttressed arguments did not go unchallenged. A profound and brilliant contemporary of Levita, the Italian Jewish scholar Azariah de' Rossi, rose to the defense of the antiquity theory. Drawing on talmudic, kabbalistic and other sources, and appealing to the genius of the Hebrew language, he contended that the consonants and the vowel-signs in Hebrew must have originated simultaneously with Adam and transmitted to and by Moses. But Moses, according to de' Rossi, preferred to eliminate the vowel-signs from the text of the

Torah in order not to restrict its meaning and to allow it to be interpreted in "seventy different ways," in accordance with the living tradition. In the course of time, however, and especially during the Babylonian captivity, de' Rossi continues, these signs were forgotten, but were restored by Ezra. Subsequently, during the period of the Second Temple and thereafter, particularly owing to the widespread use of the Aramaic language among the Jews, the signs once more were forgotten, and were finally re-established by the masoretes.[6]

The authority and antiquity of the vowel-signs were also subjects of dispute among Christian scholars. As far back as the thirteenth century, some of them rejected the authority imputed to these vowels as a malicious and wilful invention of the Jewish masoretes, calculated to corrupt the text of the Bible for their own special designs. In the fifteenth century, one of these "scholars," giving free rein to his imagination, presented a vivid and amusing account, full of malicious misinformation, of the origin of the vowels. According to him, the rabbis, roused by the success of the Church and the loss of their own revenues due to defections from their ranks, "assembled in great multitudes at the Babylon of Egypt, which is called Cairo, where they, with as much secrecy as possible, falsified and corrupted the Scriptures, and concocted about five or seven points originally invented by Ravina and Ravashe, two of their doctors. The same Rabbis also concocted the Talmud."[7]

After the publication of Levita's and de' Rossi's works on the problem of vowel-points, the Catholics and the Protestants seized upon the issue with great zeal, and a vehement controversy ensued. At first, the Protestants upheld Levita's views, finding in them a warrant for throwing off the shackles of the Church of Rome in the interpretation of the Bible. Later, however, they reversed their position, since the Catholic Church, likewise, espoused Levita's views as corroborating its exclusive authority in interpreting the Bible. Motivated by common hatred for the Jews and by hostility toward each other, the two opposing religious camps prosecuted the controversy with much heat, although oftentimes with little light. It reached its intellectual high watermark in the works of Louis Capellus, who accepted Levita's views, and of John Buxtorf, father and son, who relied on de' Rossi's arguments.

In modern times the problem of the antiquity of our vowel-system can no longer be regarded as controversial. Levita's valid arguments, reinforced and corroborated by the discoveries of the Palestinian and Babylonian systems of vocalization, have established beyond doubt the fact that our vowel-system could not have been definitely fixed before the middle of the eighth century C.E. This system was, of course, an outgrowth and culmination of numerous experimentations and inventions, which must have taken a number of centuries.

The Talmud contains references to the practice of "punctating" (*nikkud*) biblical manuscripts and to a number of special signs (*te'amim* or *ta'ame Torah, simmanim*) in some Hebrew words or phrases.[8] It is, however, fairly evident that no vowel-system to speak of existed during the talmudic period. Even the Sages were confused and uncertain about the reading of certain biblical words and their meaning.[9] It was only after the completion of the Talmud (fifth or sixth century) that definite attempts at the establishment of a system of vocalization may be noted.

The Use of Vowel-Letters in Hebrew

One of the earliest attempts to indicate vowel-sounds was, as already indicated previously, by means of the letters *aleph, he, waw, yod*. These letters, which had weak consonantal values in the early history of the language, even when unvocalized, gradually dropped their respective sounds in the unvocalized state and evolved into vocalic aids.

The first two letters to undergo this evolutionary process were the *waw* and the *yod*. Thus, words like *yom* (day) and *hurad* (was brought down) were originally written *ywm* and *hwrd,* but pronounced *yawm* and *huwrad,* in both of which the *waw* (*w*) was sounded. Similarly in the words *bain* (between) and *rib* (quarrel), the *yod* (*i*) was originally consonantal.

Gradually the consonants *waw* and *yod* lost their distinctive sound-value, but they were retained in writing for etymological reasons, as were in English the *w* in "saw" and "who" and the *i* in "nailed" after these letters had lost their original consonantal values. Eventually the muted *waw* (*w*) in *yawm* and *huwrad* coalesced with the preceding vowels, with the result that the *aw* in *yawm* yielded the same sound as the identical diphthong in "saw," while the *uw* in *hurad* evolved into the sound *oo* as in "cool." On the other hand, the muted *yod* (*i*), in the case of *bain* and *rib,* contracted in the former with the preceding *a* to yield the sound *ei,* analogously to the same diphthong in the English "nail," and in the latter with the preceding *i* to result in the sound *ee,* as in "see."

Consequently the *waw* (*w*) came to be regarded as the vowel-sign indicating the sounds *o* and *oo,* as the case may be; while the *yod* (*i*) suggested the sounds *ei* and *i.* They were, therefore, often employed even in the biblical texts as pure vowel-signs, without serving any etymological purpose.[10] In fact, evidence of the use of these letters in this manner is found in some degree even in the Mesha and Siloam inscriptions, as well as in the Lachish letters, especially at the end of words. When the Greeks adopted the alphabet in the ninth century B.C.E., they must have found these two vowel-letters already in use to a limited extent, and they took them over and employed them in their system.

The evolution of the *aleph* and the *he* as vowel-letters proceeded in a similar fashion. For example, the *aleph* in *mtz'* (pronounced *matza'*) "he found," was originally consonantal, pronounced as a glottal stop, distinctly audible as in the second syllable of the English "cooperate," or the word pair "sea-eagle"; but it coalesced with the preceding *a* after its consonantal value was dropped, yielding a long *a.* Eventually the *aleph* was taken as the sign for long *a,* as in "far," and was employed as a vowel-letter pure and simple. Hence, when one wants to signify in Hebrew the sound *a* in such words as *Paris, Bialik,* and the like, the *aleph* is employed for the purpose.

As regards the *he,* its consonantal function at the end of the word was apparently dropped early in the history of the language. In the masoretic text of the Bible, it is employed to indicate any final vowel, except *i* (= *ee*). It is never used as a vowel-sign in the middle of the word. In modern Hebrew the *he* is employed especially in loan-words to indicate a final *a* as in the case of הסטוריה (= historia, history), אפריקה (Africa), אמריקה (America). The absence of this final vowel-letter in unvocalized texts would result in considerable confusion for the reader.

Why the Vowel-Letters Were Not Adopted and Expanded

These four vowel-letters were employed quite liberally in post-biblical or mishnaic Hebrew, and they were extended to cover all the vowel-indications. The problem of vocalic aids was thus solved in the main in the case of non-biblical writings. But what about the biblical texts? When the Holy Scriptures were finally canonized (in the early part of the second century C.E.), the biblical books were provided with vowel-letters to a very limited degree. How was one to read, for example, a word like *ktb?* Is it to be read *katab* (he wrote), *kitteb* (he wrote busily), *katob* (writing), *koteb* (writes), *ketab* (writ, document), or *ketob* (write, imper.)? All these are possible vocalizations of the three consonants. Very often even the context could provide only inadequate clues. The people, especially children, found great difficulty in reading the Bible. Even the rabbis were sometimes undecided as to the reading of certain words. Something had to be done to remedy the situation.

It is certain that if the scribes and masoretes had not intervened with their zealous and systematic efforts to guard against any alterations in the received text of the Scriptures, the use of the vowel-letters would have gained currency. A thoroughgoing vowel-system would then have evolved, even as in the case of the Indo-European languages and of Mandaic. However, toward the end of the Second Commonwealth, especially after the destruction of the Temple, various religious sects emerged, who attempted to tamper with the biblical text to make it agree

וְשָׁפַֿט בֵּֿין עַמִֿֿ֜ים רַבִּֿים וְהוֹכִֿיח לְגוֹיִֿם
עֲצֻמִֿים עַדֿ־־רָחֹוק וְכִֿתְּתֹֿו חַֿרְבֹֿתֵֿיהֶֿם
לְאִֿתִּֿים וַֿחֲנִֿיֹתֵֿיהֶֿם לְמַֿזְמֵרֹֿות לֹא־יִֿשָּׂא֩
גֹּ֣וֹי אֶֿל־גֿוֹי חֶֿרֶֿב וְלֹֿא־יִֿלְמְֿדֹֿוןֿ עֹֿוד מִֿלְֿחָֿמָֿה׃

וְשָׁפַֿט בֵּֿין עַמִֿים רַבִּֿים וְהֹוכִֿיח לְגוֹיִֿם
עֲצֻמִֿים עַדֿ־־רָחֹוק וְכִֿֿתְתֹֿו חַֿרְבֹֿותֵֿיהֶֿם
לְאִֿתִּֿים וַֿחֲנִֿיֹתֵֿיהֶֿם לְמַֿזְמֵרֹֿות לֹֿא־יִֿשָּׂא֩
גֹּֿוי־אֶֿל־גֿוֹי חֶֿרֶֿב וְלֹֿא־יִֿלְמְֿדֹֿוןֿ עֹֿוד מִֿלְֿחָֿמָֿה׃

וְשָׁפַט בֵּין עַמִּים רַבִּים וְהוֹכִיחַ לְגוֹיִם
עֲצֻמִים עַדֿ־רָחוֹק וְכִתְּתוּ חַרְבוֹתֵיהֶם
לְאִתִּים וַחֲנִיתֹתֵיהֶם לְמַזְמֵרוֹת לֹא־יִשָּׂא֩
גוֹי־אֶל־גֹּוֹי חֶרֶב וְלֹא־יִלְמְדוּן עוֹד מִלְחָמָה׃

Three Vowel Systems: 1) Babylonian; 2) Palestinian; 3) Tiberian with their own views and ideas. This prompted the scribes and the masoretic scholars to exercise special watchfulness over Scriptural words and to prohibit the slightest alteration of even a jot or tittle in the received text. Under such circumstances the insertion of vowel-letters into the biblical texts was, of course, unthinkable.

Experiments with Other Vowel-Systems

But since familiarity with biblical Hebrew was steadily declining, the danger of errors in pronunciation of the sacred words was increasing, especially among the young and untrained. Other means to aid reading had to be resorted to. The scribes, and especially the teachers of the young, consequently cast about to devise some vowel-signs which would meet the pedagogic need of guiding the young pupils in the correct reading of the Torah, without, at the same time, violating the injunction of *lo toseph alaw*, "thou shalt not add thereunto," which was their watchword. Numerous devices were experimented with, and the products of these experimentations are the three vowel-systems now extant: the Babylonian, the Palestinian and the Tiberian. The first two, preserved only in a few recently discovered ancient manuscripts, are superlinear. The Tiberian system, which is now in use, is sublinear, except for one vowel-sign in the middle, *shurek* (ּו), and one above the letter, *holem* (ֹו). The names of these systems stem from the names of the places where they presumably originated. Our system, the Tiberian, is presumed to have been invented and fixed in the Tiberian academies, where the masoretes flourished around the seventh and eighth centuries C.E.

The Babylonian system seems to have operated on the principle of using vowel-letters. The practice in mishnaic Hebrew of employing the letters *aleph, waw, yod,* to indicate vocalization was extended to include the weak *ayin,* with the following results: *aleph* for *a* as in "water" (Tiberian *kametz*), *waw* for *oo* as in "food," *yod* for *i* or *ee* as in "bee," *ayin* for *a* as in "far" or "fast" (Tiberian *patah* or *segol*). But in order to avoid the violation of "thou shalt not add," the letters were placed above the consonants the vocalization of which they were meant to denote, thus leaving the textual orthography intact. A manuscript in which this type of vocalization is still preserved was recently discovered by Kahle.[11] These Hebrew vowel-letters were later supplemented with what are probably conventionalized forms of a double yod ('') sign for *ei* and a double *waw* (:) sign for *o*; and eventually, after having gone through modification and simplification in form, there evolved what is now known as the Babylonian vowel-system. This system of employing superlinear vowel-letters was also in vogue in Syriac among the Jacobites of West Syria, but they used Greek instead of Syriac letters for this purpose.

In the Palestinian system, the use of which was discovered toward the end of the last century, as well as in our Tiberian system which seems based on it, the single dot is the basic unit. The varying position, as well as the change in the arrangement and a number of the dots, determines the sound-value of the vowels in all their variations, excepting the *patah* in the Tiberian system.[12] In the Palestinian system, however, the vowel-points are all superlinear.

The following is the table of vowel-signs in the three vowel-systems (Tiberian, top; Babylonian, middle; Palestinian, bottom):

$\bar{a}$	a	e	ei	i	o	u
⊤	⊤	⊤	'⊤, ⊤	'⊤, ⊤	⊺, ⊺	⊥, ⊤
≤	⋎	, ∴	∙∙	∴	∴	⊥
⊥	=	∙∙ , ∴	∴	∴	∴	∙∙

In the Babylonian system no distinction is made between *patah* and *segol*. In the Palestinian system the *tzerei* and the *segol* are represented by the same vowel.

The development of the system of dot and line for vowels appears fairly clear; it also explains the origin of the currently used names for the vowel-signs. The earliest device to indicate vocalization was the masoretic practice of placing a dot above or below the word, as the case might be, in order to differentiate roughly between two classes of vowels. Thus a dot above, called a *mille'el* (above) represented the more "muffled" vowels, that is, vowels formed by partly rounding or closing (Hebrew *kemitzah*) of the mouth, such as the sounds *o* in "song" or "open," and *u* in "put." A dot below, designated as *millera* (below) suggested the "clearer" vowels, that is, those produced by the wider opening (Hebrew *petihah*) of the mouth, as is the case of *a* in "far," the *e* in "end," the *ei* in "sleigh," or the *i* in "pin" and *ee* in "bee."

Another, perhaps later, stage was probably the scheme of employing a horizontal line (*patah*) to indicate the "clearer" vowels articulated by the wider opening of the mouth, while the same line with a dot below it (*kametz*) represented the "muffled" or "rounded" vowels. This type of *kametz,* with a detached dot below the line, is still to be found in some old manuscripts.

The terms *kemitza* or *kamtza* (contraction) and *petiha* or *patha* (opening), employed to designate the respective vowels, are apparently abbreviations of the teachers' instructions to their pupils, guiding them in correct vocalizations. In the case of the "clearer" or more "open" vowels, the teacher would direct his pupil in the Aramaic vernacular: *petah pumakh,* "open your mouth"; in the case of the "muffled" or "rounded" vowels, he would tell him *kemotz pumakh,* "contract" or "round out your mouth." These two terms subsequently came to denote more specific vowels, the *patah* standing for *patah* (*a*) and *segol* (*e*), the *kametz* for *kametz* (rounded *a*), and *tezere* (*ei*). In the writings of the early grammarians the *segol* is called *patah katan* (small *patah*) and the *tzerei, kametz katan* (small *kametz*). Finally, the *kametz* and *patah* were further delimited to designate, respectively, the two vowels now known by these names, while the other vowels were differentiated and referred to by their own specific names.

Still another scheme preliminary to vocalization was to place in the middle of a letter a point known as a *dagesh*,[13] designed to warn the reader against the danger of a likely mispronunciation. It was, therefore, employed under the following conditions:

1. To indicate a deviation from the general type. For example: nouns ending in *ah*, of the type *shanah* (year) or *etzah* (advice), have the accent on the final syllable. Hence one would expect to have the similar looking words like *lamah* (why, wherefore), *shamah* (there, thither), and *henah* (here, hither) similarly accented. However, contrary to expectations, in these words the accent is on the first syllable. In order to warn the reader of this deviation a dot is placed in the middle of the consonants *mem* and *nun*, as the case may be, following the accented syllable.

2. Hebrew does not usually record in script the double or long pronunciation of a consonant. Instead of writing the consonant twice, a dot is placed in the middle of it to signify its double or long sound.[14] Thus, in a word like *kallah* (daughter-in-law), only one *l* (*lamed*) is written, but a dot in the middle of it symbolizes its double sound. It should be noted, however, that this indication of double consonants is merely a relic of a time when these consonants were really pronounced long or double. In modern pronunciation of Hebrew these consonants with *dagesh* have a single sound, just as in the case of the English words "battle," or "happy," where the old spelling with double letters is merely reminiscent of the period when these letters were pronounced long or double. However, careful speakers and readers, especially some Readers in the synagogue or actors on the stage, still endeavor to retain the double pronunciation in these instances.

3. The letter *he*, when it occurs at the end of words and is vowel-less, is not sounded in Hebrew; it is there merely to serve the purpose of a vowel-letter, as has been stated above. But

there are a few instances in Hebrew where this final letter *he* has consonantal value. These include several verbs[15] and all cases of accented pronominal suffixes in the third person feminine singular, for example, *malkáh* (her king) as distinguished from *malká(h)* (queen, the feminine of *melekh*). Both words look orthographically alike, except that the former has a dot in the *he* to denote its consonantal sound. This dot is generally designated in Hebrew by the term *mappik* (that which brings out), referring to its function of "bringing out" the consonantal value of the *he*.

4. There was originally, during the pre-vocalic period, a dot in all consonants following a silent or vowel-less consonant. Such vocalization is still found in some manuscripts and is attested in masoretic notes.[16] This dot, or *dagesh*, apparently served the purpose of indicating the silent pronunciation of the preceding consonant.

After the more elaborate and specific vowel indications were introduced, this type of *dagesh* became superfluous, except in the six consonants *bet, gimel, dalet, kaf, pe, taw*. These six consonants have twofold pronunciations, the original hard or explosive, and the soft or spirantized pronunciation which evolved later.[17] Since these consonants retain their explosive pronunciation after vowel-less consonants, the *dagesh* is left there in order to remind the reader of their explosive character. It was later extended in its use to include all cases where the hard or explosive pronunciation of these letters was in effect, as at the beginning of a word.[18]

The Basis and Character of the Present Hebrew Vowel-System

Our system of vocalization seems to represent the final stage in these experimentations. Vestigial remains of the various steps in the process of experimentation are, of course, in evidence in this system; but in the main it is based on the dot—its varied position and number. The scheme is as follows:

1. One dot placed below the letter (⳱) represents the sound uttered with the narrowest space of lip opening, namely *i* (as

in "pin"), or *ee* (as in "bee"). Hence the Hebrew or Aramaic name for this vowel is *hirek,* "narrow splitting" or "gnashing" (of the teeth).

2. Next in order to the *hirek* is the *tzere,* represented by two horizontal dots below the letter ( ). It is sounded by a wider opening of the mouth, *ei* (as in "sleigh"), as its name indicates, "wide splitting" (of the teeth).

3. The vowel next in the scale is the *segol,* represented by three dots below the letter in the shape of a cluster of grapes ( ), as is indicated by its name *segol* (grape cluster). It is pronounced by a further widening of the mouth; namely, *e* as in "left."

4. The vowel sounded by the widest opening of the mouth is the *patah* (opening), which is graphically symbolized by the sign of a straight line under the letter ( ). It is pronounced like the *a* in "far."

The four vowels just mentioned constitute the "open" vowels, that is, vowels articulated by varying gradations of mouth opening. The next series of vowels is articulated by a gradual contraction or rounding out of the mouth. They are as follows:

1. *Kametz.* Its symbol was a *patah* with a dot below it placed under the letter ( ). In the course of time the dot became attached to the *patah,* yielding its present form ( ). There still are, as mentioned above, ancient manuscripts extant in which the dot of the *kametz*-sign is detached from the line, or *patah*-sign, above it. The name *kametz* means "contraction" or "rounding" (of lips). This vowel was apparently pronounced by the founders of this system like the *a* in "all."

2. Further rounding or contraction of the mouth is required by the sound *holem,* "strong" (rounding of the mouth), symbolized by a dot above the letter ( ). It is pronounced *o* as in "more."

3. The "lowest" or most "muffled" vowel-signs are the *shurek* ( ) "whistling," and *kibbutz* ( ) "gathering." Its sound-value is *u* as in "full," or as *oo* in "cool," requiring almost

complete rounding or contraction of the mouth. Graphically the vowel scheme may be represented by a triangle, as follows:

open vowels   rounded vowels[19]

This vocalic triangle is based on a well-established principle in phonetics, according to which all "culture languages," without exception, must have the three vowels on the apices of the triangle, namely, *a, u, i*. These are the original or primitive vowels. The vowels on the sides of the triangle are secondary and may be lacking in one or another language. In Hebrew the four secondary vowels on the sides evolved out of the three primitive vowels—*patah, kibbutz* or *shurek,* and *hirek*—and represent mere shadings or modifications of them.

To the right of the triangle, the vowels change from the *patah* downward by a progressive rounding of the mouth and consequent muffling of the sound. To the left, the change from the *patah* downward is in the direction of the progressive narrowing of the opening of the mouth and clearing of the sound.

The vowels on each side of the triangle tend to interchange in accordance with certain specific rules. Thus in the word *kol* (all): the *k* is vocalized with *holem* when it has the accent; upon the loss of the accent, the *holem* changes to *kametz* (e.g., kol-yisraél, "all of Israel"), or to *kibbutz* (kullánu, "all of us"). Similarly, the accented *tzere* in *leib* (heart) will change upon the loss of accent to *segol,* as in *leb-yám* (the heart of the sea: Exodus 15. 9), and to *hirek,* as in *libbi* (my heart). For the same reason, the pronunciation of the *kametz* varies, as will be noted below, from the sound *a* (as in "far") in the Sephardic pronunciation, to *o* (as in "or") in the Ashkenazic, and to *u* (as in "full") in the Polish-Ukrainian pronunciation. In like manner, no clear distinction is generally made in the Sephardic pronunciation between *tzere* and *segol,* both being pronounced *e*;

while the Polish-Ukrainian pronunciation of the *segol* vacillates between *ei* when the *segol* is in an accented open syllable (a syllable ending in a vowel), and *i* (as in "pin") when the *segol* is in an unaccented and closed syllable (a syllable ending in a consonant). Thus, in words like *mélekh* (king), *kéleb* (dog), *tzélem* (image), the first *segol* is pronounced *ei* and the second *i* (for example, *méilikh, kéiliv, tzéilim*). Incidentally, the first accented *segol* is pronounced *ei* also in some Sephardic communities.

English presents an illustration of a corresponding interchange or vacillation of sounds on either side of the triangle. Compare, for example, the phonetic variations of the *e* in words like "end" and "equal," or of the *ei* in words like "eight" and "leisure" in the two different pronunciations, or the phonetic vacillations of the *a* in "far," "fast" and "fare." Similarly, on the right side of the triangle we find the transition from the Anglo-Saxon *a* in words like "ham" (diminutive "hamlet") to Middle English *oo* ("hoom") and to modern English *o* (home), which transition constitutes a basic phonetic law. Compare also the sound changes of the *o* in "democracy," "democrat," "open" and "move."

Cantilations or Accent-Signs

In addition to vowel-signs, our biblical texts are provided with cantilation or accent signs. The primary purpose of these signs was to regulate the public reading of the sacred texts, indicating the manner in which these texts were to be chanted or recited. They served as musical notations, and originally were not placed necessarily on the tone-syllable.

Eventually, however, these signs came to serve two other purposes, namely, (a) the marking of the tone or accent of the individual word and (b) as punctuation marks, designating the logical or syntactical relation of single words to their immediate surroundings in the context of the phrase or sentence. As marks of the tone or accent they are placed above or below, as the case may be, the syllable which has the principal tone of the word. In the capacity of interpunctuation, the accent-marks cover a much wider range than our punctuation marks. They indicate not only varying degrees of separation (disjunctive accents), but also varying degrees of connection (conjunctive accents). They designate distinctly the phrasing or interrelationship of the words in the sentence, and they are thus very helpful in the interpretation of the text.

Ben Asher's text of the Bible, which has become our accepted text on the authority of Maimonides,[20] was already fully equipped with vowel-signs and accent-marks. The oldest available manuscript of the Bible, comprising the Prophets, now at Leningrad and bearing the date 916 C.E., exhibits vowel-signs as well as accents, but of the Babylonian or superlinear system.

Vocalized Mishnah Texts

Not only were the Bible texts equipped with vowel and accent signs, but also the old Mishnah texts. According to the testimony of Profiat Duran, a grammarian of the fourteenth century C.E., all old Mishnah texts were provided with vowels and accents; and the chants based on these accents were employed in the study of the Mishnah even as they were in that of the Bible.[21] He also refers to fully vocalized manuscripts of the Mishnah, "which were written about three hundred years ago in the valley of Himyar (חמאר)."[22] Similarly, Azariah de' Rossi (sixteenth century C.E.) reports having seen two such manuscripts of the Mishnah which were over five hundred years old.[23] Mishnah fragments with the Babylonian, also some with the Palestinian, vocalization were discovered not long ago by Paul Kahle.[24]

Differences in the Pronunciation of Vowels

There are, as was noted previously,[25] two main systems of Hebrew pronunciation, the Sephardic and the Ashkenazic. One of the major distinctions between these two systems is the pronunciation of the *kametz*. In the Ashkenazic pronunciation, employed mainly by the Jews of Germany (hence the term

The Masoretic Text as prepared by the Ben Asher School

From S. A. Birnbaum, *The Hebrew Scripts*, Fasc. 2, 92.

Ashkenazic, since Germany is designated Ashkenaz by medieval Hebrew writers) and of a large section of Eastern Europe, all *kametz* vowels are sounded alike; namely, *a* as in "all." In the Sephardic pronunciation, used chiefly among the Jews of medieval Spain (hence the designation Sephardic, Spain being referred to in Hebrew literature as Sepharad), their descendants in Holland, England, Italy, the Balkans, North Africa, Turkey, Syria and Palestine, a distinction is made in pronunciation between *kametz* in an open syllable, or in one bearing the accent even when closed, and the *kametz* in a closed unaccented syllable. The first is pronounced *a* as in "far," for example, אָדָם; the second is pronounced as *o* in "nor," for example, אָזְנִי . The second *kametz* is called by the medieval Spanish grammarians *kametz hatuf* (hurried *kametz*).

Origin of Sephardic and Ashkenazic Pronunciations

The available evidence points to the assumption that the so-called Ashkenazic pronunciation really stems from Palestine. It was the pronunciation in vogue there during the period when the vowel-systems were established. This pronunciation may have been carried to Germany and Eastern Europe, during the Middle Ages, by the Tiberian or Palestinian teachers, whose expertness in the "proper" pronunciation of Hebrew was at that time generally recognized among the Jews.

The Sephardic pronunciation, on the other hand, may have been imported into Spain from Babylon during the eighth to eleventh centuries. Indeed, the Jewish population of Spain during that period was mainly of Babylonian origin. By the end of the seventh century hardly any of the indigenous Jewish population was left in Spain. Some had been forced to adopt Christianity, others were exterminated, while still others had fled to other countries. A number of Babylonian Jews came to Spain with the invading Arabs and Berbers in 711, and waves of migration of Babylonian Jews continued to reach Spain during the following three centuries. The internal conflicts and consequent spiritual decline of the Jewish community in Baby-

Ionia, as well as the religious persecutions there during that period, forced a number of Jewish scholars to emigrate and to seek refuge in Spain. They laid the foundation for the Golden Age of Jewish scholarship, literature and Hebraic studies. They also may have set there, according to some reliable evidence, the standard for the pronunciation of Hebrew.

These assumptions have been challenged by some modern scholars, who maintain that the "Ashkenazic" pronunciation of the *kametz* was also current in Babylonia, while the "Sephardic" pronunciation was indigenous to Egypt, Spain, France, Italy and even Germany during the early medieval period. But the evidence adduced by them is inadequate and inconclusive. The whole problem regarding the origins of the various pronunciations is far from settled, and further evidence is needed for its solution. It is, however, certain that the Sephardic pronunciation was firmly established in Spain after the eleventh century.

After the Spanish expulsion (1492), a large number of the Spanish exiles migrated to Palestine. They brought with them some wealth, and they were equipped with worldly knowledge and abundant energy. They joined a group of their countrymen, who had emigrated from Spain about a century earlier as a result of the massacres there. By virtue of both their numerical superiority and their supremacy in worldly experience and knowledge, they imposed their customs, their way of life and their language on the Jewish community in Palestine. The Sephardic influence remained in vogue until the latter part of the nineteenth century.

When the East European Jews began to immigrate into Palestine under the influence of the Zionist movement, after their hopes for emancipation had been blasted by the Russian pogroms of 1881, they found there a relatively large and influential Sephardic community, employing the Sephardic pronunciation of Hebrew. In Jerusalem, for example, there were in the year 1856 four thousand Sephardim, comprising Jews from all over the Orient, and only about 1,700 Ashkenazic Jews. By 1880, the proportion of Ashkenazic Jews increased. Their number in Jerusalem grew to 6,660, but they were still a minority as compared with 7,200 Sephardic and Oriental Jews. Furthermore, the Sephardic community enjoyed a political status, accorded them by the Ottoman rulers of the country, which enhanced their prestige in the eyes of the Ashkenazic minority. The Sephardic rabbis were vested with official authority by the Turkish government to supervise the religious affairs of the entire Jewish community of Palestine, and the Sephardic Chief Rabbi bore the traditional title (which is retained to this day) *Rishon le-Zion* (the First of Zion).

Little wonder, then, that the Sephardic group was regarded as the more indigenous and their pronunciation of Hebrew as the more original and authentic, especially since it resembled that of Arabic in a good many respects. Furthermore, the young Zionist immigrants, in their desire to cut themselves loose from the *Galut* (lands of the exile), were eager to discard the Ashkenazic pronunciation on which they were reared and which they viewed as the symbol of the *Galut* spirit. Consequently, they adopted the Sephardic pronunciation with slight modifications, due to the inveterate Ashkenazic sound-patterns of which the speakers could not rid themselves. This pronunciation has become the symbol of the Hebraic revival also in the Diaspora and is constantly gaining vogue. The establishment of the new Israeli state bids fair to make this the predominant pronunciation all over the Diaspora.

There Is No Incorrect Pronunciation

The question one often hears raised is: which of these pronunciations is correct, the Ashkenazic or the Sephardic? The fact of the matter is that such a question is totally meaningless and irrelevant. One might as well ask: which of the pronunciations of English is correct, the British or the American; the one used in London, Edinburgh, New York, Boston, Atlanta, or anywhere else? There is no pronunciation which may be sanctioned as *correct* without regard to time and locality. The pronunciation of English, for example, was different in the days of Alfred the Great, of Chaucer, of Shakespeare and of George Bernard Shaw, as it is in different localities in modern times. The same applies to Hebrew. The language was pronounced differently by Abraham, by Moses, by Isaiah, by Ezra, by Hillel, by Maimonides, and so on, just as its pronunciations have differed and still differ in different localities. Which of these is the correct pronunciation?—One is as correct as the other for the particular time and the particular locality.

The Sephardic pronunciation, which apparently stems from Babylonia, approximates closely the pronunciation of Hebrew in Palestine during the Second Commonwealth, as attested by transcriptions and the Septuagint transliterations; while the Ashkenazic pronunciation corresponds more or less closely to the Palestinian pronunciation during the period of the masoretes. It is a well-known historical phenomenon that where the language is not employed as a vernacular, it tends to be conservative and resists changes and innovations. Hence, the Hebrew in the Babylonian Talmud is generally more bookish and more classical than that in the Palestinian Talmud in its orthography, grammatical constructions and syntax. In Palestine, Hebrew must have been more or less alive as a vernacular; it therefore liberally admitted changes and modifications in these areas. Numerous examples may be cited in corroboration of this assertion.[26]

Which of these pronunciations are we to adopt? The answer cannot be given on the basis of *correctness,* but on that of expediency and status. If we regard Israel as the spiritual center of Judaism and want to establish and maintain intimate contact with that country, we should perhaps adopt the Israeli pronunciation of the language. There is, however, little doubt that, despite all attempts at unification in pronunciation, differences will eventually evolve and persist in the various localities of the Diaspora, with the result that the native Israeli will be able to identify by his "accent" the land from which the Hebrew-speaking Jewish visitor is hailing.

As a matter of fact, there is no uniform Sephardic pronunciation, just as there is no single Ashkenazic pronunciation. There are several phonetic variations in each of these pronunciations. There are wide divergencies in the Ashkenazic pronunciation among the Jews of Germany, Galicia, Poland, the Ukraine and America. There are also a number of phonetic variations in the Sephardic pronunciation.

It is certainly incorrect to maintain that the present pronunciation of Hebrew in Israel is purely Sephardic. It is, in effect, composed of both Ashkenazic and Sephardic elements, with a predominance of Sephardic features only in the pronunciation of the vowels and the letter *taw*. It would take us too far afield to discuss here the phonetic deviations in the Israeli pronunciation from that employed by the Sephardic Jews of Morocco, Gibraltar, the Balkans, or Iraq. In all likelihood, the pronunciation of Hebrew in Israel itself is bound to be influenced by all the significant immigrant groups of which its present population is composed.

CHAPTER SIX
HOW THE STUDY OF HEBREW
GRAMMAR BEGAN AND DEVELOPED

The Age of Hebrew Grammar

The medieval period in Spain is usually referred to, in Jewish literature, as "the Golden Age" in the history of the Diaspora, and with good reason. It was an age rich in poets, philosophers, moralists and scientists. Jews have always looked back on that period with pride and have found in it inspiration and stimulation.

But perhaps the greatest literary-scientific contribution of that age was in the field of Hebrew grammar. The study of Hebrew grammar was easily the most widespread pursuit among scholars and students of all fields, and the literary output in this special field has never since been rivaled or equaled either in terms of quantity or in those of quality and originality. Hence that period may reasonably be designated also as "the Golden Age of Hebrew Grammar."

Beginnings of Hebrew Grammar

Why this interest in Hebrew grammar at that time? Where did this interest spring from? What were its sources? An attempt will be made in this chapter to analyze the sources of this grammatical interest and to trace the course of its manifestation.

The tenth century marked a turning point in Hebrew and biblical studies. Original masoretic researches reached their high water-mark in Palestine in the works of Ben Asher, a famed contemporary of Saadia (882-942). The vowel-system became definitely established, with the Tiberian system predominating. Students of Hebrew then began to direct their attention to purely grammatical problems, without regard to their implications for biblical exegesis.

Occasional grammatical observations are to be found already in the Talmud and the Midrashim.[1] The masoretic notes and comments, likewise, contain a number of significant grammatical remarks. Considerable grammatical material is found in the *Sefer Yetzirah,* an anonymous ancient kabbalistic work. But it was not until Saadia that Hebrew grammar was treated as an independent science, and not merely as an aid to the clarification of biblical texts. This versatile scholar laid the foundation for the scientific movement in Hebrew philology. Although most of his grammatical works were lost many centuries ago, his observations on grammar have come down to us through the works of his successors, who quoted him extensively, especially through the commentaries and grammatical writings of Abraham ibn Ezra (1092-1167), who revered him and regarded him as the "chief spokesman everywhere."[2]

Saadia was prompted to undertake the task of writing Hebrew grammar, as he himself testifies in his introduction to his *Agron* (lexicon, dictionary), because he was irked by the ignorance of the language and by the disregard for grammatical accuracy among the Hebrew writers and poets of his day. His work was, accordingly, designed to guide and aid these writers in the correct use of the language.

One of the major contributions by Saadia in the field of Hebrew grammar was a work in Arabic, entitled *Kutub al-Lughah* (Books on the [Hebrew] Language). This book, consisting of twelve "books" or parts, must have treated Hebrew grammar extensively and comprehensively and must have exercised a tremendous influence on the early progress of Hebrew grammar. Unfortunately, it disappeared from circulation early in its career. Grammarians of the eleventh and twelfth centuries, such as Ibn Janah and Ibn Ezra, referred to it but had no direct access to it. Their information of its contents was based on secondary sources. Until recently, our only sources bearing on the contents of this book were quotations by Saadia himself in his commentary on *Sefer Yetzirah,* criticisms (*Teshubot*) of his views by his pupil Dunash ben Labrat and by R. Mebasser (Mubassir?), and a rejoinder to Dunash's criticisms by Ibn Ezra. Recently, however, the late Professor Solomon L. Skoss of Dropsie College brought to light a fragmentary text of this work, based on manuscripts available in the Leningrad Public Library, the Bodleian Library at Oxford and the Taylor-Schechter Genizah Collection at Cambridge. Skoss also succeeded in completing before his death the preparation of a book, entitled *Saadia Gaon, the Earliest Hebrew Grammarian,* in which these manuscripts are analyzed and illuminated. It was published posthumously by Dropsie College.

Reasons for Interest in Grammar

As long as the writers confined themselves to conventional themes, such as liturgical compositions and legal discourses, the available vocabularies, idioms and word-forms in the Bible and the Talmud were adequate and could be readily employed as vehicles for self-expression. When, however, the writers began to deviate from the conventional themes, whether because of the influence of the Arabic culture of medieval Spain or as a result of independent creative urges, a departure from the stereotyped linguistic pattern became essential. New words had to be coined and new word-forms had to be constructed. Since Hebrew was not the vernacular of the people, ignorance of grammar was proving a most serious handicap and threatened to corrupt the language. Even some of the grammarians of that period fell into glaring etymological errors; and they were criticized severely on that account by their colleagues.

As time went on, the philological movement initiated by Saadia gathered momentum, especially under the spur of Arabic philological pursuits and the urge for literary and religious expression in Hebrew. The rise of the Karaite sect (toward the end of the eighth century), which rejected rabbinic tradition as expressed in the Talmud and emphasized the diligent scrutiny of the Bible as a basis for its tradition, was also a significant factor in focusing the attention of Hebrew scholars on a more searching study of the languages of the Bible. The knowledge of Hebrew grammar, consequently, became a vital need. Grammatical accuracy served as a criterion for the recognition of the merits of literary and religious compositions, and grammatical knowledge constituted a badge of honor and the measure of Jewish learning and scholarship. Interest in Hebrew grammar was, therefore, not confined to professional grammarians, but gained vogue among poets, philosophers and even statesmen. The celebrated statesman and talmudist Samuel ha-Nagid (993-1056), the eminent physician and distinguished poet Judah Halevi (1086-1141), the brilliant philosopher and poet Solomon ibn Gabirol (1021-1069), and others, all concerned themselves with Hebrew grammatical problems to a greater or lesser degree and wrote about them more or less extensively. Ibn Gabirol wrote a grammatical work in verse, entitled *Anak* (Necklace).

The study of Hebrew grammar as an independent science was pursued with zeal and profundity by Saadia's immediate successors. An important lexical work by Menahem ben Saruk (910-970), entitled *Mahberet,* inaugurated Hebrew grammatical research on Spanish soil and provoked a vehement attack by a pupil of Saadia, Dunash ben Labrat (920-990), a brilliant grammarian. Dunash pointed out many errors in Menahem's work, and he advanced views which already forecast the triliteral theory,[3] later scientifically and systematically expounded by Judah Hayyuj (ca. 1000 C.E.), one of Menahem's disciples.

Nature of the Hebrew Stem

In order to appreciate Hayyuj's monumental contribution to Hebrew grammar, a word about the unique nature of the Hebrew, or Semitic, stem is apropos. Stems in Hebrew, as in other Semitic languages, from which nouns and verbs are derived, consist of consonants. Meaning, as we have seen, depends essentially on these consonants. The vowel sounds, which in Indo-European languages are generally on a par with the consonants as regards their essential role in the stem or root, play a minor part in the Hebrew word; they merely serve to indicate different shadings of the inherent meaning. Only in a few instances does English offer a parallel which may serve as an illustration. For example: in the word "sing," the change in vowels results in such modifications as "sang" and "sung," as well as in the nominal form "song." In this instance, the consonants *s,n,g,* may be said to constitute the essential parts of the stem, or the root-letters. In Hebrew and in all other Semitic languages this characteristic is regular in all words. The consonantal stem is the basis of both nouns and verbs. A change in vowels will transform an active into a passive verb, or a verbal into a nominal form. Thus the consonantal stem *ktb* will yield such forms as *katab* (wrote), *koteb* (writes), *katub* (written), *ketab* (script), and a host of other forms, in all of which the concept of "writing" is inherent. These basic consonants which are never dropped in all the modifications of the word were designated by the medieval Hebrew grammarians the *shoresh* (radix, root). It therefore became customary among Christian grammarians to refer to these letters as "radicals," or "root-letters."

Furthermore, in Hebrew and in other Semitic languages the personal pronouns are integral parts of the word and are represented, with the single exception of the 3rd person, singular in the past tense, by prefixes or suffixes appended to the stem. The so-called tense of the verb is determined by the position of these appendages. The prefixes indicate a future tense, while the suffixes indicate a past tense.[4] Thus, in *lamadta* (you learned), the suffix *ta* (an abbreviation of *attah*, "you" or "thou") attached to the stem *lmd* suggests a past tense, while in *tilmad* (you will learn) the prefix *ti* (likewise an abbreviation of *attah*) transforms this verb into a future tense.

In addition to prefixes and suffixes, infixes are sometimes inserted in the Hebrew word in order to lend it a different shade of meaning. This infix consists of doubling the second radical by putting a dot (*dagesh*) in it. Thus *limmed* (he taught or caused to learn) is but a modification of the stem *l(a)m(a)d* (learned), and *kitteb* (he wrote busily or diligently) is derived from the stem *k(a)t(a)b* (he wrote).

The stem of a word is accordingly determined by removing the prefixes, infixes and suffixes. In the majority of cases the triliteral basis of the word is quite evident. The residual number of radicals clearly amounts to three. In a good many instances, however, the number of these radicals seems to be reduced to two and even to one. Thus, for example, in *wa-yet* (Exodus 9.23) "and he stretched out" (form of the verb *natah*), the stem would be only *t,* since this letter alone remains after the prefixes have been removed. Similarly in the case of the verb *'afah* (he baked), the *f* is the only consonant which remains permanently in the various inflections and therefore appears to be the only stem-letter. Thus in *wa-tofehu* (1 Samuel 28.24), "and she baked it," the *f* is the only stem-letter that remains after the removal of prefixes and suffixes.

Hence all the predecessors of Hayyuj, with the exception of Dunash, who on occasion had an insight into the triliteral basis of the Hebrew stem, operated with the idea of biliteral and even uniliteral stems. These grammarians failed to recognize the special character of assimilated stems, such as have a *nun* as the first radical, in which case the vowel-less *nun* is dropped and assimilated to the subsequent letter, with the result of doubling it and indicating this doubling by a *dagesh* (a dot) in this letter. Thus in *yiggash* (יִגַּשׁ: he will approach), from the stem *ngsh*, the first *g* actually represents the first radical *n,* which was dropped because of its being vowel-less.[5] Nor were these grammarians able to comprehend the nature of the weak verbs, such as have one of the letters *aleph, he, waw, yod* as a radical, which is occasionally omitted in the inflections. Now these omissions follow definite phonetic principles, and the dropping of the letter in no way detracts from its essential role as a radical.

Although Dunash had a glimpse into the operation of these phonetic principles, Hayyuj is undoubtedly entitled to the credit of being the first grammarian to observe the overall pattern of triliterality in Hebrew, and he thus laid the foundation for the science of Hebrew grammar.

The theory of triliterality in the Hebrew stem (and in the stem of Semitic languages generally) is universally accepted by modern grammarians, with minor modifications. But a great many triliteral stems may be traced to a common biliteral base; indeed, according to some grammarians all triliteral stems are derived from biliterals. This is particularly evident in the case of stems that include one weak consonant (*aleph, he, waw, yod*), or when the second and third radical are identical. Thus the stems *d(a)kh(a)h, d(a)kh(a)', d(u)wkh, d(a)kh(a)kh* may all be traced to the basic root *d(a)kh,* connoting the idea of *breaking, striking.* In other instances the biliteral base is almost equally clear, especially if we take into consideration the phonetic laws which operate in the interchange of kindred consonants, that is, consonants pronounced by the same organs of speech. A series of words, all signifying the idea of *cutting, carving,* such as *katzah, katzatz, katzab, katza', katzar, katab, katal, katar, kataf, gazar, gazaz, gaza', gazam, gadad, gada', gadar, gadah,* etc., may all be traced back to a common biliteral basic root.

Differing Theories of Hebrew Stems

Although Hayyuj's view was universally adopted by the subsequent grammarians, his disciples diverged in their interpretation of the master's ideas. Nor was his triliteral theory consistently accepted. The versatile and brilliant statesman, talmudist, soldier and poet, Samuel ha-Nagid, found time amidst his multifarious duties and occupations to engage in verbal clashes on grammatical issues with the profound grammarian Jonah ibn Janah (995-1050) and to write, according to Ibn Ezra's testimony, twenty two books "of supreme quality" on Hebrew grammar.[6] The monumental works of Jonah ibn Janah, who was a physician by profession, have been preserved in the main, probably because they had been translated from the Arabic into Hebrew and had thus received official traditional sanction, as it were, while those of the Nagid were lost. Fortunately, a few fragments were recently discovered. A number of quotations from his writings are also to be found in the works of Ibn Ezra and others. But even from these fragmentary remains it is evident that he was an exceedingly ingenious grammarian. In point of fact, some of his grammatical theories anticipate some very important discoveries in Hebrew grammar recently made.

Controversy between Samuel ha-Nagid and Jonah ibn Janah

The grammatical controversy between Ibn Janah and Samuel ha-Nagid is recounted at some length in the writings of a number of medieval Hebrew grammarians.[7] Samuel ha-Nagid, apparently aroused by Ibn Janah's criticism of some of the views of his teacher, Judah Hayyuj, sent a messenger from Granada to Saragossa, the place of Ibn Janah's residence, charged with the task of challenging Ibn Janah to a verbal combat on certain grammatical issues and of exposing publicly the "fallacy" of his theories. In Saragossa, the messenger stayed at the home of a communal leader in that city, named Abu Soleiman ben Taraka, a friend of Ibn Janah. A public reception was arranged in honor of the visitor, to which Ibn Janah was invited. The latter, without suspecting the chief purpose of the gathering, accepted the invitation. During the reception, the visitor began to inveigle Ibn Janah gradually and subtly into a discussion. Some of the questions raised by him were readily disposed of and adequately answered by Ibn Janah. But others followed, and Ibn Janah, unprepared for this barrage of questions, was befuddled, and he promised to reply at some future time.

He did so and sent his reply to the visitor. The latter, however, superciliously remarked that it would be wiser for Ibn Janah to withhold his reply until the Nagid's book was published, where he would find even more serious criticisms leveled against him. This Ibn Janah refused to do. He issued his reply in book form and called it *Kitab al-Taswiya* (The Book of Reprisal). After the publication of the Nagid's attack on him, Ibn Janah retorted with a violent counterattack in a book which he called *Kitab al-Tashwir* (The Book of Confounding). Ibn Janah was very proud of this work, and he frequently referred to it in glowing terms,[8] but, unfortunately, only a fragment of it is now extant.

The points at issue in this controversy seem trifling indeed to most of us, but not so to the Jewish physician of Saragossa, or to the Jewish vizir, the Prime Minister of the King of Granada, who was in charge of all political, military and financial affairs of his country. A principle in the structure of the Hebrew language or the grammatical analysis of a certain biblical form, whether a certain category of forms belongs to one conjugation or to another, and other such matters were no less vital and all-absorbing to the vizir of Granada than some of the paramount issues relative to his official responsibilities, which he discharged scrupulously and efficiently.

The Dissemination of Grammatical Studies

Most of the works on Hebrew grammar were written at that time in Arabic and were, therefore, inaccessible to the Jewish scholars of France, Italy and Germany. But that traveling scholar, Abraham ibn Ezra, writing in Hebrew, served as the intermediary, and through his copious writings and commentaries, he popularized the ideas of the Spanish Hebrew grammarians among the Jews of non-Arabic speaking countries. The translations into Hebrew of Hayyuj's work by Moses ibn Gikatilia and of Ibn Janah's works by Judah ibn Tibbon also aided in the dissemination of grammatical knowledge among the Jews of these countries. The subsequent grammatical works of outstanding merit during the medieval period were nearly all written in Hebrew.

The Contributions of David Kimhi

These philological pursuits reached their culmination in the writings of the Kimhi family, especially those of the younger member, David (about 1160-1235), popularly called *RaDaK* (רד״ק), representing the initial consonants of the name Rabbi David Kimhi. His works, though inferior in originality and profundity to those of Hayyuj and Ibn Janah, eclipsed and almost entirely displaced the works of the earlier masters. Even so thorough a grammarian as Fr. Eduard Koenig made constant reference to David Kimhi in his monumental work, in three volumes, *Lehrgebäude der Hebraischen Sprache,* less than a hundred years ago. As an indication of the esteem in which Kimhi was held by posterity we may cite the following mishnaic dictum which was applied to his works: *'im 'ein kemah 'ein Torah,*[9] and interpreted in the sense of "without the works of Kimhi no knowledge of the Torah is possible." His comprehensiveness, simplicity, conciseness and systematic organization are chiefly responsible for the popularity of his work. His main original contribution to Hebrew grammar was the development and systematization of the theory suggested by his father, Joseph, relative to the subdivision of the vowels into five long and five short.[10]

David Kimhi is to be noted particularly for his progressive and vital attitude toward the development of the Hebrew language. Besides taking frequent cognizance of the grammatical forms and constructions found in post-biblical literature, he often sanctioned and suggested the creation of new forms and conjugations as long as they conform to the pattern of the Hebrew language and grammar. Thus he criticized the grammarians, including his own father, for objecting to usages which deviate from those found in the Bible. For example, the word *hekitz* is always employed in the Bible in the intransitive sense (that is, "he awoke"), never in the transitive (awaken or arouse). His father, Joseph Kimhi, therefore, criticized the transitive use of this verb in the liturgical formula *ha-mekitz nirdamim* (who awakens those that slumber), and he also attacked an "eminent linguist" (Moses ibn Ezra) for using this conjugation in the same sense in one of his poems. David Kimhi maintained that, since there is no other form of this stem in the transitive, it is perfectly legitimate to use it both in the transitive and the intransitive sense, even though it does not occur thus in the Bible. He also proposed the coining of new conjugations, whenever needed, if some suggestive basis for such coinage can be found either in the Bible or in the Talmud. He even sanctioned the use of forms which occur in the Talmud but are in violation of the laws of biblical Hebrew grammar.[11]

Kimhi himself made no claim to originality. In the introduction to his Hebrew Grammar he modestly assumed the role of a "gleaner after the reaper," whose task it was to compile and present succinctly and simply the voluminous scientific findings of his predecessors. But Kimhi was more than a mere compiler. He was thoroughly conversant with the entire range of Hebrew language and literature. He had a fine sense of system and organization, deep insight into the language and its structure, and splendid critical acumen. All this equipment stood him in good stead in his undertaking. In an independent and rigorous manner he examined and evaluated the rich harvest of the grammatical research of his predecessors, presenting it systematically and concisely, selecting and rejecting, advancing some original ideas and adding some grammatical material of his own.

Since David Kimhi's works mark the closing of the "Golden Era" of Hebrew medieval philology, it might be appropriate to pause here and summarize the contributions of the medieval Hebrew grammarians to the science of Hebrew grammar. Such a summary, in the space allotted here, will have to be presented in general and broad outlines and will have to include only the highlights of these contributions.

Medieval Grammatical Studies Summarized

One of the most notable and helpful contributions in the field of Hebrew grammar was the triliteral theory as presented by Hayyuj. This theory shed significant light on the nature and structure of the Hebrew language, particularly as related to the "assimilated" verbs (those which begin with the letter *nun*) and the weak verbs (those having *aleph, he, waw, yod* as one of the root-letters). Without an understanding of the character of these verbs, Hebrew writers were groping in the dark whenever they ventured to turn aside from the set models and familiar constructions found in the Bible or in the Talmud. In their ignorance of these grammatical principles, the early *paytanim* (authors of religious poems) who preceded the grammarians, and even some of the later *paytanim* who were ignorant of grammar, fell into some flagrant errors in verbal and nominal constructions. Thus one of the best known *paytanim*, Eliezer ha-Kalir (about 700 C.E.), coined freely such forms as *pan* (for *panah*, "he turned"), *as* (for *asah*, "he did"), *patzti* (for *patziti*, "I uttered," "spoke"), *bat* (for *hibbit*, "he looked"), *gad* (for *higgid*, "he said"). He simply failed to realize that all these verbs are triliterals which belong to different conjugations. He was also ignorant of the rules which govern the dropping of one of the radicals on occasion. Since he found in the Bible such forms as *panu* (they turned), *asu* (they did), *patzu* (they uttered, spoke), in all of which the suffix *u* indicates third person, plural, he inferred that the respective stems are, by removing this suffix, *pan, as, patz*. Similarly the biblical forms *hibbit* (he looked) and *higgid* (he said), in which the syllable *hi* is a prefix, suggested to him a biliteral stem *bat* and *gad*. Even such a splendid Hebraist as Menahem ben Saruk was criticized by his own disciple, Hayyuj, for employing erroneously verbal forms of this category and for failing to understand the character of these weak verbs.[12]

The significance of this theory in promoting the progress of the study of the Hebrew language can hardly be overestimated. It enabled grammarians to envisage the Hebrew language as a design in which the structure of nouns and verbs fitted in a perfect mosaic fashion. Later grammarians differed with Hayyuj in regard to minor details of this theory. Some verbs, like those having a *waw* or a *yod* as the middle root-letter, were regarded by them as having a biliteral stem. However, these are minor differences of opinion, and they do not detract from the tremendous significance of this theory in explaining the nature of the Hebrew verbs, particularly those of the assimilated and weak stems.

Another significant contribution by the medieval grammarians is the arrangement of the paradigms, that is, models of verbs and their various inflections in the different conjugations. In order to appreciate the significance of this contribution one must again recall the consonantal character of the Hebrew language, which has already been discussed. Once the nature of a given consonantal stem is understood, it is possible to construct a long series of derivative forms, all having the same basic meaning. The various semantic shadings and modifications, as well as the differences in person, number and gender, are indicated by mere changes in vowels or by additions of prefixes and suffixes, as the case may be. Thus of the stem *mzg* one may build the following variety of conjugations: (1) *mazag* (blended or mixed), (2) *nimzag* (was blended), (3) *mizzeg* (integrated, clarified or analyzed), (4) *muzzag* (was integrated, clarified or analyzed), (5) *himzig* (caused to be blended), (6) *humzag* (was made to blend), (7) *hitmazzeg* (became fused together). One may also add a number of nominal forms such as *mezeg* (mixture, temperament), *mezigah* (blending), etc.

These seven conjugations are the most common in biblical Hebrew and are known as *binyanim* (literally in Hebrew, building forms). There are also a number of other *binyanim* in the Bible which are rare and no longer functional.

All the *binyanim,* with one exception, derive their names from the form assumed in each particular conjugation by the verb *pa'al* (he did), a paradigm borrowed by the early medieval Hebrew grammarians from Arabic. The choice of this paradigm was obviously motivated by its meaning, since it connotes action or doing, and therefore most appropriately represents the verb.

The first of the *binyanim* is accordingly called *pa'al,* or more generally *kal* (light, simple), since it constitutes a pure stem, without any formative additions and therefore serves as the ground-form for all the other *binyanim.* The second is designated *niph'al,* and is frequently the passive of the *kal.* The third conjugation is known as the *pi'el* and is usually intensive in sense, while the fourth is the passive of this conjugation and is known as the *pu'al.* The fifth is the *hiph'il* and is often causative in meaning, while its passive is the sixth conjugation, the *hoph'al.* The seventh and last conjugation is the *hitpa'el*—a reflexive conjugation.

In all formations of the various *binyanim* the basic meaning is more or less in evidence. Consequently, an understanding of the nature of the *binyanim* opens up the wide vistas of the language and provides an insight into its linguistic pattern. Equipped with this understanding it is possible to get along on a comparatively small basic vocabulary and to manipulate the language with relative ease and facility.

Saadia was the first to attempt the arrangement of paradigms. He, however, confined himself only to two conjugations, namely, the first and fifth of those named in the discussion above. The standard arrangement of the seven conjugations which is in use among Hebrew grammarians, with slight modifications, to this day, is to be credited to Moses Kimhi, the older brother of RaDaK, who was also his teacher.

Very few verbs occur in the Bible in all the seven *binyanim.* But the tendency in modern Hebrew is freely to coin new formations, on the basis of existing verbal stems, in consonance with these *binyanim.* The passive conjugations *pu'al* and *hoph'al* are infrequently employed in modern Hebrew, but under the influence of mishnaic Hebrew new conjugations have gained currency, such as *nitpa'el* (a blend of the *niph'al* and *hitpa'el*), *shiph'el* (a Ugaritic and Akkadian equivalent of the *hiph'il*, also found to a limited degree in Biblical-Aramaic), and its passive forms *shuph'al* and *nishtaph'al*.

The *shiph'el* conjugation is often employed in mishnaic and in modern Hebrew, alongside the *hiph'il*, in order to indicate a variation or different shade in meaning. Thus, alongside the biblical form *he'ebid* (caused to work, or, to serve), *hiph'il* of *'abad* (worked, served), mishnaic Hebrew has the *shiph'el* form *shi'bed* (subjugated, subjected), as well as the passive forms *meshu'bad* (subjected) and *nishta'bed* (was subjected).

It is impossible to enumerate here the manifold grammatical discussions by the medieval grammarians on the various aspects of the Hebrew language. There is hardly a phase of the language which escaped their scrutiny and comment. Theirs was a labor of love. After having succeeded in unravelling some etymological difficulty, Ibn Janah waxes ecstatic and proclaims proudly: "This is one of the wonderful things we have discovered by the grace of God . . . after much labor, effort and study, and after searching day and night, so that we expend on oil (in burning the midnight oil) twice as much as other people spend on wine."[13] With selfless devotion, untiring assiduity and unremitting zeal, they applied themselves to the pioneering task of analyzing and investigating every aspect of the Hebrew language in the field of sound and pronunciation, word-formation and structure. They left a rich heritage which, unfortunately, has not yet been fully exploited, although splendid efforts in this field of research have been made by such profound scholars as Bacher, Poznanski, Joseph and Hartwig Derenbourg, Kokowzoff, and the late Solomon Skoss.

Interest in Grammatical Research Passes from Jews to Christians

The reaction which set in against the works of Maimonides toward the end of David Kimhi's days, and which the latter endeavored valiantly but vainly to offset, marked the waning of all rationalistic pursuits, including grammatical research, and of any studies outside of the Talmud. Furthermore, the deterioration of the Jewish economic and political position in southwestern Europe, resulting largely from persecution and from the internal rivalries and quarrels within the Jewish communities, led to a serious decline among Jews in general cultural interests and activities. The Jewish people, faced by an accelerated rise in jealousies and prejudices among the Christian populace and in persecutions and repressions by the Catholic Church, sought shelter in their own shell, as it were. Their interest shifted accordingly from the luxury of pursuing poetry, philosophy and grammar to the necessity of fortifying themselves by means of a better understanding of Judaism and a stronger faith in their religious destiny. This interest found its outlet in the study of the Talmud and of the mystic philosophy of the Kaballah, which began to flourish around that period.

Most of the Jewish scholars of the subsequent generations regarded the study of grammar as a waste of time, and some even saw in it a lack of piety. "Shame on those that prattle and chatter regarding the words of the Torah," cried Leon de Modena (1571-1649), "but disparage the study of grammar by claiming that the study is a waste of time! . . . This is unwise; it is merely intended to hide from us their nakedness (that is, ignorance)."[14] Even the study of the Bible began to be regarded as of secondary importance and was dwindling to such an extent that a German rabbi of the seventeenth century complained that there were rabbis in his generation "who had never in their lifetime seen a text of the Bible."[15] Apparently the Talmud and rabbinic studies absorbed their entire attention.

As interest in Hebrew grammar waned among Jewish scholars it began to flourish among the Christians. The Renaissance which, initiated in Italy, grew apace and crossed the Alps into the Netherlands, France and Germany, reached its peak during the latter half of the fifteenth and the first half of the sixteenth centuries. This mighty intellectual movement brought in its wake the Reformation which split the Christian world into two warring camps.

One of the main motives of the Reformation was to break the shackles of the Church's authority and to reassert the right of the individual to search on his own for the word of God, without the Church as intermediary. They therefore turned to the study of Hebrew as the master key to the Judaic background of Christianity, in order to discover for themselves the pristine meaning of the Bible and the original principles of the Christian faith. Many of the early leaders of the Reformation achieved considerable proficiency in Hebrew and familiarity with its literature.

The center of interest in Hebrew grammar and lexicography accordingly shifted from Jewish to Christian scholars. The father of Hebrew grammar among the Christians was the famous humanist Johann Reuchlin (1455-1522). His book, *De Rudimentis Hebraicis,* ushered in the Hebrew philological movement among the Christians. This movement was accelerated by the itinerant Jewish scholar Elias Levita (1469-1549). Through his personal contact with the Christian scholars and by means of his books, some of which were translated into Latin by his pupil, Sebastian Münster, Levita became the exponent of the Kimhian School to the Christians and he set the Kimhian stamp on succeeding grammatical works. The Christian grammarian, whose work enjoyed widest currency and influence, was Wilhelm Gesenius (1786-1842). His grammar and dictionary have appeared in numerous editions and adaptations.

The contribution of the Christian scholars to Hebrew grammar was considerable. They resumed the comparative study of Hebrew and Arabic, which had been interrupted after a promising beginning made by the early medieval Hebrew grammarians. The Christian grammarians extended these studies to include the other Semitic languages, and on the basis of these studies they succeeded in making some interesting discoveries. However, a good many of these "discoveries" had already been

made by the medieval Jewish grammarians, but had been forgotten because the works of these grammarians were not readily
accessible. Besides being unconversant with the Kimhian and
pre-Kimhian source materials of Hebrew grammar, the Christian Hebrew grammarians were also handicapped by the tendency to restrict themselves in their Hebrew studies to the language of the Bible. The language of post-biblical Jewish
literature was regarded by them as a variety of corrupted dialects, not deserving of serious study. These handicaps robbed
their work of progressive and dynamic value.

Revival of Interest in Grammar Among Jews

There was a renewed spurt of zeal for the study of the
Hebrew language and of Hebrew grammar among Jews during
the Haskalah period. A number of contributory factors stimulated and facilitated this renewed interest. There was, in the
first place, a general awakening of interest among the early
proponents of Haskalah (end of the eighteenth century) in the
renaissance of the Hebrew language and literature. Moses Mendelssohn and Naphtali Hertz Wessley issued urgent appeals
to instruct young children in the rules of Hebrew grammar.
Furthermore, in the Edict of Toleration granted by Emperor
Joseph II of Austria, Jews were permitted and encouraged to
avail themselves of the opportunities for general education extended to them. They were also urged to reform their school
system and their communal organization.

The cumulative effect of all this was soon evident. A curriculum for a new school in Vienna, prepared by three communal leaders in the year 1812, included among the subjects
for the second year the study of "Hebrew grammar beginning
with the inflections of nouns and verbs, and translation from
one language into another orally, in writing and by dictation."[16]
Isaac Hirsch Weiss (1850-1905) relates that in the elementary
school which he attended, about two hours a week were devoted
to the study of the elements of Hebrew grammar.[17]

Contributions to Hebrew Grammar during the Haskalah Period

The Haskalah movement was, however, with some rare exceptions, not productive of creative and original contributions either in the field of art or in that of science. Only two grammarians of that period made any notable and original contributions to the science of Hebrew grammar, namely, Samuel David Luzzatto (1800-1865) and Simhah Pinsker (1801-1864).

Luzzatto was a versatile scholar and author, endowed with keen linguistic insight and a passionate love for Hebrew and its literature. He was the first to make a thorough study of Aramaic, and as a result of his studies he arrived at the conclusion that both Aramaic and Hebrew stem from the same origin, but that Aramaic has preserved the original forms to a greater degree than Hebrew. He, accordingly, sought to explain many lexical and grammatical phenomena in Hebrew on the background of Aramaic, and not of Arabic, as the Christian grammarians had been attempting to do. Furthermore, he attacked the prevailing view among the grammarians of that period, who regarded the Hebrew language as a fossil tongue, preserved only in the Bible and arrested in its growth and development after the biblical period. Luzzatto contended vigorously that the Hebrew language continued to live long after that period, and that mishnaic Hebrew, far from being an artificial and corrupt dialect as maintained by most of the grammarians, was a live and dynamic tongue and constituted a normal evolutionary stage in the development of the Hebrew language.

Pinsker specialized mainly in the history of vocalization and of the Masorah. His discoveries served to clarify some obscure forms in Hebrew and to shed light on some interesting developments in Hebrew pronunciation, orthography and grammar.

For example, in both the Ashkenazic and Sephardic pronunciations, the *shurek* (‍), and the *kibbutz* (ֻ) are pronounced *oo* as in "cool." The Polish and Ukrainian Jews, however, made no distinction between the pronunciation of these two vowels and that of the *hirek* ($\leftarrow$), pronouncing all these vowels *ee* as in "bee." Thus, the Hebrew name *Shemuel* (Samuel) is pronounced by the Polish and Ukrainian Jews *Shemiel*. This difference in pronunciation is carried over also to Yiddish words. Thus, the German *butter* (English "butter") is pronounced in Lithuanian Yiddish *pooter* and in Polish-Ukrainian Yiddish *pitter*.

The pronunciation of the Polish-Ukrainian Jews is generally regarded as incorrect or corrupt. But language students cannot recognize a pronunciation employed by a large section of the population as "incorrect." How then did this difference in pronunciation arise?

As a solution to this problem, Pinsker offered a very plausible theory, according to which there was actually no pure *oo* sound in the Hebrew of ancient Palestine, but rather one resembling the German *ü* or French *u,* that is, a blend of *oo* and *ee.* This pronunciation, he maintained, was transmitted from Palestine to the Polish and Ukrainian Jews via Caucasia, the land of the Khazars, and Crimea; while the Sephardic Jews received their pronunciation of the *shurek,* or *kibbutz,* from the Babylonian Jews via Africa.[18] The Babylonian Jews, as was stated previously, are known to have exercised considerable influence on the Jews of Spain and to have laid the foundation of Jewish scholarship in that country, as a result of their immigration there during the eighth and eleventh centuries. The Sephardic influence seems to be evident in the Ashkenazic pronunciation of these two vowels by the Jews of Lithuania and other countries.

In the light of this theory Pinsker explained plausibly a great many "irregular" formations, as well as some orthographic confusions in the Bible. In corroboration of his theory he adduced proof from the Babylonian system of vocalization, of which he had made a rather exhaustive study.[19] His theory is also borne out by numerous instances in the orthography of the Bible and the Talmud, which seem to indicate a similarity in the pronunciation of the vowels *shurek* and *hirek* during the early history of the language.[20]

Pinsker also made a thorough study of the *dagesh* (the point in the middle of the Hebrew letter), the origin of which had been puzzling the grammarians. He advanced the theory that this sign had been invented by the teachers in the elementary schools, before our vowel systems were established, for the purpose of guarding their pupils against the danger of mispronunciation.[21] This plausible theory likewise sheds light on a number of difficulties in our present system of vocalization.

Modern Trends in Grammatical Studies

The trend among modern students of Hebrew grammar is to treat this subject historically and descriptively rather than prescriptively; that is, to trace the course of the development of the language during the various historical stages, within the sphere of the Semitic languages and in the light of general principles of linguistic science. Grammatical rules merely serve to describe the particular ways in which a language is employed at a given period, as well as the pattern according to which it evolves and changes. Rules of grammar are no more constant than the psychical processes governing linguistic development. An individual whim in the speech of a linguistic community may initiate deviations from the standard language which, in the course of time, are adopted by the community and become a new norm. Indeed, these deviations, or slight grammatical errors, are the milestones that mark the progress of a language.

Most of the modern grammarians, however, confine themselves to biblical Hebrew only and fail to take into account the later stages of the language evolved during the mishnaic, medieval and modern periods. Nor do they avail themselves to the fullest extent of the vast grammatical resources stored away in the Jewish, ancient and medieval writings. A truly scientific study of the Hebrew language under such limitations is hardly possible.

The notion that the life or growth of the Hebrew language was definitely arrested at a certain stage, which was followed by a period of decay and corruption, is responsible for misconceptions in Hebrew grammar among students of the Hebrew language and for some distorted views on the language. In point of fact, Hebrew never ceased to be the medium of written, if not oral, expression among the Jews, and Hebrew terms and processes of thought found their way into the various languages adopted by the Jews. The use of Hebrew in traditional houses of study and prayer has never been interrupted.

Linguistic study cannot therefore be scientific unless cognizance is taken of actual usage in all the successive stages in the process of the development of the language in question. To base the study of a language and its grammar exclusively on classical models handed down from antiquity is to violate a fundamental tenet in modern linguistics.

CHAPTER SEVEN
HOW WAS THE TEXT OF THE HEBREW BIBLE PRESERVED?

The Bible—Remnant of a Vast Hebrew Literature

With the exception of the few fragmentary documents mentioned in a previous chapter (III), the Bible remains the sole source of the early Hebrew language. A great many books now lost were written during the biblical period, some twenty of which are quoted in the Bible, such as *Sefer Ha-Yashar* (Joshua 10.13), *Sefer Milhamot Adonai* (Numbers 21.11), *Sayings of the Moshlim* (*ibid.*, 27), *Dibrei ha-Yamim le-Malkhei Yehudah* (1 Kings 14.29), *Dibrei ha-Yamim le-Malkhei Yisrael* (*ibid.*, 16.5), *Dibrei Shelomoh* (*ibid.*, 11.41), *Dibrei Nathan ha-Nabi* and *Dibrei Gad ha-Hozeh* (1 Chronicles 21. 29), *Midrash Iddo ha-Nabi* (2 Chronicles 13.22). Other books presumably composed during the biblical period are mentioned in the Talmud. These books must have been in vogue among the people, since some of the citations from them are fragmentary and even incomprehensible, as if the writer of the existing books of the Bible assumed the reader's familiarity with the context from which these excerpts were taken.

Some books written during the late biblical period disappeared in their original Hebrew form, but survive in translation; such are the books of the Maccabees and other books in the Apocrypha. One of these books, the Proverbs of Ben Sira, has been in part recovered in the original Hebrew from the Cairo Genizah (a repository of discarded Torah scrolls, books and papers), although some scholars question its authenticity as the original text.

It is safe to assume that the so-called *nebiei ha-sheker* (false prophets), some of whom are mentioned and quoted in the Bible, were literary people who wrote prophecies which were not inferior, from a literary point of view, to those included in our biblical text. But since these prophecies failed to materialize or to coincide with the accepted ethical, political, or religious standards of the authoritative Jewish leadership during the period of biblical canonization,[1] they were discarded into the limbo of spurious or "uninspired" writings. They were, therefore, "hidden away," that is, they were withdrawn from circulation and eventually disappeared. Even some of the biblical books, such as The Song of Songs, Ecclesiastes, Ezekiel, and Proverbs, were exposed to the danger of being excluded from the canon. Similarly the book of Job was subjected to scrutiny, because Job's religious motives had been challenged. Fortunately, the authority of some of the rabbis prevailed, so that these books were admitted into the canon and were thus saved for posterity. Other books, however, failed to meet the canonical standards and were excluded; they were consequently lost. Who can tell how serious this loss has been to Hebrew literature and language!

The wonder, however, is not that so many of the early Hebrew writings have been lost, but that so much has survived. The Bible, it must be remembered, is a book of great antiquity: parts of it are about thirty-five centuries old. For about three thousand years these ancient records were preserved only in manuscript form, prepared by the hands of copyists. The majority of the Bible manuscripts are of the twelfth and sixteenth centuries C.E., although there is one complete Bible manuscript dating from 1009 C.E. and another, containing the Prophets, dating from 916 C.E. (Both these manuscripts are in Leningrad.) References to other manuscripts are found in the writings of medieval scholars. The earliest scrap of Bible manuscript now extant is the Nash Papyrus,[2] probably of the first century C.E. This bit of parchment was found in Egypt some fifty-five years ago and brought to Cambridge, England, by Mr. Nash, whose name it bears. It contains the beginning of the *Shema'* (Deuteronomy 6.4-5) and the Ten Commandments in a version which is different from both that of Exodus (20. 2-17) and the one given in Deuteronomy (5.6-18). It seems somewhat of a conglomerate of both these versions, and it resembles largely the version which served as the basis of the Septuagint.

What is remarkable is the fact that all the manuscripts, regardless of the long intervals separating them, are substantially alike. Even the Samaritan text, which dates back to a very early period, probably not later than the period of Ezra (fifth century B.C.E.), differs little from our text. To be sure, a number of biblical citations given in the Talmud indicate slight deviations from our masoretic text. Similarly, a considerable number of biblical passages are quoted in medieval Jewish literature which are at variance with those found in our text. But in many instances these deviations may be explained by the fact that the rabbis and medieval scholars often quoted from memory, as is evidenced by occasional inconsistencies in their quotations.

The divergences exhibited in the manuscripts, as well as the deviations found in the biblical quotations in the Talmud and in medieval literature, are minor and insignificant, and we may regard our masoretic text as to all intents and purposes authentic. To quote Professor W. F. Albright, ". . . no comparable literary legacy from the past has come down to us so faithfully recorded and so little modified by the passage of time as the Bible."

The Rise and Purpose of the Targumim

How was this preservation of the genuine form of the biblical text achieved?

After the Jews were exiled from their native soil and their Temple was destroyed (586 B.C.E.), they began to turn to the Pentateuch and to the prophetic writings for inspiration and guidance. They would frequently gather in their meeting-places, especially on holidays and festivals, as well as on the Sabbath and on Monday and Thursday mornings (market days), to hear men well-versed in the knowledge of the Torah (Pentateuch) and the prophets read and interpret the "word of God." These neighborhood meetings, or 'edahs (congregations), which sprang up in every nook and corner, even in Jerusalem in the neighborhood of the Temple, formed the beginnings of the institution of the synagogue. Interpretations of the Torah were given in Hebrew as long as it was the spoken language. When Aramaic came into vogue, it supplanted Hebrew in the interpretations, since it was more readily understood by many in the audiences. Thus the Targumim (Aramaic translations) gradually evolved, such as the Targum Onkelos, Targum Yerushalmi and Targum Jonathan ben Uziel.[3] All the Targumim include layers dating back to a very early period, since for a long time they, too, were preserved only in oral form, and their appearance in written form centuries later was disapproved by the rabbis. When an Aramaic translation of the book of Job was brought to the attention of Rabban Gamaliel, the Elder, he ordered it immured beneath a layer of stones in the Temple, in order to put it out of circulation.[4] Even as late as the fourth century C.E., when Rabbi Samuel son of Isaac entered the synagogue and found a scribe reading from a written Targum, he criticized him on the principle of "things handed down by word of mouth must be transmitted orally, while that which is written might be written."[5]

The oldest and most authoritative of these Targumim is the Targum of the Pentateuch ascribed in the Babylonian Talmud to Onkelos the proselyte, who is said to have prepared his version under the supervision of Rabbi Eliezer and Rabbi Joshua (around the second century C.E.). Although the authenticity of this statement in the Talmud has been challenged, internal evidence does seem to point to the second century C.E. as the most likely period for the writing down or editing of this Targum.

The term *targum,* originally signifying a translation, took on a restricted meaning in talmudic and post-talmudic literature, and was applied exclusively to the Aramaic translation of the Bible. But the Targumim were more than mere translations; they actually represented the traditional interpretations of the Bible in vogue during the talmudic period, reflecting the homiletic and legal ideas as well as the folklore of that period. It was apparently in that manner that the Bible was taught and expounded to the masses and to the school children in the Aramaic vernacular most widespread during that time.

The Work of the Scribes and the Masoretes

But while the Targumim were designed to convey the meaning of the biblical texts, the original text of the Bible was not neglected. Indeed, it was studied, cherished and treated with great care and solicitude. The correct reading of the text claimed major attention and emphasis. This text was after all the source of Jewish inspiration, law and conduct. Any change in reading might entail serious consequences.

The men proficient in the correct reading and responsible for the preservation of the Bible were called *sofrim,* "scribes." They are already mentioned in the early books of the Bible (Judges 5.14), but in a secular sense, namely, as writing experts or secretaries. It was not until the period of Jeremiah that reference is made to the *sofrim* as writers or interpreters of the "Law of the Lord" (Jeremiah 8.8). Their activities must have extended during the Babylonian Captivity; and they must have been given special impetus and inspiration by Ezra, who was himself a "ready scribe" (*sofer mahir:* Ezra 7.6), "who had set his heart to seek the Lord, and to do it, and to teach in Israel statutes and ordinances" (*ibid.,* 10). He was accordingly regarded by the rabbis as almost equal in rank to Moses.

The task of these scribes was not limited to the reading, investigation and interpretation of the Bible; it included also the function of copying carefully the biblical texts and of preserving them in their original form. They were in effect the bearers of the oral tradition of the Law, as well as the guardian of its written form.

As the Oral Law progressed and expanded, the *tannaim* (teachers) came upon the scene, whose function it was to study and investigate the Torah, as well as to teach the Oral Law in the advanced academies. The task of the scribes was accordingly restricted to copying and teaching the Scriptures in the synagogue and the elementary school, which was designated *Bet- ha-Sofer* (the House of the Scribe) or *Bet- ha-Sefer* (the House of the Book).

The scribes were expected to be thoroughly familiar with the authentic manuscripts of the Bible and to study the biblical texts in the minutest detail, even to the extent of counting the number of words and letters. This process of counting words and letters in the biblical texts was resorted to, when need arose, even in the advanced academies. To cite an example: a question was raised in the Academy as to whether the letter *waw* in the word גחון (Leviticus 11.42) marked the midpoint in the number of the letters in the Pentateuch. The rabbis did not move from their seats, we are told, until the matter was settled by a count of letters in the scroll of the Pentateuch which was brought in for that purpose.[6]

According to a talmudic statement,[7] there were kept in the Temple Court three scrolls of the Torah, which are respectively designated as the *ma'on,* the *za'atutei* and the *hi'* scrolls. One of them had the reading *ma'on* (Deuteronomy 33.27) and two the reading *me'onah,* "dwelling place"; one contained the reading *za'atutei* (Exodus 24.5) and two the reading *na'arei* "young men"; in one *hi'* (in place of *hu'*) was found nine times, and in two, eleven times.[8] The minority reading in all these cases was discarded, and the majority reading was adopted. The official text may have become established after the Maccabean victory,[9] and must have served as the model or archetype for the scribes, the copyists and the teachers. Oral tradition guarded the transmission of the scriptural words with utmost vigilance. Veritable "fences" (*seyagim*) were established by means of marginal notations and diacritical marks (dots), meant to ward off the slightest change or innovation in spelling which had not been sanctioned by tradition. The biblical injunction of *lo' toseph 'alaw* (Deuteronomy 13.1), "thou shalt not add thereto," was the guiding principle. Typical of this attitude is the admonition given by Rabbi Ishmael to Rabbi Meir, who was a scribe by profession, warning him to be very careful in his work, for the omission or the addition of a single letter might mean the destruction of the whole world.[10]

The three different manuscripts referred to above, each containing a number of variant readings, were very likely at the basis of our masoretic text, of the Samaritan Pentateuch (the text preserved by the Samaritans to this day), and of the text used by the Alexandrian translators of the entire Bible into Greek (the Septuagint). The variations found in any of these manuscripts were caused largely by incompetent copyists and partly, too, by the ulterior motives of the sects or parties to which the copyists belonged. Since the Bible was used by all sects and parties as a source of inspiration and doctrine, the rise of various parties during the Second Commonwealth, such as the Samaritans, Hellenists, Sadducees and Christians, must have motivated numerous falsifications and corruptions in the biblical texts. This evil was doubtless disconcerting to the scribes and prompted them to redouble their zealous efforts to guard the original texts. Manuscripts were studied, compared and evaluated. Those which were credited with some degree of authenticity were taken into account. Readings that were common to most of these manuscripts received the stamp of authenticity.

Variant readings were recorded in the margins. Certain expressions in the text which were regarded in the light of the ethical or theological standards of the times as vulgar or obscene were rendered euphemistically, a synonym or equivalent milder in tone or implication being used. Archaic formations which were no longer understood or recognized were emended. But these emendations were not incorporated in the text, since the sacred text was not to be tampered with. They were merely noted down in the margins by the technical term *Kere* (קרי), "to be read," as against *Ketib* (כתיב), "what is written," that is, the word or expression found and left in the text. Words or expressions which required special comment were provided with some device for calling the attention of the reader to them, such as dots at the top or at the bottom of a letter or a word.[11]

The dot, because of its inconspicuous form, was apparently regarded as too "harmless" or insignificant to infringe upon the precept of *lo' toseph*. In point of fact, the dot had been in use, according to Ludwig Blau, in the ancient manuscripts in the orient, as well as among the Romans. It was designed to call to the reader's attention certain words or letters in the text which were suspected of being misplaced or extraneous. Blau suggests that these dots were already employed in the three Torah texts of the Temple Court, mentioned above, to indicate the suppression of discarded readings. Instead of expunging extraneous or unacceptable readings from the sacred texts, the scribes may have resorted to the much "safer" and more reverent procedure of leaving the rejected readings in the text, but with the designation of dots above or below the readings. Since these Temple texts were obviously based on much older manuscripts, the view of the rabbis, that these dots are traceable all the way back to Ezra, is not at all implausible. They apparently served the purpose of indicating variations in reading or in spelling, as well as of calling attention to dubious readings or spellings which lend themselves to homiletical or midrashic interpretations.

Ten places provided with such dots in the Bible are men-

tioned in the Talmud.[12] Ezra's motive for pointing these instances is quaintly explained as follows: Ezra figured that in
case Elijah the Prophet comes to criticize him for what he has
written down, he will reply, "I have already provided these
instances with dots." But if Elijah says, "Your written text is
correct," the dots could be removed.[13]

Similarly, in the book of Numbers (10.35-37), there are
several verses which were designated in the Torah texts of the
talmudic period by dots above and below the letters in order
to indicate its irrelevant character. "The Holy One blessed be
He provided this portion with signs above and below in order
to indicate that this is not its proper place,"[14] for it really belongs, by its context, in the first chapters of this book.[15] This
section in our masoretic Text is marked off by an inverted
nun (‫ נ‬) at the beginning and at the end, almost like modern
parentheses. The *nun* is construed by Ludwig Blau as the initial
of *nakud* (pointed), and refers to the dots which had been in
the text originally above and below the letters in this section,
but which were later eliminated to prevent confusion resulting
from the letters and dots running into one another. The inver-
sion of the *nun* was a precautionary device against the danger
of regarding it as a part of the text.

In the course of time, especially at the close of the talmudic
period, a body of rules and regulations relative to the copying
of the biblical texts evolved, and the work of the scribes became
further specialized. The teaching functions, formerly exercised
by the scribes, were taken over by special elementary teachers
(*melammedei tinokot*), while the scribes devoted themselves
to the study of manuscripts and the different deviations in the
versions which had accumulated in the course of transmission.
The designation of *sofer* (scribe) was accordingly replaced by
that of *masorete* (an authority on the *masorah* or traditional
version),[16] and was retained only for the copyist.

Masoretic activity must have been in progress all through the
talmudic period and several centuries thereafter. There is, however, scant documentary evidence available that might shed light

on its extent, especially during the early part of the post-talmudic period. We do know, however, that after the Bar Kokhba debacle (135 C.E.), a number of masoretic scholars fled from Palestine to Nahardea in Babylonia and pursued their studies there. Divergences in biblical readings between the schools of Palestine and Babylonia can be traced as far back as the period of Rab Joseph (died in the year 323 C.E.) and even farther back to that of Judah ha-Nasi (2nd century C.E.).

With the advent of Christian supremacy in Palestine, the center of all Jewish learning, including masoretic studies, was shifted to Babylonia, where the academies of Sura and Nahardea flourished. Babylonian scholarship and authority continued to hold sway until about the seventh century, when under friendly Moslem rule Palestine again took over the leadership in masoretic studies. The masoretic records of the Babylonian schools were known as the Eastern Masorah (*madinha'ei,* in Aramaic); those of the Palestinian academies were referred to as the Western Masorah (*ma'arba'ei*). The differences between the two masorahs are generally trivial and are limited chiefly to the Prophets and the Writings—the books read less extensively and less frequently than the Pentateuch.

After the systems of vowels and accentuation had become established, a new specialty emerged, constituting a further ramification of the masoretic activities, namely, that of the *nakdanim* (vocalizers). They concerned themselves primarily with the study and the careful copying of the vowels and the accents, while the masoretes were engaged chiefly in the copying of the text and the writing down of the vast body of masoretic notes and comments that had accumulated in the course of the centuries.

Scant as is the available evidence, it is fairly obvious that masoretic studies were pursued uninterruptedly both in the Babylonian and Palestinian academies, despite all handicaps, during the post-talmudic period. Biblical manuscripts were carefully examined and copied, variant readings were noted, and a whole masoretic apparatus evolved and took shape. Brief masoretic notes were written down on both sides of the biblical texts and were designated as *Masorah Ketanah* (little or minor Masorah). More extensive notes were recorded at the top or bottom of the texts and are known as *Masorah Gedolah* (big or major Masorah). Later on, toward the end of the masoretic period, these notes were collected in special books, some of which are still extant. One of them, *Dikduke ha-Te'amim,* is the work of a Tiberian masorete of the tenth century C.E., named Aharon ben Moshe ben Asher, the lineal descendant of an old family of prominent masoretic students. This book already deals with grammatical as well as masoretic problems. It therefore represents a transitional stage between the activities of the masoretes and those of the grammarians.

Ben Asher's masoretic text has been adopted as our authentic traditionally accepted text on the authority of Maimonides.[17] Another masoretic authority, whose readings are recorded in the masoretic notes, is Moshe ben Naphtali, but very little is known about him beyond the fact that he also lived in Palestine, probably in Tiberias. Fragments of texts recently discovered, containing variations from our text, are ascribed to this masorete.[18]

In sum: owing to the tireless efforts and careful watchfulness displayed by the scribes and by the masoretes who succeeded them, we now have a fairly uniform and authentic text of the Bible both in consonantal form and in vocalization. These scholars, most of them probably also humble teachers in the elementary grades, counted every word and letter, noted variant readings, recorded emendations, drew up lists of irregular spellings, and devised a system of notations by means of points and figures above, inside and below the letters to indicate vowels, variations in the pronunciation of consonants, accentuation, phrasing and pauses. In this manner a system of safeguards was built up for the preservation of the scriptural text through what we designate as *Masorah* (traditional transmission), that is, readings regarded as authentic or legitimate by tradition and thus transmitted from generation to generation. Our traditionally accepted text is the resultant of all these efforts, and to it

we refer as the Masoretic Text.[19] "We have given," declared
Josephus, "practical proof of our reverence for our own Scriptures. For, although such long ages have now passed, no one
has ventured either to add or to remove or to alter a syllable."[20]
This statement by Josephus, written some two thousand years
ago, is still true today.

The Subdivisions and Final Form of the Traditional Text

Originally the biblical texts were written in continuous form,
without any attempt at subdivision into chapters or verses. But
as early as the talmudic days, the scribes or copyists began to
subdivide the texts into verses. The Pentateuch was also subdivided, for liturgical purposes, into one hundred fifty-four or
one hundred sixty-seven portions (*sedarim*), which were to be
covered in ritual use in the course of three years. This subdivision is of Palestinian origin, while according to the Babylonian
arrangement, which is of a later date, the Pentateuch was subdivided into fifty-four portions (*parashiot*), the reading of which
was to be completed annually. The Babylonian supplanted the
Palestinian system and has been generally adopted. The subdivision of the Hebrew Bible into chapters did not occur until
the fourteenth century C.E. and was taken over from the Christian Bible.[21]

With the adoption of the officially accepted text, interest in
masoretic studies began to wane and was replaced by grammatical researches. The masoretic notes were faithfully copied in
later manuscripts of the Bible, but chiefly as embellishments
and rather through force of habit, or because of tradition, than
for purposes of elucidation. In numerous cases these notes were
incorrectly copied, betraying a growing misunderstanding of
their significance and purpose. But in the sixteenth century
(1524-5 C.E.) Jacob ben Hayyim submitted the masoretic materials to a fresh and critical evaluation and, as a result of his
studies and examination of available manuscripts, he edited the
so-called Rabbinic Bible (*Mikra'ot Gedolot*) with marginal
notes. He also prepared an alphabetic arrangement of the maso-

הפטרת ראה

אבן עזרא   פרשת שפטים   רש"י

תולדות אהרן

בעה"ם

רמב"ן   ספורנו

A Page from the Rabbinic Bible

retic notes, which he appended at the end of the texts. These appended notes are denoted *Masorah Sophit* (Final Masorah).

The Jews as "the People of the Book"

The Jews have been referred to, since the days of Mohammed, as "the people of the Book," and appropriately so. The Book, or the Bible (Greek *biblia,* plural form of *biblion,* books), occupies a central place in Jewish life and tradition. Its original texts were guarded most zealously and scrupulously. The rabbis, the exponents of the living Jewish tradition, while admonishing against tampering with the original text of the Bible, displayed nevertheless considerable latitude with regard to interpretation. They were, however, opposed to translations, for a translation imposes on the text a fixed and stereotyped interpretation. The Torah was likened by them to "a hammer that breaketh the rock in pieces (Jeremiah 23.29), that is, just as [the rock] is split into many pebbles, so also may one biblical verse convey many meanings" (Sanhedrin 34a).

The Bible is to the Jews not a mere compilation of ancient writings, representative of an ancient civilization, ancient modes of thoughts and beliefs. Nor is it treated by them as just another sacred book to be placed on a shelf as an object of reverence and to be used merely for solemn recitative reading. The Bible has been to the Jew a dynamic book, a living fountain, the mainspring of Jewish civilization, a book that has grown and evolved in the creative imagination of the Jewish people and has been brought near to our own times by the "mouth" of Jewish tradition and reinterpretation. The prophetic spirit that animates this Book is the life-blood coursing through the best of Jewish literature and tradition of all time, and it is as fresh and timely today as it was in antiquity. The biblical legends, the aggadic (sermonic) and halakhic (legal) interpretations, as well as the modern "literalist" commentaries, are all regarded as part and parcel of the traditional Jewish Bible. They all represent the attempt on the part of Jewish tradition to adjust the biblical content to the changing conditions and needs of the times. The essays of Ahad ha-Am and A. D. Gordon, the poetry of Bialik and Chernichovski, and the narratives of Mendele and Agnon—all radiate the spirit of the Bible, colored and modified by the living stream of Jewish tradition.

The typical Jewish attitude toward the Bible may be best illustrated by the following talmudic legend: When Moses went up to heaven he found the Holy One blessed be He sitting and providing tittles for the letters of the Torah. "Why all this bother?" Moses asked. "There will arise a man," God answered, "after many generations, who will deduce manifold laws from each of these tittles." "Show me this man," Moses requested. "Turn around," God said. Moses did so, and he saw rows of scholars engaged in discussions. He took a seat at the end of the eighth row and listened, but he did not understand what the scholars were arguing about. He felt downhearted. But suddenly he heard one of the disciples ask Akiba how he arrived at a certain law. Whereupon he heard Akiba replying: "This is one of the Sinaitic laws of Moses." Then Moses' mind was set at rest.[22]

Moses, according to this legend, did not object to the fact that implications, incomprehensible to him, were drawn from his words. Indeed, he was happy about it. He realized that change and adjustment are essential to a living and eternal Torah, as long as they stem from the original source. The traditional Jew is concerned not merely with the literal meaning of the words of the Bible, but also with the interpretations put upon them by the creative Jewish tradition throughout the ages. "This little Book," Bialik has been quoted as saying, ". . . has said everything there is to be said. Everything is implied and anticipated in it. Whatever one should like to put into words has already been said in it."[23] This is a kind of paraphrase of the succinct statement by the ancient sage Ben Bag-Bag: "Turn it and turn it over again, for everything is in it . . ."[24]

The Bible is also the fountainhead of the Hebrew language. It has set the pattern for Hebrew structure and grammar. Its vocabulary, idioms and locutions still retain their pristine freshness and potency, and modern Hebrew writers continue to turn to the Bible as the main source and model for style and diction. One cannot conceivably grasp all the subtle allusions and overtones, all the stylistic nuances, and all the idiomatic niceties of the classical, the modern and even of the contemporary Hebrew writers, without a familiarity with the Bible. To be sure, a large number of new words and expressions have been added to and incorporated in the Hebrew language, but the biblical pattern is still focal and predominant. Very little of the biblical vocabulary and structure have been discarded as archaic or obsolete. It is significant that this ancient text has always been and remains to this very day the central subject in the Jewish curriculum, in Israel as well as in the Diaspora. In this respect the Bible is a unique book. No other book of such antiquity has occupied, in its original form, a similar position.

PART THREE

How the Language Was Preserved

CHAPTER EIGHT
HOW DID THE HEBREW
LANGUAGE GROW?

The Aramaic Dialect Among the Jews

As stated in a preceding chapter (Chapter II), Aramaic, or some primitive form of it, was the language of Abraham and his kinsmen, but it was gradually displaced by "Canaanitic" Hebrew. Abraham's descendants in Canaan already spoke a pure Hebrew. Thus, when Jacob and Laban concluded a covenant of peace after a heated argument regarding Jacob's flight from Laban's house, they both gathered stones, piled them up and, in accordance with an ancient oriental custom, proclaimed the cairn a testimony or monument of the peace treaty. Jacob, the Hebrew, called the monument in Hebrew gal-'ed (a cairn of witness); while Laban, the Aramean, designated it by the equivalent name in his native dialect yegar sahaduta (Genesis 3.47). Later, the prophet Jeremiah, in addressing himself to the Jews living in Babylonia, employed a whole Aramaic verse (Jeremiah 10.11), in which he bade them tell the idol worshippers in Babylonia that the idols were helpless, futile and doomed to perdition. The reason for rendering this verse in Aramaic is that this language was then popular in the Near

East, and it must have gained wide currency among the Hebrews, especially those residing in the Babylonian exile.

It should be recalled that there were many Jewish colonies and settlements, during the period of the exile and thereafter, in Babylonia, Egypt and other Near Eastern countries, where Aramaic was spoken. Palestine itself, especially Jerusalem, contained during the Second Commonwealth a number of settlements of Jews from the Diaspora, particularly Babylonia. Furthermore, the capital city was frequently visited by merchants, students, scholars and pilgrims from Aramaic-speaking countries.

For this reason, considerable portions of Daniel and Ezra, two of the latest books in the Bible, were written in Aramaic. It is even possible, as some scholars suggest, that these books were written outside of Palestine, perhaps in Persia, where Aramaic was in vogue. For the same reason the so-called *Targumim* (translations and interpretations of the Bible written in Aramaic), as well as parts of the Talmud Yerushalmi (the Jerusalem Talmud) and the *Midrashim* (rabbinic comments and homilies on the Bible) were written in Aramaic. The Aramaic portions of the Babylonian Talmud, on the other hand, belong to another branch of Aramaic, which may be designated as a Jewish modification of Eastern Aramaic.

The urgency of spreading the knowledge of the Torah among the Jewish masses must have dictated to the Jewish scholars of that period the employment of Aramaic, the language used in some localities by the masses, for purposes of instruction and interpretation. Traditional Judaism has always endeavored to bring the masses of the people in possession of the Word of God, and not to allow it to become the monopoly of the professional clergy or priesthood. In their synagogues or *edahs* to which reference was made above (p. 142), they would listen to the reading of selections from the Torah or the Prophets, while the *Torgeman* (the official interpreter) would translate the selections into Aramaic. The *Torgeman* was enjoined to stand in deferential posture some distance away from the desk where stood the reader of the Hebrew text. A clear and sharp distinction was to be maintained between the words of the original text and those of the translator. In point of fact the rabbis discountenanced the writing down of these translations, in order to preserve this distinction in the minds of the people. Never was the translation meant to be regarded with the degree of authority accorded to the original Hebrew text. In the course of time, however, it was found necessary to write down these translations. They underwent several editions and recensions, and they were finally widely accepted among the Jews and designated as *Targumim* (translations).

Thus we find the Hebrew people in close contact with the Aramaic language both at the dawn of their history and toward the end of the biblical stage in their career, and even beyond that stage. Our traditional prayerbook contains several significant prayers written in Aramaic, such as *Kol Nidre, Kaddish,* and others. Indeed, some of the rabbis regarded Aramaic with reverence. Rab, the founder of Jewish learning in Babylonia (third century B.C.E.), maintained that Aramaic was the language used by Adam and that, accordingly, it preceded the Hebrew language.[1] Rabbi Hanina observed that the reason the Jews were exiled to Babylon, rather than to any other country, was that the Babylonian language (Aramaic) was akin to the language of the Torah.[2] This attitude toward Aramaic was not, however, shared by other rabbis. Rabbi Judah ha-Nasi, for example, remonstrated against its use in Palestine, while a Babylonian Amora of some three generations later, Rab Joseph, was equally opposed to its use even in Babylonia.[3] Both Rabbi Judah and Rabbi Johanan (third century C.E.) went as far as to object to praying in Aramaic.[4] As a matter of fact, the Aramaic language was sometimes dubbed *leshon hediot* (the language of the ignorant),[5] pointing to the fact that the people whose vernacular was Aramaic and could speak no Hebrew were not held in high esteem.

The close relationship between Hebrew and Aramaic, due to linguistic kinship as well as to ancestral tradition, undoubtedly facilitated the adoption of Aramaic by the Jews. Not only are the major portions of Daniel and Ezra written in Aramaic, but even the Hebrew books of the Bible of the same period are marked by a strong Aramaic complexion. This is particularly true of the books of Esther, Song of Songs, Ecclesiastes, and a number of contemporaneous Psalms. The language of these books thus constitutes the transitional stage between the classical Hebrew of the pre-exilic books of the Bible and the mishnaic Hebrew, of which rich resources are stored away in the Talmud, Midrashim, and liturgical compositions.

Hebrew Vernacular Remains Intact

It is clear, however, from a study of the "transitional" and mishnaic Hebrew that the Aramaic influence did not impair the distinctive character of the Hebrew language. The Aramaic words and constructions, some of which may have been imported by the Abramides and injected into the "Hebrew" of the Canaanitish period, were absorbed and assimilated by the Hebrew language. It is a well-established principle in linguistics that the nature of a language is determined not by its words, but by its grammar and structure. Languages borrow words, but do not generally borrow grammar from one another, or do so only to a very limited degree. The majority of words in the English language are Roman. They have come into the language through the influence of French after the Norman conquest. Yet English is regarded as a Germanic language by virtue of the fact that its grammar is generally Germanic.

Mishnaic Hebrew—a Normal Evolutionary Hebrew Vernacular

Other features of the so-called mishnaic Hebrew cannot be traced to the influence of either Aramaic or any other Semitic language. They are, nevertheless, genuinely Semitic and may have found their way into the language through the channels of the other dialects employed in some parts of Palestine even in the pre-exilic period. An excellent example of this Hebrew is to be found in the book of *Shir ha-Shirim* (Song of Songs), the content and style of which possess the virility and artless simplicity of the pre-exilic period, whereas its language is closely akin to that of the Mishnah. It seems quite unlikely that such poems could have been written during the insecure and troublesome post-exilic period, or that they would have been admitted into the biblical Canon had they been written in that period. The Jewish mind was then too preoccupied with religious matters to permit of excursions into the province of erotic and idyllic poetry. There are also other evidences testifying to the early origin of this book.

It must, therefore, be assumed, as has already been pointed out (p. 48f.), that alongside the literary classical style there existed a simple conversational style, employed especially by the peasants and simple folk of the backwoods, particularly in the northern part of Palestine, where these erotic pastoral idylls must have been in vogue. It is inconceivable that even in Jerusalem, the average man in the street, even during the heyday of the classical biblical period, spoke the noble and majestic prose typical of Amos and Isaiah, or even of Genesis and Deuteronomy. More probably, men like Amos and Isaiah, after writing down or delivering their lofty and noble messages in the classical style, addressed their acquaintances or members of their family in the simple conversational dialect, including colloquialisms and slang, current among the rest of the people. This non-classical style must have gained currency during the exilic and post-exilic periods, owing especially to the unsettled and transmigratory conditions of the people of those days.

It often takes centuries for a new word-coinage to take root and be widely employed. Little wonder, then, that many of the so-called mishnaic words, grammatical forms and syntactical constructions, are already in evidence in the Bible, to a greater or lesser degree.

Differences Between Classical and Vernacular Hebrew

Numerous examples could be cited to illustrate the difference between the classical and the conversational Hebrew forms. But for the sake of simplicity and brevity only a few such examples will be mentioned.

1. Classical or biblical Hebrew has an intricate design of expressing time of action or state in verbs. Unlike the Indo-European language, biblical Hebrew, as well as other Semitic languages, makes no time-distinction (that is, past, present and future) in the verb forms. The tense-idea in these languages is related not to the *time,* but to the *kind* of action. The difference in tense is determined by whether the action, in the mind of the speaker, is completed or uncompleted. The completed action is expressed by a form which we call Perfect, the uncompleted action by a form designated as Imperfect.[6] The Perfect may thus denote also action which is represented as accomplished, or absolutely definite, even though it is continued into the present time, or is even still in the future. Thus when God asks Cain about his brother, Cain replies in the Perfect form, *lo yadati* (Genesis 4.10) in the sense of *I absolutely do not know.* Similarly when Ephron wants to assure Abraham that he will give him the field and the cave of Makhpelah in order to bury Sarah therein, Ephron says *ha-sadeh natati lakh* (*ibid.,* 23.11), the literal translation of which is "the field I gave to you," as if to convey the impression that the field is already in Abraham's possession, even before the matter of payment was negotiated. In both cases the Perfect tense is employed because the speakers intend to lend emphasis and conviction to their statements. The Imperfect, on the other hand, may indicate action in the past of a continuous and recurrent nature, although more frequently it refers to action in the future. Thus Elkanah, the father of the prophet Samuel, when he pleads with his wife Hannah to desist from weeping and fasting on account of her childlessness, says to her *lameh tivki we-lameh lo tokhli* (Samuel 1.8). The Imperfect is employed here, but the sense of Elkanah's plea is *Why do you go on weeping? And why do you persist in not eating?*

The Present tense is generally expressed in biblical Hebrew by an adjectival form. No special form for it exists in Hebrew.

Actually, to quote the medieval grammarian Ibn Janah, the Present is merely an assumption; it has no reality. It is merely, he maintains, a line of demarkation between the past and the future and may be compared to a point in geometry which is indivisible. An act has temporal reality only in terms of past and future.

Post-biblical or mishnaic Hebrew discards all these intricacies. It operates on the same tense-pattern as the other Indo-European languages. The tense-idea (past, present and future) is definitely and clearly established. The Perfect is employed to indicate past action or status, and the Imperfect, future action or status. The trends in this direction are, however, already in evidence in the Bible, from which numerous instances indicative of these trends can be quoted. Apparently the inadequacy of the rather cumbersome classical tense-construction was felt already during the biblical period, and attempts to experiment with the time-idea in the use of tenses were already in progress.

2. In representing a series of past events or actions, a narrative in biblical Hebrew is generally introduced by a verb in the Perfect tense and is followed by an Imperfect tense with a prefixed *waw* (meaning "and"), for example, *we-hanahash hayah . . . wa-yomer . . . wa-tomer* (Genesis 3.1). A literal translation into a European language of this would yield "and the serpent *was* . . . and he *will say* . . . and she *will say* . . . ," which, of course, would make no sense. Similarly an Imperfect tense is followed by a verb in the Perfect with a prefixed *waw* to indicate events or actions in the future, for example, *yehi . . . we-hayu . . . we-hayu* (*ibid.,* 1.14 f.), a literal translation of which into a European language would likewise sound cumbersome and meaningless. Mishnaic Hebrew dispensed with this intricate design. The tenses are clearly and consistently differentiated in temporal terms even as they are in European languages and as we find them already in a number of instances in the Bible, for example, *'anah dodi we-'amar* (Canticles 2.10) *"my beloved spoke and said"* (for the classical construction *'anah dodi wa-yomer*), or *kiyyemu we-kibbelu* (Esther

9.27) *"they ordained and undertook"* (for the classical construction *kiyyemu wa-yekabbelu*).

3. The use of the definite article *ha* (the) is also on the wane in certain constructions of mishnaic Hebrew. Biblical Hebrew would render "this boy" by *ha-yeled ha-zeh,* with the definite article *ha* attached to each of the two words. The literal translation of this expression would be "the boy the this." But in mishnaic Hebrew this expression would be simplified by discarding the definite article in both words, thus yielding the simple form *yeled zeh* (this boy). This trend is likewise already to be found in the Bible as *yom ha-shishi* (Genesis 1.31: the sixth day) for the more classical *ha-yom ha-shishi.*

4. In the Imperfect or future tense in biblical Hebrew the plural feminine, second and third person, differs from the corresponding masculine forms. For example, in the verb *shamar* (he watched), the plural masculine forms are *yishmeru* (they will watch), *tishmeru* (you will watch). The corresponding form in the feminine for both persons is *tishmornah,* a rather cumbersome form. In mishnaic Hebrew this feminine form was dropped and the "masculine" forms were employed for both genders. But traces of such simplifications may be found in the biblical texts, especially in the allegedly later books of the Bible, such as Canticles, Ecclesiastes and Esther. In Canticles, for example, ten instances occur in "mishnaic" forms of the feminine plural Imperfect over against three "biblical" forms. Modern conversational Hebrew, as well as spoken Arabic, likewise discarded the distinctive feminine plural form of the Imperfect. The Hebrew Language Academy in Israel has in effect sanctioned officially this simplified usage.

5. Since the verb, in classical Hebrew, does not operate within the framework of time, it is understandable why a temporal clause, like "when he spoke," is rendered in biblical Hebrew by one word, composed of an inflected gerund and a prefixed *b* (in) or *k* (as, like); namely, *b'dabro* (in his speaking), or *k'dabro* (as his speaking). The equivalent in classical Hebrew of the clause "when Moses spoke," for example, would

be *k'daber Moshe* (as the speaking of Moses), or *b'daber Moshe* (in the speaking of Moses). No further indication of time would be necessary. Mishnaic Hebrew dispenses with such constructions and employs the simple temporal equivalents of the Indo-European languages.

6. In order to affirm something emphatically, biblical Hebrew repeats the verb. Thus when God instructs Adam (Genesis 2.16) that he may eat freely of every tree in the garden, the Hebrew phrase employed is *akhol tokhel* (literally, eating thou eatest). When He subsequently warns Adam not to eat of the tree of knowledge, "for on the day thou eatest thereof thou shalt surely die," the latter expression is represented in the biblical Hebrew text by the phrase *mot tamut* (literally, dying thou diest). No such construction is to be found in mishnaic Hebrew. The simple constructions employed in the Indo-European languages are, in such instances, similarly used in mishnaic Hebrew.

7. The concept of possession is expressed in biblical Hebrew by means of suffixes and by modifications of the nominal form. For example, the noun *dabar* (word) changes to *debar ha-melekh* (the word of the king), *debari* (my word), *debarkha* (your word). In mishnaic Hebrew an independent symbol is employed, as in the European languages, to indicate possession, namely, *ha-dabar shel ha-melekh* (the word of the king), *dabar shelli* (my word), *dabar shelkha* (your word), and so on.

8. A number of biblical words took on entirely different meanings in mishnaic usage. Thus the verbs *kanah* and *lakah,* which in biblical usage mean, respectively, "bought" or "possessed," and "took," adopted in mishnaic usage the respective meanings of "acquired possession" and "bought." The verb *pasal* is employed in biblical Hebrew in the sense of "hewed" or "carved," while in mishnaic Hebrew it is used in the meaning of "disqualified" or "abrogated." Modern Hebrew prefers the biblical usage in the case of *kanah* and *lakah,* perhaps because of their high frequency in the Bible, while in the case of *pasal* both biblical and mishnaic usages are in vogue.

Differences Recognized by the Rabbis

The differences between the biblical and the mishnaic Hebrew were already recognized by the rabbis of the talmudic period. The former is referred to as *leshon Torah* (the language of the Torah), the latter as *leshon hakhamim* (the language of the learned), or even *leshon benei Adam* (the language of the people, or the vernacular). Thus Rabbi Assi, a Babylonian Amora of the third century C.E., upon his arrival in Palestine found Rabbi Johanan, while instructing his son, using the plural *rehelim* (lambs). Whereupon Rabbi Assi remonstrated, asserting that the correct plural form is *rehelot*. When Rabbi Johanan adduced in defense of his usage the example of Genesis 32.14, Rabbi Assi asserted that a distinction must be drawn between *leshon Torah* and *leshon hakhamim*, implying thereby that the latter must be given priority in usage.[7] On the same principle the mishnaic verb *mazag* (blending of wine) is given preference in usage to the biblical synonym *masakh*.[8]

Similarly, the following question was raised by the rabbis:[9] If one makes a vow to refrain from eating that which is *mebushshal*, is he allowed to eat anything that is roasted or seethed? Rabbi Johanan was of the opinion that in the case of vows the term *mebushshal* is to be taken, in accordance with "popular usage" (*leshon benei Adam*), namely, connoting also that which is roasted and seethed. Rabbi Josiah, on the other hand, argues that the term *mebushshal* is to be taken, in the case of vows, in the biblical sense (*leshon Torah*), according to which the term is restricted only to that which is cooked. The person making the vow, employing the term *mebushshal*, is therefore permitted to eat anything roasted or seethed. There were, however, certain localities in Palestine, even at that time, according to the Talmud, where the biblical term *tzeli* was still in use to indicate roasted meat, while *mebushshal* continued to be applied only to cooked meat.

Some scholars would infer from the term *leshon hakhamim*

(literally, the language of the learned) that mishnaic Hebrew was an artificial and academic language, just like Latin during the Middle Ages. This is, however, an extremely unlikely interpretation. It is inconceivable that the rabbis, in instructing the youth, would reject grammatical forms found in the Bible in favor of artificial forms current in the dialect of scholars. Such a dialect would, in any event, tend to preserve classical models of grammar.

As a matter of fact, the term *leshon hakhamim* does not actually mean the "language of the learned," but rather the language in which the Talmud, namely, the words or discourses of the *hakhamim,* was written, which was certainly not merely a literary or academic language. A synonymous term for *leshon hakhamim* is *leshon Mishnah,* namely, the language in which the Mishnah was written. Similarly, the Aramaic language is designated in the Talmud as the language of the *Targum,*[10] because the Targumim were written in it. The term *targum loshen* (language of the *Targum*) for Aramaic is also preserved in Yiddish tradition. The Jews of Kurdistan, whose vernacular is Aramaic, refer to their language as Targum.

It is significant that the rabbis placed mishnaic Hebrew on a par with biblical Hebrew, designating both as *leshon ha-kodesh* (the holy language). An apparently early Mishnah (Sotah VII, 2) contains a list of formulae to be recited in *leshon ha-kodesh.* The list includes beside the recitation of *bikkurim* (Deuteronomy 26.1-11), *halitzah* (*ibid.,* 5-10), and others mentioned in the book of Deuteronomy, also that of *birkat kohanim* (the priestly blessing) and *birkat kohen gadol* (the blessing of the high priest). The last two formulae are not found in the book of Deuteronomy, or anywhere else in the Bible. It is extremely doubtful whether the term *birkat kohanim* mentioned in the Mishnah has reference to the priestly benediction found in Numbers 6.22-27; but it is certain that no basis for the *birkat kohen gadol* can be found in the Bible. Yet the language in which these two formulae were recited is entitled *leshon ha-kodesh.* It is inconceivable that the rabbis would have accorded such prestige to an artificial academic dialect.

Injections of Middle East Languages into Mishnaic Hebrew

Mishnaic Hebrew is, of course, richly colored by Aramaic, but no more than was Aramaic, especially Judeo-Aramaic by Hebrew. The two languages are closely related and lived side by side for centuries. A mutual influence under such circumstances was obviously inevitable. Even biblical Hebrew shows evidence of being influenced by Aramaic both in vocabulary and, to a more limited degree, in grammatical and syntactical construction. In view of the widespread use of Aramaic as an international language in the Near East during the period of the Second Commonwealth, the increased influence of this language on mishnaic Hebrew is to be taken for granted. But mishnaic Hebrew still possessed the capacity to assimilate and integrate this influence into its own system. To all intents and purposes, the grammar and structure of mishnaic Hebrew remain Hebraic.

Although Assyro-Babylonian or Akkadian had been eclipsed and superseded by Aramaic as the *lingua franca* of the Near East, it was still alive during the Babylonian captivity and for a number of years thereafter. It is therefore not surprising to find in mishnaic Hebrew a number of Assyro-Babylonian words, especially in the legal area; such as *get* (legal document, bill of divorce), *shetar* (document), *mashkon* (security, pledge), *nedunia* (bride's gift, dowry), but also *nahtom* (baker), *shewalya* or *shulya* (apprentice), *taggar* (merchant).

But Aramaic and Assyro-Babylonian were not the only languages from which mishnaic Hebrew borrowed vocabulary. The vernaculars of the peoples with whom the Jews came in contact during that period—the Persians, the Greeks and the Romans—are all represented in the dictionary of mishnaic Hebrew, to a greater or lesser degree, and some of these loanwords have survived also in modern Hebrew. Thus such common Hebrew words as *raz* (secret), *pitgam* (edict, saying), *dat* (law, religion), *gizbar* (treasurer)—all stem from the Persian and are already found in later books of the Bible.[11] The proportion of words of Greek origin is relatively extensive. Among them are such widely used words as *hikhriz* (proclaimed, announced), *basis* (basis), *ambati(a)* (bath tub), *arnak* (purse), *watik* (keen, steady, earnest), *zug* (pair), *'akhsania* (inn), *signon* (style), *defus* (mould, printing press). The influence of Latin, although not equal to that of Greek, is evident in words like *aspeklaria* (window pane, mirror), *blorit* (plait, locks), *gardom* (gallows, scaffold), *kappandria* (short cut), *sargel* (a ruler), *simta* (a narrow path, alley) and *safsal* (bench). All these words were, however, incorporated into the language and Hebraized in form. They were inflected in accordance with Hebrew grammatical principles to such a degree that their foreign origin is not at all recognizable by the average Hebraist. Few will be able to identify the Greek stems in such regular Hebraic conjugations as *hit'akhsen* (lodged), *ziwweg* (paired, joined in wedlock), *bisses* (based, founded), *hidpis* (printed). Nor will many a Hebrew scholar detect the Latin noun *regula* in the normal Hebrew conjugation *sirgel* (drew lines). All these are now regarded as genuine Hebrew words.

Capacity for Original Creativity in Mishnaic Hebrew

Mishnaic Hebrew was not restricted in its growth and development to loan-words. It was capable of sprouting its own linguistic shoots and of creating a large number of original coinages, which have become an integral and indispensable part of the language. Such new coinages as *efshar* (possible), *achshaw* (now), *hotem* (nose), *ella* (but, only, except),[12] *ilan* (tree), *afilu* (even), *bishbil* (for, for the sake of), *kedei* (in order that), displaced almost entirely the respective biblical equivalents *ulai, attah, af, ulam* and *ki-'im, etz, gam, ba'abur, lema'an.*

Furthermore, mishnaic Hebrew discarded some of the biblical conjugations and evolved new conjugations in their place.

Passive conjugations of the type *muzzag* (*pu'al*), and, to a certain extent, even *homzag* (*hoph'al*) and *nimzag* (*niph'al*), were dropped and replaced by a new conjugation *nitmazzeg* (a combination of *niph'al* and *hitpa'el*). Thus, instead of *kubbal* (was received), mishnaic Hebrew employs the form *nitkabbel*. The present tense *memuzzag* (mekubbal) was, however, retained.

Other new conjugations which gained currency in mishnaic Hebrew were *shiph'el* and its passive forms *shuph'al* and *nishtaph'el*. The *shiph'el* conjugation, which is already found in Ugaritic, Akkadian and to some extent in Aramaic, is the equivalent of the *hiph'il* in biblical Hebrew. It was probably introduced in mishnaic Hebrew under the influence of Aramaic. Thus *shi'bed* (from the stem *'bd*, serve), "subjugated," corresponds to the biblical Hebrew *he'ebid* (*hiph'il* of the same stem) but the latter form is also employed in the sense of "caused to work," "compelled to labor" and "wearied." The new form was therefore coined in order to avoid ambiguity. We have accordingly a new category of verbs and nominal formations in mishnaic Hebrew of this conjugation and its derivatives, such as *meshu'bad* (subjugated), *shi'bud* (subjugation), *nishta'bed* (was subjugated); *shihrer* (liberated, stem *hrr*), *nishtahrer* (was liberated), *shihrur* (liberation); *shi'mem* (made dull, bored, stem *'mm*), *nishta'mem* (was bored), *shi'mum* (dullness, boredom), and the like.

But it was not only in the realm of vocabulary and grammar that mishnaic Hebrew displayed its vitality and creativity; it also produced a number of new graphic and homespun idioms which attest the popular character of this language as the vernacular of the peasantry and simple folk. To cite just a few examples, a person who risks his money in a precarious venture is said to "have placed his money on the horn of a deer" (*hinniah me'otaw al keren ha-tzebi*), since the deer is very likely to run away and disappear. When an individual suspected of hostility offers his assistance, his offer is rejected with the saying *lo mi-dubshakh we-lo me-'uktzakh* (I want neither your honey nor your sting). The expression *pashat et ha-regel* (he stretched out his foot) is applied to a person who fails to keep a promise or to discharge a responsibility, and instead of stretching out his hand and paying his debt he stretches out his foot. He who ravishes a woman must marry her, according to the Talmud, however much he may dislike her, for "he must drink out of the earthen (offensive) vessel he has chosen" (*shoteh ba'atzitzo*). The expression *nistahafah sadkha* (your field has been ruined by a flood) implies the idea that "it is your hard luck, no one else is to blame." These and many other such expressions have the earmarks of an earthy simplicity, which is not at all characteristic of an artificial scholarly or literary style.

The injection of all these non-classical elements and new linguistic coinages rendered the Hebrew language richer in vocabulary and more adaptable to the daily needs of secular and conversational usage. There was hardly a phase of human endeavor and pursuit of that period which was not given expression in mishnaic Hebrew. The "newer" Hebrew was inferior to the classical Hebrew in vigor, solemnity, succinctness, picturesqueness and poetic imagery; but it was endowed, instead, with simplicity, exactness, flexibility and richness of vocabulary.

CHAPTER NINE
HOW THE HEBREW LANGUAGE HAS
KEPT ABREAST OF CHANGING NEEDS

The Growth of Hebrew During the
"Golden Era" in Spain

The mishnaic Hebrew was in the main adopted by subsequent
Hebrew writers of prose, while the classical Hebrew served
as the model for poetic expression even during talmudic and
medieval periods. A vast literature, talmudic, midrashic and
liturgical, was written in mishnaic Hebrew. During the Spanish
period, the so-called Golden Age in the diaspora history of
Jewish literature and of the Hebrew language, which lasted
about three centuries (tenth to thirteenth), the Hebrew language was enriched with many new forms and terms. The chief
contributions in this respect were made by the Tibbonids
(Judah ibn Tibbon and his son Samuel), who translated from
Arabic into Hebrew philosophical and grammatical works
written by such outstanding men as Bahyah, Ibn Gabirol, Judah
Halevi, Ibn Janah, Saadia, and Maimonides. Their style became the model of scientific Hebrew during the Middle Ages.
The grammarians of that period, on the other hand, pursued
with unparalleled zeal and keen insight the study and investigation of the Hebrew language, and unraveled its intricacies,

rendering it a ready and wieldy instrument for self-expression. Thus was blazed the path for the creative poets of that period, who soon "began to chirp" in novel metrical forms and on original diversified themes. The legacy in the field of Hebrew poetry, philosophy and philology which that period left has been an inexhaustible source of inspiration and guidance to subsequent generations.

The Spanish period stands out as a beacon in the history of the Hebrew language and literature. The Spanish Jewish community of the Middle Ages enjoyed for a good many years the blessings of economic and political freedom and of unhampered cultural pursuits no less than does the modern Jewish community in the United States. But while maintaining close contact with the people of the land and making themselves acquainted with their language and their literature and sometimes even surpassing them in that knowledge, they, nevertheless, did not neglect their own language and literature. For a period of some five centuries the Spanish Jews pursued the study of the Hebrew language and its literature with a zeal and a love which has not since been equaled. They wrote a glorious chapter in the history of Judaism, which will continue to serve as a source of pride as long as Judaism lives. They did write some of their philosophical and philological works in Arabic largely because the Hebrew language lacked at that time an appropriate terminology in these literary fields; also because Arabic was then the language of the learned, just as Latin was later, and it was natural to resort to that language when thinking about philosophic or scientific problems. But they never forgot that the Hebrew language is the most effective, nay, the sole medium for the creativity and full self-expression of the Jewish soul. Hence they wrote their poetry and liturgical compositions exclusively in Hebrew. Furthermore, they were constantly seeking, with boundless interest and zeal, to investigate the language and to coin new words and expressions in order to increase its effectiveness as a medium of Jewish self-expression even in the field of scientific research. The names of the poets Judah Halevi and Gabirol, of the philologists Hayyuj and Ibn Janah, of the grammarians and commentators Ibn Ezra and RaDaK, and of the philosophers Maimonides and Crescas will always occupy a dominant place in the constellation of Jewish creative writers and thinkers.

The Spanish period enriched the Hebrew language. A number of new words coined during that period, especially in the field of philosophical and philological terminology, have become an integral part of the language. Hebrew could not conceivably be employed in modern times without such words as *merkaz* (center), *aklim* (climate), *kotev* (axis), *hishta'el* (coughed), *ophek* (horizon), *tib'i* (natural), *mlakhuti* (artificial) and the whole grammatical terminology, which were originated in the main by the Tibbonids. Some of these words are directly borrowed from Arabic, while in others the Arabic influence is distinctly evident. These words are now taken for granted as legitimate and indispensable members of the Hebrew language. But the purists of the period must have looked askance at the process of adding "indiscriminately" the suffix *ut,* characteristic ending of abstract Hebrew words, to the interrogative words *eikh* (how?), *kammah* (how much?), *mah* (what?), resulting in such "monstrous" coinages, after the model of Arabic, as *eikhut* (quality, literally *howness*), *kammut* (quantity, literally *howmuchness*), *mahut* (nature, literally "whatness").[1] However, the Jewish intellectual horizon widened, creative Jewish experiences expanded and deepened, and the need for self-expression called for the coinage of new terms and linguistic forms to keep up with the progress of the Hebraic mind.

Close to three thousand philosophical and scientific terms were coined during the Middle Ages by the Tibbonids and others. Only about eighty of these terms, or about two and a half per cent, are words and stems borrowed directly from Arabic. A good many of the other terms were coined by a process of loan-translations, that is, by borrowing the Arabic words and their concepts, and then translating these words into the respective Hebrew etymological equivalents, thus giving the original Hebrew words an entirely new meaning.[2]

To illustrate: the English word *conscience* was borrowed directly from the Latin *conscientia,* where it originally meant "knowledge," but later assumed the connotation of moral judgment and feeling applied to conduct in terms of standards of right and wrong. When this Latin word, in its new connotation, was translated into German, the term *Gewissen* (derived from *Wissen,* "knowledge," with *ge* as the equivalent of *con,* as in "conscience") was employed. On the same principle, the Arabic equivalent *damir* (originally "hidden" but later "conscience") was rendered in Hebrew by the biblical *matzpun* (hidden place). Similarly, the Arabic *hadd,* originally signifying "limit" or "boundary," came to be used in Moslem philosophical literature also in the sense of "definition." Hence the concept "definition" was rendered in Hebrew by the word *geder* (fence)—an approximate etymological equivalent of the Arabic word *hadd.* The majority of medieval Hebrew coinages originated along these lines.

Special mention should be made of Maimonides' contribution to the growth of the Hebrew language. Although he wrote mainly in Arabic, he was a masterful Hebrew stylist and manipulated the Hebrew language dynamically and creatively. His chief contribution was manifest in his attempt to convert talmudic Aramaisms into Hebraic forms. In his *Mishneh Torah,* where talmudic sources are paraphrased, abridged and simplified, Maimonides consistently endeavored, whenever possible, to translate Aramaic words and phrases into Hebrew. By a slight modification in form, Maimonides Hebraized the Aramaic words and thereby enriched the Hebrew language with new coinages. Thus the Aramaic *ma'abarta* or *ma'aborta* (*Tefillin* holder, also ferry boat; Men. 35a) and *shuma* (estimate, appraisal) were converted by Maimonides into the Hebraic forms *ma'aboret* (*Hilkhot Tefillin* III, 1) and *shumah,* which he declines as a regular feminine form (*Hilkhot Ishshut* V, 9).

Rashi's Contribution to the Development of Hebrew

It is important to bear in mind at this juncture that the Spanish Jews were not alone in their lively interest and creative efforts in the field of Hebrew literature and language during the Middle Ages. The Jews in the rest of the world were likewise zealous in their pursuit of Jewish studies and Hebraic learning. The foremost and most popular Hebrew scholar and writer of the medieval period outside of Spain was Rabbi Shlomo Yitzhaki, who is better known by the abbreviation RaSHI.

Rashi was born (1040) in Troyes, France, and there he died (1105). He wrote commentaries on nearly the entire Bible and Talmud. The popularity of his commentaries is due mainly to his ability to integrate his interpretations of the Bible with midrashic tales and rabbinic expositions. Although he apparently knew French well and employed it extensively in his commentaries when citing equivalents of certain Hebrew words and expressions, his Hebrew is nevertheless free from any foreign influences and displays a matchless ease and charm. He enriched the Hebrew language exceedingly by extending the meanings of numerous old words and expressions, by constructing new word-combinations, and by coining new words and word-forms. He is credited with having coined over thirteen hundred new words on the basis of biblical and talmudic stems. Some of these words are part and parcel of modern Hebrew and could not be dispensed with, as, for example, *hatzlahah* (success), *badhan* (jester), *haskamah* (consent), *yahadut* (Judaism),[3] *peredah* (departure), *bi'ur* (commentary), and the like. Some of the words coined by Rashi have been restored only recently, such as *hablagah* (self-restraint) and *hagannah* (protection).

Yet it cannot be gainsaid that the literary interests and the creative horizon of the Jews outside of Spain during the Middle Ages were generally rather limited and circumscribed within the confines of Bible, Talmud and liturgy. The Jews of Spain, however, exhibited a much more universal range of literary interests and activity, and they are therefore justly credited with being the initiators and creators of the "Golden Age" in medieval Jewish literature.

The Expansion of Hebrew in Paytanic Literature

Our account of the medieval contribution to the development of the Hebrew language would be incomplete without mention, however brief, of a type of literature in vogue during that period, known as *piyyut* (probably from the Greek *poieteis*, "poet"). The writers of the *piyyut* were designated as *paytanim* (Aramaic *paytana*, "poet").

The *piyyutim* (poetic compositions) are liturgical or synagogal poems, in which were articulated the experiences of the Jewish people: their sufferings, yearnings, hopes, fond memories of past glories and aspirations for their speedy restoration. The *piyyutim* are incorporated into the ritual of the Sabbath, high holy days, holidays and festivals. Some of the *piyyutim* were apparently composed for the purpose of edification and instruction. It is assumed by some that the *piyyutim* originated to serve in place of midrashic lectures and addresses, which were forbidden at one time by the Byzantine emperor. Since prayers were permitted, the liturgical form of instruction served as a convenient subterfuge.

In form, the *piyyutim* were cast in a conventional mold or pattern. Originally the writers operated with alphabetical acrostics at the beginning of the verse in varied orders; such as the usual alphabetical order (*aleph, bet, gimel, dalet*), the inverted order (*taw, shin, resh, koph*), or a combination of both (*aleph, taw, bet, shin*). In some instances the name of the author was indicated by the order of the initial letter in each line. Some of the later poems employ meter and rhyme. This is particularly true of the *piyyutim* composed in Spain, where the intricate pattern of Arabic prosody in vogue served the Hebrew *paytanim* as a model. Many of these poems were set to music, and their meter was therefore an essential element.

The rise of the *piyyut* literature can be traced to the early Gaonic period in Palestine (seventh century). It is probable that the later *paytanim* were influenced in their literary compositions and musical settings by the troubadours and minnesingers who flourished from the eleventh to the latter part of the thirteenth century, principally in the South of France, Catalonia, Aragon, Germany and northern Italy. It was during that period and in those localities that most of our *piyyutim* were composed.

The language of the *piyyutim* is of great significance in the study of the development of the Hebrew language. Besides utilizing talmudic and midrashic sources, the *paytanim* coined a large number of words formed on the models and from roots to be found in these sources. A great many of the new formations were wild aberrations from the standpoint of Hebrew grammar and were the target for violent attacks by Saadia, Ibn Ezra and others. Some of the *paytanic* coinages were discarded, but others gained currency and were incorporated in the language. Among the best known of these coinages in modern Hebrew are *meretz* (energy), *miklahat* (shower; cf. Saadia, *Hoshanot*), *lahan* (melody), from which is derived the modern term *malhin* (composer), *piryon* (fertility; Shabtai, *Ofan Pesah*).

The *paytanic* school began with Yose be Yose (sixth century) and reached its earlier climax in the works of Eliezer ha-Kalir (probably seventh century). It began to wane toward the end of the eleventh century, but the tendency toward versification persisted in all aspects of literary self-expression: in philosophy, grammar, liturgy, and the like. These versifiers were, however, eclipsed by the bright poetic luminaries who appeared on the horizon in Spain between the tenth and thirteenth centuries.

The Scene of Hebrew Development Shifts to Italy, Germany and Eastern Europe

After the Spanish period, the next milestone in the development of the Hebrew language and literature was the Haskalah period, generally regarded as the period of the renaissance of modern Hebrew literature. Moses Hayyim Luzzatto (1707-1747), a mystic-poet, born in Padua, is credited with having inaugurated the new trend. Luzzatto's work marked in effect the culmination of an unbroken chain of a Hebrew literary tradition which flourished in Italy since the days of Immanuel ha-Romi, a contemporary of Dante, who also wrote a book of poetic visions of the other world (*Mahberot ha-Tofet we-ha-Eden*), patterned after the Divine Comedy. This tradition was in the main under the influence of the Sephardi poetic tradition. But none of the poets in Italy, with the exception of Immanuel, achieved any great heights of poetic creativity or influence.

After several centuries of comparative literary sterility, the Hebrew language and literature received at the hands of Luzzatto a fresh start and a new lease of life. He wrote in a pure and simple biblical style with masterly skill and artistry. He was followed by Mendelssohn (1729-1786) and his disciples, who started the publication of the first modern Hebrew journal *Ha-Meassef* (The Compiler), in which they preached the gospel of spiritual and cultural emancipation and de-ghettoization. This magazine, founded in 1784, continued as a monthly, although irregularly, for fifteen years and exerted a considerable influence on the development of the Hebrew language and literature. Its publication was resumd in 1809 and continued to 1811.

Mendelssohn, as well as some of the members of his entourage, were sincere in their desire to revive the Hebrew language and to make it an effective instrument for modern literary expression. Mendelssohn himself wrote a beautiful Hebrew with a strong biblical coloring. So did his chief collaborator, Naphtali Herz Wessly (1725-1805). However, some of Mendelssohn's later disciples were more interested in assimilation than in the Hebrew language. It devolved upon the adherents of the Haskalah in Eastern Europe, Austria and Russia to resume the thread of linguistic and literary progress.

The eastern Haskalah was primarily interested in the enrichment of Judaism and Jewish life by a transfusion of worldly knowledge and universal culture. Hence its adherents persisted in the use of the Hebrew language as a means of expression and communication of their ideas. They were eager to see the spread of "enlightenment" (*haskalah*) among Jews, but within a Hebraic framework. They thus brought about a renascence both of the Hebrew language and of Hebrew letters. However, the revolt of the Haskalah writers against what they called the "rigorism" and "narrow-mindedness" of Rabbinism and the Talmud prompted them to frown upon mishnaic or medieval Hebrew, which was symbolic, in their minds, of rabbinic thought and life-patterns. They preferred, instead, to restore and to revive biblical Hebrew also in the writing of prose. But only the great literary masters, such as Abraham Mapu (1808-1867), succeeded in recapturing the grandeur and idyllic beauty of the old classical models. In the case of the majority of the writers, these attempts degenerated into a hodge-podge style, a sort of mosaic of biblical expressions and turns of speech, lacking spontaneity and virility. Instead of mastering the biblical style and making it serve the purposes of literary expression, these writers often became subservient to it and forced their thinking and feeling into the classical molds. Under such circumstances no creative achievement in language or in literature could be expected. Twenty centuries of linguistic development cannot be erased with impunity to cultural growth and progress.

Some curious examples may be culled at random from the writings of the Haskalah authors to illustrate their slavish adherence to biblical stereotypes. In describing blighted trees that will no longer bear fruit, or whose fruit will be rotten and poisonous, Kalman Shulman, one of the most popular authors of that period, uses a mosaic of biblical phrases which yield the following literal translation: The trees will yield no fruit, and even the trees that will not cease from yielding fruit (Jeremiah 17.18) their fruit will be wild grapes (Isaiah 5.2) . . . and all that devour them shall be held guilty (after Jeremiah 2.3). In bewailing the desolation of the Holy Land, the same author gives vent to his emotions in an ensemble of biblical phrases, constituting an appeal to the reader, a literal translation of which would run as follows: Can thy heart endure (Ezekiel 22.14) and its thoughts not be broken off (after Job 17.11), on the day when thine eyes look right on (after Proverbs 4.25) how cruel strangers rule over it (probably after Isaiah 1.7) with great dominion (Daniel 11.3) . . . ?

These writers were especially befuddled when confronted with the need of translating or naming things and creatures for which no apparent name is found in the Bible. They resorted to all kinds of circumlocutions and descriptions within the framework of biblical phraseology in order to meet this need. Thus, a nightingale is rendered by the phrase *noten zemirot ba-laylah* (one who gives song at night), after Job 35.10. For a parrot the biblical phrase *maggid le-adam mah seho* (one who declares to man what is his talk, actually *thought*: Amos 4.13) is employed. The term "admiral" is translated by Joshua Steinberg, the grammarian and lexicographer of that period, by *moshel be ge'ut ha-yam* (he who rules the proud swelling of the sea: Psalms 89.10). The expression *bamat yishak* was employed to denote a theatre. This expression found in Amos 7.8, literally means *the high place of Isaac,* where the word *yishak* (for Yitzhak) is used to symbolize the people of Israel. But by a play of words this name was interpreted in the sense of *sihek* (he played, or acted), with the result that *bamat yishak* came to signify a platform or place where a play is performed. All these and even more ludicrous circumlocutions are rendered in modern Hebrew by single words, frequently drawn from talmudic or later Hebraic sources.

Perhaps one of the most extravagant of these circumlocutions was employed to indicate a microscope. No less than two biblical phrases were drawn upon for this purpose, namely, *zekhukhit asher ba'adah ha-ezob asher ba-kir* (after 1 Kings 5.13) *ke-erez ba-lebanon yisgeh* (Psalms 92.13), a literal translation of which is as follows: a glass through which the hyssop which is on the wall will grow like a cedar in Lebanon.

Modern Hebrew has one word for microscope, namely, *mag-delet* (literally, an enlarger)—a newly coined word from the stem *gdl* (big, or grow).

But the writers of the Haskalah period (and this was true of the readers as well) regarded all Hebrew outside of the Bible as inauthentic. In fact, the above-mentioned Kalman Shulman, when asked to translate a book from German into rabbinic Hebrew, replied boastfully: ". . . I am capable of creating expressions in the Hebrew language and of investing every subject with Hebrew garments, so that I am not compelled to avail myself of the rabbinic language."[4]

Yet, it would be unfair to assert that the Hebrew of the Haskalah period lacked creative vitality. As a matter of fact, despite the halting and cumbersome attempts to meet the changing needs, the Hebrew of the Haskalah period was not barren of new coinages that have survived in modern usage. To be sure, most of them stem from biblical sources. Biblical words or composites of such words were employed, to which new meanings were attached in accordance with the needs. Thus evolved such modern usages as *anokhiut* (egoism, from the biblical *anokhi*, "I"), *bikkoret* (criticism, or review of a book; originally, investigation), *ketobet* (an address; originally, inscription), *tappuah adamah* (potato; literally, apple of the earth), *yemei ha-beinayim* (Middle Ages; literally, the days of between), *mesillat ha-barzel* (railroad; literally, the path of iron), *nekuddat re'ut* (point of view; literally, point of sight), *mekhonah* (machine; originally, base, but adopted for its present meaning because of its phonetic resemblance to "machine" in the European languages). Even the modern use of the biblical *hashmal* (a shining substance: Ezekiel 1.4) in the sense of "electricity," is to be traced to the Haskalah period. The Haskalah poet laureate Judah L. Gordon was the first to employ it in this modern sense on the basis of the Septuagint translation *electron* (amber, also an alloy of gold and silver).

The fact of the matter is that the Haskalah period discharged a very important function in the development of the modern

Hebrew language. In the first place, the emphasis on secularism, on integration into the milieu and on identification of the Jew with the civilization and culture of his environment, impelled the literary protagonists of Haskalah to search for and experiment with new themes and literary patterns. Consequently, these writers had to resort to novel linguistic coinages and media of expression. The language and style employed in dealing with theological, exegetical and liturgical themes were inadequate for their purposes. Secondly, the Haskalah writers redirected the attention of the Hebraists to the rich and dynamic resources of the biblical language, which had remained largely untapped and neglected. They thus paved the way for what has probably been the most prolific period of the Hebrew language and literature since the times of the Bible.

A real synthesis of both biblical and mishnaic styles, which actually incorporated linguistic features of all periods in the history of Hebrew literature, resulting in a style possessing the vigor and grandeur of the one and the clarity and simplicity of the other, was ushered in by such literary artists as Shalom Jacob Abramowitch (Mendele Mokher Sefarim: 1836-1917) in narrative prose, Asher Ginsburg (Ahad ha-Am: 1856-1927) in the essay, and Hayyim Nahman Bialik (1873-1934) in poetry. These writers used the Hebrew language with consummate skill, and they introduced a new Golden Age in the history of the Hebrew language and literature. Not since the days of Judah Halevi and Ibn Gabirol had Hebraic creativity enjoyed such efflorescence. Poets, novelists and essayists made their appearance, some of whom wrote with exquisite beauty and matchless diction. The names of Chernichovski and Schneur, Peretz and Brenner, Berdichevski and S. Y. Agnon, among others, will live forever in the annals of Hebrew literature.

CHAPTER TEN

HOW HEBREW EVOLVED AS A MODERN VERNACULAR

How Hebrew Has Met the Exigencies of Modern Life

Modern Hebrew has gained tremendously in richness, clarity, virility and flexibility as a result of the new Golden Era initiated by the above-mentioned classics of modern Hebrew literature. But even the "synthetic" Hebrew of that period fell far short of meeting the needs of a modern spoken vernacular. The language was too literary; it lacked the artless and earthy simplicity as well as the everyday vocabulary needed for vernacular usage.

Consequently, when Eliezer Ben Yehudah and his associates launched, some seven decades ago, the idea of reviving the Hebrew language as a spoken tongue, especially in Palestine, they became aware of its inadequacy to meet the exigencies of modern life in conversational usage. They accordingly began casting about for devices to meet these exigencies, and a number of new coinages resulted. Since that time a large number of new words found their way into the language. During the last twenty-five years some ten thousand words have found their way into the language, and this number is increasing daily. some of these new coinages show evidence of the influence of

European languages, in which most of the modern Hebraists have been trained; others are modeled after the pattern of Arabic, the language spoken by the majority of the population prior to the establishment of the State of Israel. A large number, however, of these new coinages actually stem from ancient Hebrew sources; they had fallen into discard through centuries of disuse, but have now been unearthed by tireless workers in the field.

What is the general pattern of these changes? What are the sources out of which the language has been expanded in the modern period? A great many of these modern word-coinages are Hebraized forms of words, stemming from Indo-European languages. For example, such words as *tilphen* (telephoned), *tilgreph* (telegraphed) and the like are freely coined, where no Hebrew equivalent could be found. This is in keeping with the practice of all living languages. Thus in mishnaic Hebrew the verb *hit'akhsen* (received hospitality) was derived from the noun *'akhsania* (Greek *xenia* "hospitality"). In the same manner *'ir meukhleset* (a populated city) is coined from the noun *'okhlos* (Greek *ochlos* "population"). The same process of assimilation may be found in English, where the noun "jubilee," borrowed from the Hebrew, was converted into a verb by affixing to it the English verbal ending *ate,* thus yielding "jubilate."

Incidentally, in borrowing words from another language, the grammatical structure of Hebrew is followed, but the Hebrew sound pattern is generally ignored. Thus the form *tilphen* is structurally a normal grammatical Hebrew form, but according to the Hebrew phonetic pattern the form should be pronounced *tilpen.* Were that done, however, the phonetic relationship of this word with the word *telephone* would be rendered vague and loose. Hence the original phonetic pattern of the loan words is generally retained in such cases. The same is true in the case of *meballef* (a bluffer, is bluffing) instead of *mevallef* according to the Hebrew phonetic pattern.

Another form of borrowing operative in the process of word-coinages is that of loan-translations which was discussed above

(p. 174f.). In this process a word in its secondary meaning is translated into Hebrew by a word corresponding to the original meaning of the borrowed word, thus lending the Hebrew word a meaning which it did not have originally. For example, the English word "convince" stems from the Latin *convincere* which meant originally *to overcome* or *conquer*. It is in this sense that the English *convince* is still used by Shakespeare. It later took on an additional meaning, namely, that of persuading by argument or evidence. The Hebrew equivalent of "convince" in its original meaning is *hikhni'a* (*hiph'il* of the stem *kn'*). But modern Hebrew, in order to avoid ambiguity, refrained from attaching a secondary meaning to the word *hikhni'a*. It accordingly went one step further and restored to the mishnaic parallel form of the *hiph'il*, namely, the *shiph'el* conjugation, thus coining the form *shikhna'* in the specific sense of the modern "convince." We now have then such words as *meshukhna'* (a person who is convinced), *nishtakhna'* (became convinced), and the like. Similarly, *shihzer* (of the stem *hzr*), in the sense of "reconstruct," was coined alongside of *hehezir* (brought back, restored); also *shikkem* (of the stem *kum*), in the meaning of "rehabilitate," alongside of *hekim* (raised, established). The nominal formations *shihzur* (reconstruction) and *shikkum* (rehabilitation) are, of course, normal developments. This process was also operative in mishnaic Hebrew (see above, p. 170).

An important source for new word-coinages is popular etymology. For example, in the English words "democracy," "diplomacy," and many others, the letter *c* in the ending *cy* evolved by a phonetic change from *t* (compare "democrat," "diplomat," etc.). But what about the word "normalcy," introduced by the late President Harding? What is the basis for the *c* in this word? It could not have evolved from "normal." Evidently the word is grammatically incorrect and was coined under the influence of false or popular analogy of such words as "democracy," according to which the ending *cy* was wrongly assumed to be a suffix. However, the word has taken root in the language despite the grammarians and purists, and it is now accepted as legitimate. There are many other such words in English which come into being by the same process.

This principle of popular etymology was already in evidence in biblical Hebrew and is widely operative in mishnaic Hebrew. Thus nouns like *tehillah* (beginning) and *terumah* (gift, contribution) originate, respectively, from the stems *hll* and *rwm*. The initial letter *t* in these words is therefore a prefix and does not belong to the stem. But in mishnaic Hebrew the *t* is taken as part of the stem, thus yielding the new verbal stem *thl* (for example, *hithil*, "began") and *trm* (*taram*, "contributed"), since the forms *tehillah* and *terumah* were regarded as analogous to those of *ketibah* (writing) and *yeshu'ah* (help), in which the initial letter is an integral part of the stem.

In modern Hebrew such forms are freely coined. Thus, the noun *tenu'ah* (from the stem *nu'*, "to move") signifies motion or movement, as well as vowel. In the latter sense, the term was coined by the medieval grammarians after the Arabic *harakat* (movements, also vowels which put the consonants into motion), to which the Hebrew plural form *tenu'ot* corresponds exactly. A new verbal stem was accordingly assumed, namely, *tn'*, where the prefixed *t* of *tenu'ah* was incorporated in the stem, from which resulted a *hiph'il* form *hitni'a* in the meanings of "put into motion," "started the motor of a car," as well as "vocalized." The term *matne'a* (a starter of the motor in a car) was, therefore, directly and logically coined on the analogy of the form *mafte'ah* (a key) from the verbal form *patah* (opened).

An interesting case of popular etymology is the name of the largest and most modern city in Israel, Tel Aviv. This name is already found in the Bible (Ezekiel 3.15) as a designation of a place in Babylonia where the Judean exiles settled. Why was this name selected for this modern city in Israel?

When Theodor Herzl published his famous Zionist novel, *Altneuland*, in 1903, depicting the building of the new Jewish State and the ideal society evolving in the old-new Jewish homeland, he selected the name *Altneuland* for the new State, since this name symbolizes both the old (German, *alt*) and the new (German, *neu*). The book was subsequently translated by Nahum Sokolow into Hebrew, and he chose the biblical name *Tel Aviv* as the most appropriate equivalent of the German title *Altneuland, tel* (mound, ruin) indicating *old,* while *aviv* (spring) symbolizes the new. This name was accordingly also selected by the builders of the new city.

But, as Ahad ha-Am already pointed out in his critical analysis of Herzl's book, the name *Altneuland* employed by Herzl is based on a misinterpretation. Herzl took this name from an ancient synagogue in Prague, called *Altneuschul.* This synagogue was built, according to an ancient legend, by the exiles from Jerusalem, who brought with them stones from the Temple and had them immured in the foundation of the synagogue. But they did so on condition (Hebrew, *'al-tnai*) that when the Messiah will come and rebuild the Temple, the synagogue should be torn down and the stones restored to their former place in the Temple. The real name of the synagogue was therefore *Al-Tnai Schul,* which by popular etymology was misinterpreted as *Alt-Neu Schul.*

Many new coinages in modern Hebrew stem from the normal organic structure of the language. Each of the Hebrew conjugations, with the exception of the passive conjugations *pu'al* and *hoph'al,* are capable of yielding nominal forms freely. These forms evolve from the regular gerund and infinitive formations of the respective conjugations.

Thus, the nominal form of the type *ketibah* (writing, script), *behirah* (choosing, choice) is the characteristic gerund derivative of the *kal* or simple conjugation *katab* (wrote) and *bahar* (chose), respectively. Two nominal types, with a slight differentiation in meaning, may be constructed from the *pi'el* and the *hiph'il* conjugations. For example, the *pi'el* form *kibbel* (received) yields the two nominal types *kibbul* (receiving, accepting, acceptance) and *kabbalah* (receipt, reception). The former is the normal gerund of the *pi'el,* especially in mishnaic Hebrew, while the latter is the regular infinitive of the *pi'el* in Aramaic.

Similarly, the nominal types *hebdel* (difference, distinction) and *habdalah* (separation, division) are built from the *hiph'il* form *hibdil* (separated, divided, stem *bdl*). Both these nominal forms have evolved from regular infinitives of the *hiph'il*. The first is the normal infinitive in Hebrew (*habdel-hebdel*), while the second is the regular infinitive formation in Aramaic. These forms are employed sparingly in biblical Hebrew, but are used extensively in post-biblical Hebrew, probably under the influence of mishnaic Hebrew and Aramaic. In modern Hebrew they are freely coined as need arises.

In some instances, where one nominal type of the *pi'el* or *hiph'il* already exists and a need arises for a word with a slightly different shade of meaning, this need can be readily met by coining the parallel nominal type in the same conjugation. For example, the noun *bakkashah* (request, wish), derived from the *pi'el* form *bikkesh* (required, sought, desired) is already found in the Bible and is used extensively in later Hebrew. But the exigencies of the times required a word also for the concept of "a demand" (of goods or merchandise), the cognate form *bikkush* was accordingly adopted for this purpose and is widely in vogue in modern Hebrew.

But what about a word for the term "supply," the complementary antonym of "demand," in the area of marketing, where the principle of supply and demand operates? The Hebrew literary sources failed to provide such a word. However, since the mishnaic word *hatztza'ah*, a nominal derivative from the biblical *hiph'il hitztzi'a* (proposed, presented, offered) has been adopted in modern Hebrew to denote the idea of "a proposition" or "a motion," the parallel nominal derivative from the *hiph'il*, namely, *hetztza'* (already coined by Maimonides [*Hilkhot Berakhot*, xi, 3] in the sense of "formulation"), has therefore been introduced to signify the concept "supply." Thus the Hebrew language possesses now two new coinages for the terms "supply" and "demand" in marketing, namely, *hetztza'* and *bikkush*, respectively.

In the same manner, the noun *sikkun* (risk) is now extensively employed alongside the more common *sakkanah* (danger), derived from the *pi'el sikken* (endangered). Similarly, the cognate forms *heskem* (agreement) and *haskamah* (consent) were built from the *hiph'il* form *hiskim* (agreed, stem *skm*).

Whenever a further extension or shading of meaning is required, one of the nominal formations of the *hiph'il* lends itself to phonetic modifications in order to meet the need. Thus the form *habhanah* (discrimination, stem *bhn*) evolved into *abhanah* (diagnosis), from which a new verb, *ibhen* (diagnosed), is coined. In like manner, *hakhzabah* (denial, stem *kzb*) yields a parallel form *akhzabah* (disappointment), which gives rise to a new verb *ikhzeb* (disappointed).

The other two conjugations, the *niph'al* and *hitpa'el,* likewise lend themselves to the building of nominal formations. Nouns in the abstract sense may be constructed by affixing an *ut*-ending to the Infinitive form of each of these conjugations. Thus, the noun *hibbadlut* (differentiation, isolation) was formed by affixing the *ut*-ending to the *niph'al* Infinitive *hibbadel* (to be different or separated), while the *hitpa'el* Infinitive *hitbaddel* (to detach or separate oneself) serves as the basis for the noun *hitbadlut* (self-separation, isolation), by affixing the same ending.

Incidentally, it is possible to construct nouns in Hebrew generally by affixing the *ut*-ending to an adjective or noun. In this fashion evolved the abstract nouns *shelemut* (perfection) from the adjective *shalem* (perfect), *takkifut* (power, resoluteness) from *takkif* (mighty, resolute), *sifrut* (literature) from *sefer* (book), *samkhut* (authority) from *semekh* (support), *sokhnut* (agency) from *sokhen* (agent), and the like.

There are certain word-formations or nominal patterns, which are typical of specific functions or activities. For example, there is a special formation which denotes a person engaged in a certain activity as an occupation, preoccupation, or vocation. This formation is evident in a number of biblical and mishnaic nouns such as *tabbah* (cook, stem *tbh*), *naggah* (an ox wont to gore, stem *ngh*), *gannab* (thief, stem *gnb*), *naggar* (carpenter, stem *ngr*), *hazzan* (beadle, cantor, stem *hzn*). This opens the way to forming nouns on the same analogy from virtually every verb, or even noun, as need arises. Hence, a host of new coinages of this type have made their appearance in modern Hebrew, and their number is constantly increasing, such as *tzallam* (photographer, stem *tzlm*), *rashsham* (draftsman, registrar, stem *rshm*), *passal* (sculptor, stem *psl*), *kannar* (violinist, from *kinnor* "violin"), *ramman* (grenadier, from *rimmon* "pomegranate," "grenade"), and the like.

Another formation is typical of *instrumental* nouns. Such formations are characterized by a preformative *mem,* as in the biblical forms *martze'a* (awl, stem *rtz'* "pierce"), *masmer* (nail, stem *smr* "bristle up"), *malben* (brick-mould, stem *lbn* "make bricks"). Many such formations were coined in mishnaic and medieval Hebrew. In modern Hebrew we find such new coinages as *mabreg* (screw-driver, stem *brg* "screw"), *mahbet* (bat, tennis racket, stem *hbt* "beat"), *matzlemah* (camera, a feminine form, of the stem *tzlm*), *mabded* (isolator or insulator), stem *bdd,* and so on.

A type which is prolific of new coinages is that of indicating physical defects or diseases. The biblical and mishnaic examples are *dalleket* (inflammation, stem *dlk*), *shahefet* (wasting away, tuberculosis, stem *shhf*), *tzalleket* (scar, stem *tzlk*), *yallefet* (scab, scurf, stem *ylf*) and *yabbelet* (wart, ulcer, stem *ybl*). Diseases identified in modern times are generally rendered in modern Hebrew by nouns of this formation. Thus evolved words like *katztzeret* (asthma, stem *ktzr* "short"), *nazzelet* (head cold, catarrh, stem *nzl* "flow"), *addemet* (measles, stem *adm* "red"), *tzahebet* (jaundice, stem *tzhb* "yellow"), *sha'elet* (whooping cough, stem *sh'l,* "cough"), and a host of others.

Another basis for new coinages is the blending of two words or parts of words. Thus, in English, words like "electrocution," "goodbye," "chortle" are, respectively, blends of "electric" and "execution," "God be with you," "chuckle" and "snort." In modern Hebrew, likewise, we find such newly coined words as *ramzor* (traffic light), which is a blend of *ramaz* (beckon) and *or* (light). Similarly, *zerakor,* or *zarkor,* (projector) is a blend of *zarak* (throw) and *or* (light). The term for "thermometer" is *madhom*—a composite of *madad* (measured) and *hom* (heat), and *kolno'a* (sound pictures) is a blend of *kol* (sound) and *no'a* (motion). A peculiar blend is *tapuz* (orange), which is composed of the word *tapuah* (apple) and the first letter of the word *zahab* (gold).

Such blends are sometimes envisaged as independent stems, which may serve as a basis for the different conjugations. Thus an adjectival form *metzubrah* (moody, dejected) is now in vogue, which is, in effect, a *pu'al* form, in the present tense, of the stem *mtzbrh*. This stem originates from a blend of the two nouns *matzab* (condition, state) and *ruah* (spirit). When a person is dejected or moody he is said to be *metzubrah*.

A very interesting coinage is the verbal form *idken* (brought up to date), which is derived from the expression *ad kan* (up to here, up to this point). Something which is ultra-modern or up to date is accordingly designated by the normal adjectival form *adkani*. The two words *ad* (until, up to) and *kan* (here) were thus blended, in the popular mind of the speakers, into one, evolving into an adjective by the addition of the normal adjectival suffix *i,* as in *hofshi* (a free man) from the *hofesh* (freedom). The next step in the process was to coin a quadriliteral verb *idken*. Thus, for example, the sentence "he brought the dictionary up to date" would be rendered in modern Hebrew by *hu idken et ha-millon,* and "a person possessing most recent information"—by *ben adam me'udkan*.

Still another source for new coinages is the practice of taking a familiar stem and adding prefixes or suffixes, thus forming nouns denoting modern terms and concepts. Thus from the stem *klt* (absorb) we derive *taklit* (phonograph record); from *zmr* (sing, play) we get *tizmoret* (orchestra); from *gdl* (grow) we have *magdelet* (microscope); from *brk* (shine, lightning)— *mibrak* (telegram); and so on. The possibilities are obviously limitless.

Influences from Yiddish and Other Languages

Since Yiddish has been the mother-tongue of most of Israel's population, it is to be expected that numerous traits of that language should be found in modern Hebrew, especially in spoken Hebrew. Yiddish has indeed made deep inroads both lexically and stylistically. Through the channels of Yiddish, German elements have made their way into the language. A typical example in spoken Israeli Hebrew is the word *kumzitz*. It is a composite of the two Yiddish (German) words *kum* (come) and *zitz* (sit down). The word originated with the old *Shomrim*, "night watchmen" in Palestine, forerunners of the *Hagannah*, who during the long tiresome nights of vigil used to welcome one another with the words "*kum zitz* (come, sit down) and let us while away a few minutes," all then chatting congenially, chanting and singing some of the lyrics and romantic tunes of that period. The word has now come to connote a "picnic," a rest after a long hike, accompanied by refreshments and fun. The word has even been verbalized and has assumed verbal inflections, in accordance with Hebrew grammar, as in *kumzitzanu* (we took a jolly rest) during the *tiyul* (hike).

The number of Yiddish words that have invaded spoken Hebrew in modern Israel would be too large to list. Only a few of them can be mentioned here: *nebikh* (poor thing), *shpritz* (spout) from which evolved also a verbal form *le-hashpritz* (to squirt or cause to squirt), *izen* (iron, that is, strong or excellent), *shwitz* (sweat) of which the nominal form *mashwitz* (a pretentious or overbearing person) was coined.

Nor is spoken Hebrew free from the influence of Yiddish syntax. It is not at all unusual to hear such Yiddishisms as *attah tzohek mimmenni* (literally, "you laugh from me," corresponding to the Yiddish *du lakhst fun mir*) instead of the correct Hebrew construction *attah tzohek li* (literally, "you laugh to me," but in the sense of "you laugh at me"); or *hi nora yafah* (literally, "she is terribly pretty") for the correct form *hi yafah meod* (she is very pretty), in which case the word *nora* (Yiddish *shreklikh*) is employed as a superlative, like the English "awful" in such colloquial usage as "awfully pretty." Similarly, the expression *mithashshek li* ("I have a desire"; "I desire") is a literal Hebrew translation of the Yiddish *es glist zikh mir* (literally, "it desires itself to me").

Another typical example of Yiddishisms is equally startling: The Yiddish word *nood(j)en* (to disgust, bore) stems from a slavic origin. But under the influence of the Hebrew language, the very soul (Hebrew *neshamah*) is supposed to be involved in such mental or emotional states as that of being bored or disgusted. Thus there evolved such Yiddish expressions as *er farnood(j)et mir di neshomoh* (literally, "he bores or disgusts my soul"), which is readily rendered in Hebrew by *hu menadned li al ha-neshamah*. Incidentally, this construction may have been suggested by the Hebrew stem *nidned* (shook, rocked).

A few more typical Yiddishisms found in spoken Hebrew in Israel may be mentioned: *ani ohez mimmennu* (literally, "I hold from him," but in the sense of "I think highly of him"), *eifoh attah ohez?* (literally, "where do you hold?" that is, "where did you stop?"), *hu' oseh li et ha-mawet* (literally, "he makes me the death," but in the meaning of "he annoys me to death"), *zeh yikkah harbeh zman* (this will take a long time); all of which are translations from the Yiddish, respectively, *ikh halt fun im, vu haltstu?, er makht mir dem toit, dos vet nemen a lange tzeit* (incidentally, an exact equivalent of the English).

The Russian language, in which most of the East European immigrants, especially those of the second and third *aliyas,* were brought up, also left its impress on the conversational language, perhaps via Yiddish. Thus, the adjective *katanchik,* composed of the Hebrew *katan* (small) and the Russian diminutive suffix *chik,* is frequently employed in the daily parlance in Israel to describe something tiny, as in *tzerifon katanchik* (a tiny little hut). Similarly, a considerable number of words ending in *nik,* likewise a Russian suffix indicating belongingness to a certain group, locality, party, etc., in the masculine gender, also invaded the Israeli dialect, such as *kibbutznik* (a man belonging to a *kibbutz*), *mapamnik* (a man belonging to the Mapam party). The corresponding suffix in Hebrew, signifying belongingness, is *i* for the masculine and *it* for the feminine, for example, *tzioni* (a Zionist, masc.) and *tzionit* (a Zionist, feminine), *bostoni* (a Boston man) and *bostonit* (a Boston woman). The Russian masculine suffix *nik* would have to change in the feminine, according to the Russian pattern, to *nitza*. This, however, does not generally occur. Instead, the suffix *nik* is incorporated in the word, and the Hebrew feminine suffix *it* is appended, thus yielding the feminine forms *kibbutznikit* and *mapamnikit*, rather than *kibbutznitza* and *mapamnitza*.

The English language, too, has left its mark on the conversational Hebrew of modern Israel. The presence of the British in Palestine as the mandatory power over a period of nearly three decades could not but affect the Hebrew speech there. Thus, when something goes awry or a mishap occurs, the situation is described as having developed a *punture* (puncture). A redhaired fellow is referred to as a *gingi* (British *ginger*). *O.K.* and *yes sir* are commonly interjected in modern Israeli Hebrew speech. Besides, a great many words have been imported from America into Israel together with the objects and ideas which they symbolize. An American will readily recognize in modern Israeli parlance such words as *sweater, jeep, garage, nylon, tractor, bateriah* (battery), and a great many other words, with a slight modification or Israeli accent.

Even the English or American idiom can be detected in modern Hebrew, especially in the spoken dialect. The English or American mental pattern can readily be identified in such Hebrew expressions as *etmol abadti kemo klum* (I worked yesterday like anything), *hu' oseh same'ah* (he is making merry), *ha-bahurah meflartetet itto* (the young lady is flirting with him), *hu' meshuggah ahareha* (he is madly in love with her), *shuk shahor* (black market), *hitztalbut derakhim* (crossroads), *we-od eikh!* (and how!) in accentuation of a statement, an expression in vogue also in other European languages and in Arabic. In reply to a query "Did you like that?" an Israeli might answer: *Lo tob we-lo ra* (neither good nor bad), "fifty fifty." A common expression in Israel is *hu' sidder oto* (he fixed him), that is, taught him a lesson, got even with him, or did something harmful to him.

It should be noted parenthetically that Yiddish exercised a considerable influence not only on spoken Hebrew, but also on literary Hebrew. The greatest masters of the modern Hebrew literary "Golden Age" in Russia were not free from this influence. They were, after all, rooted in that language, since it was their vernacular from early childhood. A number of distinct Yiddishisms can be found even in the works of such outstanding Hebrew classics as Mendele and Bialik.

Mendele, who was able to wield both Yiddish and Hebrew with equal facility and dexterity, succeeded in creating on the basis of Yiddish some interesting and masterly Hebrew idioms and expressions, which retain the charm and flavor of both languages. Thus, for example, a fantastic and incredible story is characterized in Yiddish by an expression which may be rendered in English by "a cow flew over the roof and laid an egg." In translating this expression into Hebrew, Mendele does not use the Hebrew equivalent of cow (*parah*), but an obscure talmudic term *koi,* a species of deer, about the genus of which the rabbis were uncertain.[1] He chose the term because of its phonetic resemblance to the Yiddish word for cow (*kooh*). Similarly, Mendele employs the word *bulbusim* in the sense of *potatoes.*[2] The word *bulbus* is found in the Talmud and is borrowed from Greek. In the Talmud, however, it is used in the same meaning as in English, namely, a bulbous root of an onion. The use of the word in the sense of "potatoes" is a direct influence of the Yiddish.

One more interesting example from Mendele—the interjection *beh* in Yiddish generally connotes the idea of "I don't care to talk to you," or "what is the use of wasting words on you,

you won't understand anyhow." Mendele uses this interjection quite frequently and even constructs a verb *babe'a*[3] on the analogy of the Yiddish verb *beben*.

Numerous examples can also be cited from Bialik's writings. Bad-tempered or sour-faced people are designated as *hamutze tzelem*,[4] a translation of the Yiddish expression *zoire penimer*. *Kabtzan rimmah*[5] refers to *a very poor man*, who lives amidst vermin and worm-eaten objects. This is likewise a direct translation from the Yiddish *a veremdiger kabtzan*. To desire *a telerel fun himmel* (a little plate from heaven, that is, the moon) means in Yiddish to ask for the unattainable. Bialik uses the Hebrew equivalent *ka'arat raki'a*.[6]

The Yiddish expression *lecken honig* (literally, "lick honey," in the sense of having a good time), is very likely to be traced to the influence of the story of Jonathan (1 Samuel 14. 26-29), who felt refreshed after tasting of the honey which he had found. This expression was brought back into the Hebrew language by Bialik, when he described his bitter lot in a personal and national sense among the foreign nations and peoples, in his famous poem *Al Saph Bet ha-Midrash* (On the Threshold of the House of Study): *lo ariti ya'arot debash* ("I did not gather any honeycombs," that is, I did not fare well).

Similarly, Bialik does not hesitate to Hebraize the Yiddish verb *shnorren* (to go begging) and to lend it a Hebrew grammatical and idiomatic inflection, when he uses toward the end of his well-known poem *Be-Ir ha-Haregah* (In the City of Slaughter) the expression *we-khd'asher shnorartem tishnorru* (beggars you were, beggars you will remain).

There is an interesting linguistic development in modern Israeli speech traceable to the influence of the European languages. Hebrew, as is well known, does not possess auxiliary verbs indicating future tense, such as the English "shall" and "will." Instead, a pronominal prefix is attached to the verbal stem indicating futurity. Thus, "you will learn" is rendered by *tilmad*, where the pronoun, 2nd person, *ti* is prefixed to the stem *lmd* (learn). It is impossible, therefore, to say in Hebrew "I shall," "you will," etc., independently of the main verb.

But the modern Hebrew-speaking Israelis will not be daunted; they found a way out of this difficulty. In addition to the auxiliary tense-prefixes, the Hebrew verb can also take a conjunction-prefix *she* (that), as, for example, *shetilmad* (that you should learn or study), where both *she* (that) and *ti* (tense-prefix) are attached to the verb *lmd* (learn or study). Thus, the teacher tells the pupil "I want you to study (*shetilmad*) your lesson tomorrow," whereupon the pupil replies (if he so desires): *"be-vadai sheh"* (of course, I shall). The particle *sheh* can, accordingly, represent the idea of auxiliaries in all forms of person and number (I shall, you will, they will, etc.). It may, furthermore, correspond to our American "O.K." One little bully, for example, belabors his little playmate. The latter threatens to go home and report the beating to his big brother (*she'aggid le'ahi*). *"Sheh!"* ejaculates the bully swaggeringly, as if to say: "O.K., go ahead! I should worry."

Incidentally, the Imperative form is on its way out in the modern vernacular of Israel. It is generally replaced by the Future form, although in shorter formations, such as *kum* (get up), *zuz* (move) this usage is less common. Thus, instead of the Imperative *ketob* (write), the Israeli speaker is more likely to say *tikhtob* or rather *shetikhtob* (literally: "you will write" or "that you will write"). This is a sort of intermediate form between the simple Imperative, which implies a command and the lengthened Imperative (*kotbah*), or the Imperative supplemented with *na* or *be-bakkashah,* indicating a plea. This form is also used to express an obligation or necessity, like the English "shall" or "should." This vernacular usage has its precedents in biblical Hebrew syntax.[7]

The influence of Arabic on modern Hebrew in Israel should, of course, be taken for granted. Arabic was, in the first place, the language of the majority of the inhabitants of the country. In the second place, it is, of the modern living languages, the most kindred with Hebrew. The influence of Arabic on Hebrew during the Middle Ages has already been mentioned. Among the new words borrowed from Arabic, which have become integral parts of the modern Hebrew language, are the following: *adib* (polite), *muz* (banana), *mahson* (store, magazine), *nadir* (rare), *ta'arikh* (date), *sabbon,* originally Latin, *sapo* (soap), *retzini* (serious).

Strong influences of Arabic, especially spoken Arabic, are especially in evidence among the young native Israelis. As a matter of fact, some young Israeli authors, who write realistically about modern Jewish life and recent experiences in Israel, seem often to go out of their way to inject Arabisms into the lingo of their characters. This is particularly true of those who want to cut their ties with European Jewish life and to emphasize the indigenous oriental milieu of Israel. Some words like *chizbat* (tall talk, fairy tale), *mabsut* (all right, happy), *ya habibi* (oh, my dear), *ya ba'* (oh, father dear) as an expression of grief, *zift* (literally, "tar," but signifying something that is no good or putrid), *jamah'ah* (crowd, group), *kef* (a good time, an urge), probably of Turkish origin, are not at all uncommon in the parlance of young Israelis.

Some of these words are Hebraized and inflected in accordance with the principles of Hebrew grammar. Thus one may hear and read in the ultra-modern Hebrew of Israel such expressions as *hu mesapper chizbatim* (he is telling tall stories), or *chizbatnu kol ha-laylah* (we were telling fairy tales all night long), *ha-mahazeh hayah zifti* (the play was putrid), *ha-ne'um hayah mezuppat* (the speech was rotten), *hitkayyef li la-lekhet le-kolno'a* (I had an urge to go to the movies). In reply to a question *mah shlomekh?* (how are you?) a young lady would reply *ani mabsutah halas* (I am very fine, happy). To the young Israeli *tzabras* such Hebrew sounds perfectly natural.

It may be interesting to observe, however, that the influence of Arabic, as compared with that of Aramaic, on standard Hebrew is negligible. Despite the fact that both Aramaic and Arabic belong in the same family with Hebrew, all being Semitic languages, and despite occasional historical contacts of the Jews and the Arabs, only about thirty or forty Arabic words have been incorporated in modern classical Hebrew, while thousands of Aramaic words are now part and parcel of the language. Even some of the words introduced by the Tibbonids in their translations from Arabic failed to survive. The intimate historical relationships between Hebrew and Aramaic during the early creative life of the two languages, and the fact that a large proportion of our literature (the Talmud, the Midrash, and others) was written in Aramaic may account in a large measure for the stronger influence of Aramaic on Hebrew.

Other Organic Changes in the Language

Still another important source for new words in modern Hebrew is the capacity of old words in a language to take new meanings. In Chaucerian English, for instance, the word "clerk" meant "priest" or "scholar." It has an entirely different meaning in modern English. Similarly in modern Hebrew there are numerous words that have taken on meanings different from their original meaning. Thus the biblical word *hashmal* (a shining substance) has taken on in modern Hebrew the meaning "electricity," *nasi* (a prince, a chief) has come to mean "a president," *mokesh* (a snare, trap) now means "a mine," and the *paytanic* word *meretz* (strength or rapidity) is employed in modern Hebrew in the sense of "energy." One can readily imagine the confusion of an Israeli youngster studying the first chapter of the book of Ezekiel, where the prophet describes his visions in which he saw "the color of *hashmal*."

Words, like people, are subject to whims of fate. As an interesting illustration one may cite the case of the word *tzionut* (Zionism). Originally a very respectable word, symbolic of a moving ideology, it has recently fallen into disrepute among the younger generation in Israel. The young Israelis look down disdainfully upon the official Zionists who preach the ideals of Zionism but who do nothing concrete, in their opinion, to implement these ideas in their personal lives. Consequently, the word *tzionut* has come to symbolize Zionist claptrap, pretentious idealism, or just high-falutin and tedious talk. A long-winded speaker holding forth on any subject whatsoever is characterized as speaking *tzionut*. Such is the fate of words!

The chief reservoir for new words in modern Hebrew is to be found in the ancient literary Hebraic sources, such as the Bible, the Talmud and the Midrashim. It should be recalled that these sources dealt with every aspect of human life: domestic, political, agricultural, legal, industrial, and the like. The Hebrew language still possessed at that time dynamic creativity, and the new vocabularies were normally coined as the need for them arose. In the course of time, however, as Hebrew ceased to be the normal medium of oral expression and communication, many words in vernacular usage fell into desuetude. Jewish scholars concerned with the revival of Hebrew as a spoken language undertook, therefore, to scan these sources and to bring these forgotten words back into circulation.

There is also a trend, in the process of language development, in the opposite direction, namely, of dropping certain common words, for no apparent reason, and replacing them by more or less synonymous words. Thus the common biblical word *shab* (returned) tends to disappear in conversational usage in Israel and is replaced by its talmudic synonym *hazar*. Similarly the biblical words *ayyeh* (where) and *maddu'a* (why) are replaced respectively by the biblical synonyms *eifoh* and *lammah*; while the mishnaic *hammah* (sun) and *lebanah* (moon) are displaced by the biblical equivalents *shemesh* and *yareah*, perhaps in order to avoid confusion in the mishnaic usage of these two nouns with their adjectival meanings, namely, *hammah* (warm) and *lebanah* (white). But why was the mishnaic usage of the verbs *lakah* and *kanah* in the respective meanings of "bought" and "acquired possession" discarded in modern Hebrew in favor of the biblical usage, namely, "took" and "bought," respectively? The reason in this instance and in other similar instances is not entirely clear.

It should be recalled that the history of the Hebrew language differs from that of other languages in one respect. In the other languages ancient usages become obsolete and are discarded. They are subjects of interest only to philologists and students of ancient literature. In Hebrew, however, such usages are subjects of study in the elementary schools. Nearly every Jew of the past generations in Eastern Europe was more or less conversant with the *humash* (Pentateuch), which comprises the most ancient texts of the Bible. Since the modern Israeli vernacular evolved out of the background of the early pioneers and settlers, who were in the main of East European origin and well versed in the Bible, it should cause no wonder that they showed preference in some cases for biblical usage rather than for mishnaic or medieval usages, with which they were less familiar. Furthermore, some of the popular classics of modern Hebrew literature, such as Frishman, Bialik and Chernichovski preferred generally the biblical style, and their influence on the modern Hebraists has been tremendous.

Pristine Character of the Language Must Be Guarded

New word-coinages, grammatical changes and borrowing, such as are described above, are essential to growth and progress of languages. A living language, like all organic matter, is subject to the Law of Change. Since language is the best single index to the characteristics of a culture, changes in the people and its culture must be reflected in the structural, phonetic and semantic changes of the language. A language cannot remain static and live, any more than a people or a culture can do so. A language that is completely standardized and rejects modifications and innovations, whether in vocabulary or grammar, is a dead language, the symbol of an extinct culture.

Changes may, however, move in the direction of progress and growth, or in that of disintegration and extinction. Wholesome changes must be evolutionary; they should sprout out of the stem of the language and within its structural framework. Foreign injections and graftings are not necessarily detrimental to the language, but they must not exceed its digestive capacity. The random and excessive invasion of such foreign influences was responsible for the extinction of many oriental and occidental languages and civilizations. Nations, cultures and languages do not generally die as a result of military defeat or physical destruction, but rather in consequence of their inability either to resist the impact of alien influences or to assimilate them. In some instances the languages and civilizations disappeared completely; in others they gradually lost their identity, but in the process of disintegration furnished the seed or the fertilizer for the germinations of new civilizations and languages. It was in this manner that the Romanic languages and cultures emerged out of Latin and Vulgar Latin.

"Correctness" in language is, to be sure, determined by the majority of the native population using it as a vehicle of self-expression and communication. In the case of spoken Hebrew, therefore, usage can hardly be regarded as a criterion of "correctness," since Hebrew is not the mother-tongue of the majority of the people employing it. Indeed, the present disproportionate influx of immigrants into Israel, using a multitude of tongues, threatens to jeopardize the normal growth and development of the Hebrew language. Spoken Hebrew in Israel often evinces symptoms of dangerous adulteration. Hebraists trained on models of classical, both ancient and modern, literary Hebrew are often jarred by some of the "illicit" grammatical and syntactical coinages that have crept into the Hebrew speech of modern Israel.

There are, however, good reasons to hope that the excessive intrusions of alien influences will eventually be curbed, and that the Hebrew language will succeed in reasserting its pristine character and in regaining its normal power of growth. For one thing, the traditional Jewish attitude toward the "book" and respect for literary authorities are admittedly widely in vogue in Israel. Literacy and literary interests are predominant there on a scale unequaled in any other country. Furthermore, the authority of the Hebrew Bible and later Hebrew classics, which are studied in the Israeli schools, even in the elementary grades, should serve to safeguard the purity of the language.

There are other conservative forces, which try to guide and direct the normal development of the Hebrew language; such are the stage, the radio, the public forums and the press. The outstanding newspapers in Israel carry special columns where problems of usage are discussed by well-known authorities.

But the most important single authority, whose verdict upon usage is held generally in high esteem, is the Hebrew Language Academy. This institution, formerly known as *Vaad ha-Lashon* (Language Committee), was reorganized immediately after the establishment of the State. It was formally recognized by the *Kneset* (parliament) and endorsed by the World Zionist Organization. The Academy is composed of prominent Israeli scholars, poets and prose writers, and it concerns itself with matters dealing with all aspects of life in the new Jewish State. With the emergence of the State new fields of activity have opened up, calling for the Hebraization of their terms, such as jurisprudence, international treaties and military affairs.

All these influences, it is hoped, will exercise some restraint on the development of the language and will keep it more or less within the framework of the classical models in syntax and grammar, while allowing, at the same time, a reasonable latitude in the creation of new words, in the application of new signification to old ones, and in the adaptation of the language to the changing circumstances of civilization.

Eliezer Ben Yehudah's Role in the Revival of Hebrew as a Vernacular

One of the workers, to whom more credit is due than to any other single person for the modern revival of Hebrew as a spoken tongue and for enriching its vocabulary, is Eliezer Ben Yehudah (1858-1922). A sickly man, but possessed of boundless enthusiasm, zeal and persistence, he labored valiantly by propaganda and example, against many odds, for the revival of spoken Hebrew. In these efforts he was often discouraged and ridiculed, condemned and persecuted; but he did not flinch. The crowning achievement of his efforts was the preparation of a Hebrew thesaurus, which he began in 1910 and apparently in the main completed just before his death. An editorial committee, headed by Professor N. H. Tur-Sinai of the Hebrew University, Jerusalem, is continuing the preparation of this work for publication. Fifteen volumes of this thesaurus have thus far appeared, and one more is due to appear. In this work Ben Yehudah scanned the whole range of the vast literary sources throughout the ages in order to enlarge the Hebrew vocabulary and make it serve modern needs. The name of Ben Yehudah will forever be connected with the revival of spoken Hebrew.

The Status of Hebrew Until the Maccabean Period

The rebirth of the Hebrew language in modern times has often been referred to as one of the great miracles of our day. Few people realize that as a matter of fact Hebrew had never died.

Time was when the notion prevailed that Hebrew ceased being a living language after the destruction of the First Temple. During the Babylonian exile, it was assumed, the Hebrew language had been gradually forgotten and displaced by Aramaic, the language widely employed throughout the Near East at that time. The first to state this explicitly and to reproach the Jews severely for having abandoned their language was Saadia. The Hebrew language flourished, according to him, up till the exile from Jerusalem to Babylonia in the days of Zedekiah. "In the year 101 after the destruction of the city of our God (485 B.C.E.)[1] we began to abandon the Holy Tongue and to employ the languages of alien nations. . . . Our heart breaks because of all this; for the Holy Speech, our source of strength, was removed from our mouth, and the vision of all its prophecies and messages became to us like the words of a sealed book . . ."[2]

This charge was reiterated time and again by Jewish scholars, poets and grammarians. A little over a century ago Abraham Geiger asserted in the introduction to his *Mishnaic Grammar* that "since the time of the Second Temple the vernacular of the Jews in Palestine was Aramaic . . . Hebrew had accordingly ceased to be a living language. It remained, however, like Latin in medieval times, a religious vernacular of scholars during the period of the Temple and also about two centuries thereafter . . ." Mishnaic Hebrew was, according to him, only "a later literary modification of Hebrew, after the language had ceased to live in the mouths of the people."

Geiger's view was severely criticized by Graetz and S. D. Luzzatto, among others. Both scholars point to Geiger's failure to grasp the dynamic quality and popular character of mishnaic Hebrew. Indeed, any student of modern linguistics who has examined the language of the Mishna will concede that this language bears all the earmarks of a typical vernacular employed by peasants, merchants and artisans. It is a vigorous tongue; it is concise, flexible, simple and direct. Its vocabulary covers every aspect of trade, craftsmanship and profession, and it bears no trace of circumlocution or periphrasis characteristic of dead or purely literary languages. It possesses creative vitality and virility. It produced new word-coinages, it lent new connotations and shades of meaning to old words, and it created new idioms and turns of expression. None but a living language, spoken by a peasantry and simple folk, could evince such characteristics.

Yet, some modern scholars still adhere to the view of Saadia and Geiger. Such an assumption is utterly without foundation. It is quite inconceivable that the exiles who, according to the psalmist, "sat down by the rivers of Babylon, weeping as they remembered Zion," would in so short a time abandon their language and adopt the language of their hated captors as their vernacular. A language is too intimately interwoven with the experiences of a people, especially when these experiences are articulated and incorporated in cherished literary compositions, as was undoubtedly the case of the Judean exiles in Babylonia.

The prophets who flourished during the Babylonian captivity,

Ezekiel and the so-called Deutero-Isaiah, who were quick and ready to denounce whatever transgression they found among the exiles, never refer to the abandonment of the Hebrew language by the exiles. Should it be argued that neglect of the Hebrew language was not regarded by these prophets as a transgression, it would be difficult to explain why, a century later, Nehemiah, a favorite of the royal court of Persia, coming from a less cohesive Jewish community, was so wrought up when he found that the children of mothers from Ashdod or from Ammon and Moab were unable to speak a pure Hebrew. Where did he acquire his zeal for Hebrew conversation and his expert knowledge of its purity? Certainly not in the royal court of Persia, or in the Persian circles where he must have moved.

The conclusion is, therefore, inescapable that Hebrew speech was not only in vogue among the exiles of the Babylonian captivity, but that it flourished also at least a century or more later in Persia, and especially in Palestine. Nehemiah imputes the use of a corrupt Hebrew speech only to the children of non-Hebrew mothers. These must have constituted a small minority, for in the book of Ezra (10.18-43) a complete list of those who married foreign wives is given, which includes seventeen priests, ten levites and eighty-six "Israelites," a total of one hundred and thirteen men. Even though this number must have increased during Nehemiah's brief absence from Palestine, he could not have found upon his return a very substantial proportion of such intermarriages.

The Hebrew Vernacular during the Maccabean and Tannaitic Periods

Most scholars agree that Hebrew persisted as the Jewish vernacular in Palestine up to the Maccabean period.[3] Is it conceivable, however, as they contend, that it began to die out after that period? If the Jews were able to preserve their vernacular under alien domination, during a period of unsettled political and religious conditions, they would certainly have been expected to do that after having regained national, cultural and religious independence, when the authority of the biblical writings over Jewish life was growing, and Jewish education, elementary and advanced, was gaining vogue.[4] No nation under such circumstances abandons its national language. History can record no such instance.

Some scholars point very aptly to the use of the mishnaic word *herut* on the Hasmonean coins as evidence that mishnaic Hebrew was the vernacular of Palestine during the Maccabean period. Had Aramaic been then the spoken language, the Maccabean princes would have used either biblical or Aramaic words on their coins; they would not have employed words from an artificial dialect of scholars.[5] In further corroboration of this, one may refer to the ethical sayings of *Pirke Abot* and to the Aggadic-homiletical literature of the *Mekhilta, Pesikta, Sifra* and *Sifre,* all of which are to be considered as popular literature and were written in mishnaic Hebrew. So were the prayers and the numerous aphorisms and proverbs in the Talmud and Midrashim.

Aramaic, as the *lingua franca* of the Middle East, obviously exercised a considerable influence on mishnaic Hebrew, especially in regard to vocabulary. However, it is not always possible to determine which words are directly borrowed from Aramaic, and which are genuine Hebraic coinages, taken from the daily vernacular, that for some reason or other have not been incorporated in the literary texts of the Bible. It is certainly inconceivable that the seven or eight thousand vocables found in the Hebrew Bible constituted all the words that were current in the language during that period, just as it would be absurd to assume that the 25,000 words used by Shakespeare or the 12,000 words employed by Milton represent the total vocabulary in vogue in their respective periods. Even the close to 30,000 words—an unusually high number—used by James Joyce in *Ulysses,* fall far below the number of words recognized by the average reader. The size of the recognition vocabulary of college students has been estimated to be between 150,000 and nearly 200,000.[6] In any event, the influence of Aramaic on Hebrew was no greater than that of French on English after the Norman conquest, yet English remained a distinct Anglo-Saxon language.

There is other well-substantiated evidence to the effect that Hebrew was widely employed as a spoken tongue through the period of the Second Commonwealth, especially in Palestine. One can certainly not discount the fact that certain Hebraic usages were designated by the rabbis as *leshon benei Adam* (the language of the people, or the vernacular). Nor is it possible for anyone with a linguistic sense to assume that the numerous proverbs and aphorisms in the Talmud and Midrashim were mere translations from Aramaic or any other language. Most of these proverbs are couched in such concise, pithy and poignant Hebrew phraseology, such as would be conceivable only as the product of an indigenous Hebrew-speaking population and civilization. Incidentally, the number of the Hebrew proverbs included in the Palestinian Talmud are almost twice that of the Aramaic proverbs.[7]

On the basis of the available evidence it seems fair to conclude that the Jews were generally conversant, during the period of the Second Commonwealth, especially its latter part, with both languages. Sometimes they used one, sometimes another, and at other times they shifted from one language to the other, probably unconsciously and unaware of the fact that they were speaking two different languages simultaneously. It should be recalled that the two languages are closely related, and only the more educated speakers could then differentiate clearly between them. Statements which are delivered half in Hebrew and half in Aramaic are too numerous to be cited. In the midst of a long conversation between Rabbi Johanan ben Zakkai and the daughter of Nakdimon ben Gurion, in perfect Hebrew, we find, without any apparent reason, an Aramaic injection of but one short phrase.[8] A great many Aramaic words must have been current, during that period, among the Jews, especially in Galilee and the Diaspora.

After the destruction of the Second Temple (70 C.E.) and especially as a result of the ill-fated revolt of Bar Kokhba

(132-135), hundreds of thousands of Jews perished by famine and massacres, and many were exiled. The number of Hebrew-speaking Jews must then have dwindled considerably. But even later, toward the end of the second century, in the days of Judah the patriarch, famous editor of the Mishnah, Hebrew was still spoken by the masses of the people as well. In the home of the patriarch, Hebrew was spoken by all members of the household. In some instances, young scholars hailing from all parts of the country and from Babylonia, where spoken Hebrew was not in vogue, would come to his house to listen to the living speech of the domestics, in order to discover the meaning of some obscure Hebrew words or expressions. Sermons in the synagogue were delivered in Hebrew even after that period. Witness the various compilations of the Midrash, comprising sermonic comments and legends by the Tannaim (Mishnah teachers) bearing on the Pentateuch. The prayers composed during that period, and likewise intended for the masses, were also written in a living Hebrew.

The Jewish Vernacular in Alexandria

There was one important Jewish community during the Second Commonwealth, outside of Palestine, where the Hebrew language fared badly, namely, the Alexandrian community. This community may be traced back to about 600 B.C.E., when the Babylonian conquerors of Egypt hired thousands of mercenaries from Syria and Northern Palestine to guard the frontiers of Egypt against invasion by the Ethiopians. The Israelite mercenaries were joined later by exiles from Judea after the destruction of that country by Nebukhadnezzar, the mighty ruler of Babylonia. The Jews of Egypt were also given permission to build a temple there and to offer up sacrifices to God. This temple was later destroyed by the native Egyptians, about 410 B.C.E., and the Egyptian Jews sent appealing letters, written in Aramaic, to the high priest in Jerusalem and to the Persian governor of Syria to help them rebuild their temple.

The vernacular of the Egyptian Jews was undoubtedly

Aramaic, the language of the Babylonian conquerors and of some of the native population at that time, with some sprinkling of Hebrew. Later, when the country came under the political and cultural sway of the Greeks under Alexander the Great and the Ptolemies, the Jewish community had no qualms of conscience about abandoning the Aramaic language—an adopted tongue, anyway—and replacing it by Greek, the language of the new, benevolent rulers of Egypt.

A large number of Jewish captives were brought into Egypt by the Ptolemies between the third and second centuries B.C.E. They too came largely from Northern Palestine and Syria, where Aramaic was gaining vogue, and they did not possess any great knowledge of, or zeal for, the Hebrew language. They, therefore, readily submitted to the influence of the native Egyptian Jews and were assimilated with them.

The Hellenistic Greek employed by the Jews of Egypt was, of course, different from the Greek of the literary classics. It was colored by a great many admixtures, especially from Aramaic. Naturally the Aramaic vernacular did not die out overnight. During the process of its gradual eclipse, it left its traces on the newly adopted language, especially in regard to syntax and idiom. Judeo-Greek resembled in some respects the later vernaculars employed by Jews, such as Ladino (Judeo-Spanish) and Yiddish (Judeo-German). However, instead of the Hebraic complexion of these later vernaculars, Judeo-Greek had a strong Aramaic coloring. Since the Egyptian Jews were still devoted to Judaism, they had to resort to their Greek vernacular as the medium for the teaching and study of the Torah. Thus evolved the Septuagint translation of the Bible, which was generally discountenanced by the rabbis, but which the Jews of Egypt regarded as virtually on a par with the original Hebrew Bible.

The city of Alexandria, founded by Alexander the Great in the year 331, became the center of life and culture of the Egyptian Jews. In fact, Alexandria became a great center of Hellenistic culture and civilization for the entire Greek world. As a commercial port it also became one of the most active centers of commerce in the world and attracted many Jewish settlers, who eventually formed a prosperous and significant Jewish community during the Second Commonwealth.

The Alexandrian Jewish community enjoyed a considerable degree of political liberty and economic equality. The Egyptian rulers of that period treated the Alexandrian Jews with respect and extended to them all sorts of privileges and benefits. The Jews took advantage of their auspicious position. They built numerous synagogues and school houses, some of which were distinguished by their size and magnificent architecture. Because of their favorable political and economic status, the Alexandrian Jews were regarded by the other Jewish communities of the Diaspora and even by the Palestinian Jews as pillars of Judaism. Many of them did indeed devote themselves to the study of the Bible and Judaism, and they produced an extensive literature of their own. But they committed one serious error: they came to regard the Greek version of the Bible as the Torah and the Greek language as their language. They recited their prayers in Greek. They adopted Greek as the language of their culture and religion. Their greatest sage, Philo, did not, in all likelihood, know much Hebrew. They succumbed to the fallacy of a dichotomy between content and form, between language and culture. They attempted to transfer the "content" of Judaism into a Greek "vessel," and they thereby doomed themselves to assimilation and ultimate extinction. They influenced to a very considerable extent the rise and development of Christianity, but they left hardly an impress on the history and development of Judaism.

There were close to a million Jews in Alexandria at the beginning of the Christian Era.[9] Yet, when Cyril and his monks undertook to cleanse the city from the unbelieving Jews in 412 C.E., there were only some 40,000 Jews left there to be liquidated. In the course of about four centuries, the Alexandrian Jews had apparently destroyed themselves. By cutting themselves loose from the original fountainhead of Jewish religion and culture they exposed themselves wide open to the corroding influence of assimilation and conversion.

The Babylonian Jewish Community Contrasted

The Babylonian Jewish community stood out in sharp contrast to Alexandrian Jewry, with regard to the attitude toward Hebrew and its influence on the history of Judaism. The Hellenistic colossus swept away or absorbed all the nations and cultures of the ancient East, but was stopped short by the small, militarily and politically weak Jewish nation in Palestine; as well as by the Jewish groups outside of Palestine which identified themselves spiritually with that nation. The reason was that Palestinian Jews and those similarly-minded refused to admit a dichotomy between content and form, culture and language, or Torah and Hebrew.

The Babylonian Jewish community was equal, if not superior, in numbers and in cultural influence to the Alexandrian community. During the period of the Second Commonwealth, the Babylonian Jews, likewise, enjoyed political, religious and economic liberties. But they adhered closely and faithfully to the study of Judaism from the original Hebrew sources. They contributed such outstanding men as the great Hillel, who obtained the foundations of his vast scholarship in Babylonia. Students and scholars frequently came from Babylonia to Palestine to attend the academies there and to sit at the feet of the great teachers in order to perfect their education. Babylonian Jews used to go in large numbers to visit the Temple in Jerusalem.

The extent to which the course of Jewish history has been affected by this intimate relationship between the Diaspora and Palestine during that period may be illustrated by the example of Abba Arikha, better known as Rab (master, teacher), as he is always referred to in the Talmud. Rab (about 175-247) was one of the most distinguished pupils of Rabbi Judah ha-Nasi. After having completed his studies in Palestine, Rab returned to Babylon, where he established the Academy of Sura. This academy which began as a modest school blossomed into full flower under the spell of Rab's magnetic personality and rich erudition. It attracted eventually over twelve hundred students, young and old, and lasted for 800 years. The Sura Academy, together with the academy at Nahardea, which was later (around the year 260) transferred to Pumpedita, gradually supplanted the declining academies in Palestine. Babylonia consequently became the spiritual center of Jewish life among all the lands of the dispersion.

Eventually both Alexandrian and Babylonian Jewries were wiped out, as a result of persecution, riots and massacres. Cultural assimilation failed to save the Alexandrian Jews from the scourge of economic, religious and political jealousies, just as it failed in the case of the German Jews of our own days. Despite the fact that the Jews were among the founders of Alexandria and that they were culturally the equals, if not the superiors, of the Greek inhabitants, they could not escape the stigma of "unwanted foreigners" and were ultimately destroyed. But while Alexandrian Jewry disappeared without leaving any contribution to Hebrew literature and culture, the spiritual vigor and creative achievements of the Babylonian Jews have influenced Jewish life to our own day. The Babylonian Talmud will remain forever a living monument of Babylonian Jewry. Even while gasping its last, its scholars emigrating to Spain, during the eighth to the eleventh centuries, laid there the foundation for Jewish scholarship which flourished so gloriously during the Spanish "Golden Era" of Jewish literature.[10]

There is indeed ample evidence to indicate that the Hebrew language did not die out as the vernacular of the Jewish masses till several centuries after the destruction of the Second Temple, not only in Judea but even in Galilee, where Hebrew scholarship was not flourishing, and in Babylonia. Thus we are told that Rabbi Judah ha-Nasi, once came to Akko in Galilee, where he found the people kneading their dough with swamp water. When asked for an explanation of this strange and forbidden practice, they told him that a scholar had instructed them to do so. Actually the scholar had taught them to use *mei beitzim* (liquid of eggs), which they misconstrued to mean *mei bitz'im* (swamp water).[11] Similarly, a Babylonian Amora of the third century C.E., Rab Matna, told the people that in kneading *matzah* for Passover they must use only water that was kept overnight (*mayim she-lanu*). But the people misunderstood him. They thought that he had forbidden them to use any other water except that which belonged to him, interpreting the expression employed by him (*mayim she-lanu*) in the sense of "our water." The misunderstanding resulted not from ignorance of the language, but from the ambiguity of the word *she-lanu,* which may be taken both in the sense of "our" and of "was kept overnight," whereupon the next day they all brought their vessels to him in order to have them filled with water. Rab Matna then found it necessary to translate his injunction into Aramaic, where no such ambiguity existed.[12] Such misunderstandings were possible only in Hebrew.

An interesting story is related in the Talmud[13] about a Babylonian man who came to Palestine and married there a Palestinian girl. The husband spoke a Babylonian Aramaic, which his wife generally misconstrued. One day he asked her to bring him two *botzinei* (young pumpkins). When she brought instead two candles,[14] he told her in exasperation to go and break them on the *baba* (the door). Misunderstanding him again she went ahead and broke them on the head of Baba ben Buta (a contemporay of Akiba), who happened to be sitting in the neighborhood interpreting the Torah. When Baba asked her in Aramaic "why did you do that?" she answered him in Hebrew "my husband commanded me to do it." Thereupon Baba proceeded to speak to her in Hebrew, exonerating her from blame for her conduct and bestowing a blessing on her.

This woman was evidently a simple person and no scholar. She was apparently more or less unilingual. The only language she was conversant with was her native vernacular—Hebrew—which perhaps included a sprinkling of Aramaic words current in the Hebrew vernacular of Palestine. Her husband must also have been unilingual, but being a Babylonian, his native vernacular was Aramaic.

There were undoubtedly numerous instances of laxity in the

use of Hebrew during the Second Commonwealth, especially after the time of the compilation of the Mishnah (around 200 C.E.), when the usage of Hebrew in daily speech began to wane, and the rabbis deemed it necessary to warn the people against their dereliction. Time and again they exhorted them to persist in the use of spoken Hebrew. "As soon as a child begins to talk," states one rabbi, "his father should speak to him in the Holy Tongue and teach him Torah. If he does not speak to him in the Holy Tongue and teach him Torah, it is as if he buries him." Another rabbinic statement asserts that "whoever is permanently settled in Eretz Yisrael and speaks the Holy Tongue is assured of belonging to those who will live in the world-to-come." Nevertheless, spoken Hebrew was soon largely restricted to the learned classes, and the tongue began to be regarded as "the language of scholars" (*leshon hakhamim*).[15] The records contain statements by scholars extolling the Hebrew language as the most suitable for speech and prayer. Very significantly the rabbis asserted: "The Judeans who were careful in the use of the language (Hebrew) succeeded in preserving the Torah; the Galileans who were not careful in the use of the language failed to preserve the Torah."[16] The Aramaic dialect is known to have flourished particularly among the Galileans, who were generally regarded as culturally inferior to the Judeans. Certainly the language continued to be employed as the chief medium for literary creativity. The prayers and hymns written during the close of the talmudic period (fifth century) and later bespeak a living mastery of Hebrew.[17]

Hebrew as a Vernacular during the Medieval and Renaissance Periods

But fluency in the employment of spoken Hebrew did not die out. We are told that the beautiful young wife of Moses son of Enoch (tenth century), the Babylonian talmudist who was the founder of talmudic scholarship in Spain, fearing dishonor at the hands of her captor, the Moslem admiral Ibn Rumahis, addressed herself to her husband in Hebrew, inquiring whether those who commit suicide by drowning will be entitled to resurrection. When her husband, replying in Hebrew, reassured her in this regard, she threw herself into the sea.

Indeed, it may be safely assumed that there were always somewhere in the world, especially in Eretz Yisrael, individuals or even groups, who could and did employ the Hebrew language effectively in oral usage. According to Ben Asher (tenth century masorete), the Hebrew language was alive during his days "in the mouths of men, women and children."[18] Solomon ibn Parhon, a Spanish philologist of the twelfth century, pleads with his readers in the introduction to his lexicon not to judge him harshly in case they find any errors or obscurities in his Hebrew style. The people living in Arabic-speaking countries, he apologizes, all use one language, that is, Arabic, and all travelers understand it. Hence they find no need for employing Hebrew and becoming adept in its use. It is different, however, Parhon continues, in the case of the German and Italian Jews. "The Christian countries employ a diversity of tongues, and when travelers arrive there they do not understand the native language. That is why the native Jews are forced to converse in the Holy Tongue, which explains their superior proficiency therein."

There is evidence, which Professor Joseph Klausner reveals,[19] pointing to the fact that Hebrew was the vernacular of the Jews of Eretz Yisrael in the fifteenth century C.E. In a book of travels by a German knight of that century, Klausner reports finding an account of the author's contacts with Jews of Jerusalem, among whom were a number of learned men from Italy and Germany. The book contains transliterations of the "Jewish language" spoken by the Jews of Jerusalem, which the author heard and copied in the course of his contacts with them. This "Jewish language" was Hebrew, and it contains a number of words and expressions "all taken from the simple conversational language." Among them are such words as *gebinah* (cheese), *hometz* (vinegar), *tarnegol* (hen), *merhatz* (bath house); expressions like *mah shemo?* (what is his name?), *kammah titten li?—ani etten lekha zahub* (how much will you give me?—I shall give you a gold coin); also such erroneous expressions as *tob boker* (good morning) and *tob laylah* (good night), in which the adjective precedes the noun after the fashion of European languages; and even some vulgar and unchaste expressions. Such words and expressions can hardly be regarded as "bookish," or the kind that would be in vogue among the scholars and the learned classes of that period.

This is not at all surprising. Palestine, and especially Jerusalem, was during that period the center of attraction of Jews all over the world. According to Obadiah of Bertinoro, the famous commentator on the Mishnah, in a letter to his brother in 1489, there were in Jerusalem Jews from Aden, Syria, Italy, Spain and Germany. What language of intercommunication could they have employed besides Hebrew, with which they were all more or less conversant, through their study of the Bible, the prayerbook and rabbinic literature? In Jerusalem, Bertinoro reports having delivered sermons in Hebrew twice a month, "for most of them understand the Holy Tongue . . . They praise and extol my sermons. They listen to my words, but they do not practice accordingly."[20]

But even outside Eretz Yisrael we find evidence of a living and effective usage of the Hebrew language in oral expression, during the sixteenth and seventeenth centuries, in such countries as Italy and Holland. Thus Azariah de' Rossi (1514-1578), the brilliant Italian Jewish scholar and the father of modern historical and literary criticism, asserts: "Though we are conversant with the Italian language, the numerous members of the intellectual class of our people meditate, speak and write in the Holy Tongue."[21] A scholar of the following century, Sabbetai Bass (1641-1718), presents in the introduction to his bibliographical work, entitled *Siftei Yeshenim,* a vivid and interesting account of conditions in the Etz Hayyim Academy at Amsterdam, where Menasseh ben Israel and Spinoza received their early education. In the fifth grade of that school, he reports, "no other language is employed beside Hebrew, excepting that the Laws are interpreted in the foreign tongue."

In his book, *Kab ha-Yashar,* which enjoyed great popularity among the masses of the past generations, both in the original Hebrew and in the Yiddish translation, Zevi Hirsh Kaidanover (died in 1712) denounces his Jewish countrymen, in Germany, who neglect the Hebrew education of their children. Instead of teaching their young children "everything in the Hebrew language, so that they might accustom themselves to the conversational use of the Holy Tongue," he complains, "the new-fangled people train their young children to speak French and other languages." One may infer from these strictures, which are directed against "many people who act improperly" in this regard, that a goodly number of Jewish parents in Germany, during the sixteenth and perhaps seventeenth centuries were not "new-fangled people" and persisted in educating their children in the oral or conversational practice of the Hebrew language.

Cecil Roth,[22] culled significant data testifying to the habitual use of spoken Hebrew during the Middle Ages as a medium of communication between native and foreign Jews. He cites from the *Book of the Pious,* a volume which reflects Jewish life in Germany during the twelfth century, anecdotes such as the following: One elder "attributed his longevity to the fact that when a stranger who did not understand his own language stayed in his house, he never spoke to him in Hebrew in the bath-house or in any similar place." Another story is that of a "pious Jew who, taken as captive into a distant land, was saved by two Jews whom he heard speaking Hebrew together." In another place "we are told of the sage, who, speaking Hebrew, advised a physician not to disclose the secrets of his art to a priest."

All these anecdotes are related casually, as if the practice of speaking Hebrew is to be taken for granted and deserves no special attention. They were apparently ordinary, commonplace occurrences.

On the basis of the available evidence, it may be assumed that Jewish migrants the world over—and they were numerous—during the Middle Ages, traveling from country to country and speaking different languages and dialects, could have only Hebrew as their common medium of intercommunication.

This would explain how, for example, a German scholar like Asher ben Jehiel (1250-1328), the exile from Germany, could communicate with his disciples or colleagues in Toledo, Spain, and revive talmudic scholarship there. They had at first no other common language but Hebrew.

Nor did the potency of Hebrew as a means of intercommunication in the Jewish world diminish during the period subsequent to the Middle Ages. Indeed, the Jews knew and spoke the respective vernaculars of the countries where they resided, but Hebrew remained their *lingua franca*—the bond that united them throughout the world. When David Reubeni, the Messianic adventurer from Arabia, came to Italy in 1524, he spoke Hebrew only, and pretended to understand no other language. He traveled about Europe and apparently managed to make himself understood and to gain considerable popularity for himself and for his ideas by means of the Hebrew language.

Records are also available which indicate that proficiency in speaking Hebrew continued, in some localities at any rate, almost up to modern times. The German Kabbalist, Isaiah Hurwitz (1570-1628) who, on his journey to Palestine at the beginning of the seventeenth century, stayed over at Aleppo, Syria, informs us about the Jewish community there as follows: "I was treated during my sojourn there with as much esteem and respect as in the community of Prague. Their soul longed for my instruction; and morn and eve they came to my door. Their speech is only in the Holy Tongue; and whenever I lectured there, I did so in the Holy Tongue likewise."[23] Nor is there any reason to doubt that this proficiency in spoken Hebrew lasted for a long time beyond that period, for intensive Jewish education was universally pursued throughout the Jewish world, all through the seventeenth, eighteenth and, with few exceptions, nineteenth centuries.

Hebrew Persists as a Living Vehicle of Intercommunication

Even as recently as a century ago (1849) an East European rabbi, Moshe Yehoshua Zelig, Rabbi of Hazenpot, Latvia, exhorted his children as follows: "If possible, as soon as your children begin to talk, educate them in the Hebrew language and train them in the practice of using it as a mother tongue. Urge also your descendants in all generations forever to act likewise."[24]

On the Sabbath of the 26th of Nisan, 1821, a Hebrew teacher named Aaron Rosenbach, one of the contributors to the Hebrew periodical *Ha-Meassef,* established by Mendelssohn and his disciples, delivered an address in Hebrew in Cassel, Germany, which he later published in pamphlet form under the title *Ruah Da'at we-Yir'at Adonai* (the Spirit of Knowledge and the Fear of the Lord). The pamphlet contains two prefaces, one in Hebrew and the other in German. In his Hebrew preface he denounces those who have neglected the Hebrew language and have become alienated from it. He then declares that the delivery of this address in Hebrew was not motivated by a desire for personal glory or financial gain, but merely by an urge to demonstrate that the Hebrew language is capable of serving as an effective and adequate instrument for expressing all our modern ideas and wishes.

Even more recently, Ben Yehudah relates how he practiced conversing in Hebrew in Paris before departing for Eretz Yisrael.[25] He met there an acquaintance, George Selikowitz, a well-known Hebrew and Yiddish journalist, who had just returned from Algeria, where he acquired fluency in Hebrew conversation in the Sephardic pronunciation among the Jews of that country.[26] Ben Yehudah also tells of his own experiences in Algeria, where his physicians in Paris had advised him to go after he had fallen ill.[27] Although his illness forced him to interrupt his medical studies, he expresses his gratitude for the opportunity offered to him during his stay in Algiers to employ Hebrew for conversational purposes normally and naturally, "especially with the elders and the scholars . . . some of whom spoke Hebrew fluently." There he acquired facility in the use of conversational Hebrew to such an extent that there were times when he felt that Hebrew was his "natural vernacular."

But aside from the fact that spoken Hebrew continued to be

employed in many Jewish communities, the language had never ceased to live in the "mouth" of Jewish tradition and to dominate the mental pattern of the Jews. To be sure, the pulse of the language continued to beat normally and uninterruptedly throughout the ages in the synagogues and in the houses of study. But it was retained until quite recently in Eastern Europe also for secular purposes, such as business and general correspondence, bookkeeping, and the like. "Every community," maintains Roth, "had its notary who drew up wills, contracts for betrothal, deeds of sale, articles of apprenticeship, and similar documents in Hebrew . . ."

". . . Through the seventeenth and eighteenth centuries, the sumptuary laws for communal taxation at Mantua (to cite only one place) were drawn up and circulated in pure Hebrew. Since the most implicit obedience was requisite, and was indeed enforced by every sanction available, the use of the 'sacred tongue' for the purpose was plainly no antiquarian diversion. It was assumed that every member of the community could understand every intricate detail." But the community of Mantua was not exceptional in this regard. Virtually in every Jewish community during that period public enactments and negotiations were recorded in Hebrew. Indeed, in some instances, big non-Jewish business establishments had to engage Hebrew secretaries in order to take care of the Hebrew correspondence of their Jewish clientele.

The Life of the Language Continues Unchecked Subterraneously

Reference has already been made to the numerous Hebrew words and expressions that persisted in the various vernaculars and dialects employed by Jews. But even the Hebrew idiom frequently injected itself into the everyday speech of the Jews and gave the non-Hebrew words a Hebraic twist.

The Jew, in his traditional environment, was steeped from early childhood in the study of the Bible, the Talmud and later Hebraic sources. The Hebrew language must have become to him something like second nature—an integral part of his mental make-up. His thoughts and feelings were cast into Hebraic molds, as it were. The most ignorant Jew in the Jewish ghetto, such as Tevyeh the Milkman in Sholom Aleichem's stories, had a stock of biblical and talmudic phrases at his tongue's end. These he sometimes misunderstood or misquoted, but the Hebrew sounds were alive in his mouth, and he could roll Hebrew words and expressions off his tongue with facility.

Little wonder, then, that the Jewish mode of thinking was influenced by the Hebraic idiom; and instead of using, for example, the equivalent, in his own dialect, of "it occurred to me," the Hebraically minded Jew would most naturally slip into the equivalent Hebrew idiom and say in Yiddish *s'iz mir aufgegangen auf'n gedank.* The words are Germanic, but the idiom is Hebrew. This was quite normal, for long before the Jewish child attained mental maturity capable of conceiving the idea represented by this idiom, he was already exposed to such expressions, in his Hebraic studies, as *'alah 'al libbi, 'alah 'al da'ti, salka 'ad-dati.* It was, therefore, quite natural for him to translate the Hebrew idiom into Germanic words.

To cite another illustration, the Yiddish expression *er redt glatt in der velt arain* is applied to a person who jabbers and chatters incongruously or at random. The literal translation of this expression is "he speaks plainly into the world"—a totally meaningless sentence. The German language offers no clue to the source of this Yiddish idiom. But in talmudic Hebrew we find the word *be-alma* in the sense of "merely," "in general" or "indefinitely." This word is composed of the preposition *be* (in) and *alma* (world, or eternity, remote past or future). Since talmudic learning was in vogue and the Hebraic mind-pattern was predominant among the traditional Yiddish-speaking Jews, it was only natural for them to cast the concept of *be-alma* into the Germanic mold *"in der velt arain"* (into the world), rendering the word *alma* in the sense of the familiar Hebrew equivalent *olam* (world). The word *glatt* (plainly) was added for emphasis.

Similarly, when a Jew wanted a simile to illustrate rapidity or haste, immediately his mind wandered back to the biblical phrase so familiar to him *pahaz ka-mayim* (Genesis 49.4) "hasty, or unstable as water," and promptly he translated it back into his Germanic dialect, thus coining the phrase *schnell wie a wasser*. Something insignificant or unsubstantial is characterized as *"a nechtiger tog,"* which is a literal translation of the Hebrew *yom etmol* and is suggested by the verse in Psalms 90.4, "For a thousand years in Thy sight are but as yesterday when it is past." Examples of this type could be readily multiplied.

Even in grammatical structure Yiddish is tinged with a decided Hebraic tint. Aside from the fact that the Hebrew words retain, in the main, their distinct grammatical construction, there are a number of non-Hebraic words in Yiddish which are inflected in accordance with the Hebraic method. Thus, for example, the plural Hebrew ending *im* is sometimes affixed to nouns of non-Hebraic origin, as in the case of *doctoirim* (sing. *doctor*) "doctors" or "physicians," *poierim* (sing. *poier*) "peasants," *taivolim* (sing. *taivel*) "devils," also *shoostoirim* (sing. *shooster*) "shoemakers" (in a derogatory sense).

The Hebraic influence is, of course, responsible for the rise of such dialects as Ladino in the Levant and Yiddish in northern Europe. It would appear that the vital Hebrew bloodstream, checked by environmental circumstances in its normal verbal channels, sought to divert its path and to find a temporary subterranean outlet, as it were, in the verbal channels employed by the Jews. It continued, in this manner, to flow beneath the surface of the vernacular framework producing, as a result, new dialects. The process began by employing the familiar Hebrew characters in writing the vernacular and by incorporating Hebrew words and phrases, as well as by encasing Hebrew thought-patterns in the words of the vernacular. The Jew, mentally habituated to the Hebraic constructions, could not help, in many instances, modeling upon them expressions in the vernacular. According to Roth, "the first clause in the code drawn up by the Western Synagogue, London, in 1809, though its syntax was Teutonic, contained upwards of 90 per cent of Hebrew words and phrases. This indeed was exceptional. But the language used in her memoirs by Gluekel von Hameln, the German Jewish Pepys, contained 25 to 33 per cent Hebrew." Yiddish has assimilated over seven thousand, and perhaps close to eight thousand Hebrew words, expressions and concepts.

These dialects attest to the vitality and predominant influence of the Hebrew language. But at no time were they given the status of Hebrew in the life of the Jewish people. They were viewed as handmaidens in relation to Hebrew, which was regarded as the Princess. In fact, the traditional name with which Yiddish was designated among the Jews was *Ivri-Taitch,* that is, Hebrew-Deutsch (German).

To be sure, the modern revival of the Hebrew language is a significant phenomenon. Anyone with a sense of language and history, regardless of national or religious sentiment, would be thrilled to hear the majestic sounds and syllables of ancient Hebrew roll off the tongues of little children spontaneously and naturally. But one must not lose sight of the greater and more striking wonder of a language that persisted as a functional organ and not as a museum exhibit for a period of two thousand years under the most adverse conditions, deprived of a geographical *milieu* and in the midst of an all-prevailing majority culture. History can record no parallel case.

Supreme efforts have been made in liberated India and in Ireland to revive and re-establish the respective national languages, but without success. The official language of India is still English, the language of the former conquerors; while in Ireland, the national Gaelic tongue, although theoretically regarded as the official language, has in effect failed to make any real progress as a vernacular; and English, the language of the "historical enemy" is still in vogue. Yet, the native population in these countries, unlike the Hebrew people, has never been expatriated. In the light of all this, the signal success of the Hebrew language as a vernacular appears all the more remarkable.

The fact of the matter is that Hebrew never died; those instrumental in the modern revival of Hebrew did not have to create a new language. They merely had to refurbish and put to modern use some of the words, expressions and idioms that have lived for centuries in literary forms, as well as in the mental patterns of the Jewish people.

PART FOUR

How the Language Meets Modern Needs

CHAPTER TWELVE
THE STRUGGLE FOR REVIVAL

The Rude Awakening

The Russian pogroms of 1881 led to a rude awakening and disillusionment among the "emancipated" Jews, the so-called *Maskilim*. Their hopes of bringing about mutual understanding between Jew and non-Jew by a process of spiritual emancipation were brutally destroyed by these pogroms. At long last the "enlightened" young men and women realized that anti-Semitism is not motivated by the "superstitions" and the unique, or exotic, manners and mannerisms of the Ghetto Jews. The pogroms were rather aimed directly against the emancipated Jews who had discarded the ways, the beliefs and the language of their parents.

A period of "heart-searching" and penitence ensued. The ardent advocates of Haskalah among the Hebrew writers, like the poet J. L. Gordon and the novelist Perez Smolenskin, who had previously thundered against Jewish fanaticism and clannishness, now began to change their tactics. They now turned their wrath against the common enemy, and their attitude toward their fellow-Jews took on a more conciliatory and even comforting tone.

At the same time a number of young men and women, among

231

them students in the Russian universities, drew the logical conclusions from these events and decided to return to Eretz Yisrael and to settle there. With the aid of Hovevei Zion, the forerunner of the Zionist organization later founded by Herzl, they laid the foundations of the first colonies: Rishon le-Zion, Zikhron Yaakob, and Rosh Pinah, as well as Petah Tikvah, which had been initiated earlier (1878) by a group of young Jerusalem Jews but had failed to make headway until the arrival of the immigrants from Russia.

Ben Yehudah and the Multiplicity of Languages

Among the new arrivals in Eretz Yisrael during that period was a sickly young man named Eliezer Ben Yehudah, to whom reference has already been made. His name was originally Perlman, but he changed it to Ben Yehudah after deciding to go to Eretz Yisrael. Ben Yehudah, who abandoned his medical studies in the Sorbonne in Paris because of ill health and because of his ideological reorientation, was destined to become the prime mover in the efforts to revive Hebrew as the vernacular of the Jewish people in Eretz Yisrael.

The use of Hebrew for conversational purposes was not entirely novel in the Holy Land. The Sephardic Jews, coming from Spain, Turkey and various oriental countries, and the Ashkenazic Jews, who arrived mainly from eastern Europe, had no language in common except Hebrew. To be sure, the Hebrew spoken by them must have been quite bookish, artificial and grammatically inaccurate; yet, it was the language of intercommunication and must have been mutually understandable. Thus, at a meeting of the twenty-eight elders convoked in Jerusalem on the initiative of Dr. L. A. Frankel, to discuss the founding of the Lämel School in 1855, the proceedings were conducted entirely in Hebrew.

The founding of the Lämel School in Jerusalem was motivated to a considerable extent, although not primarily, by a desire to strengthen Austrian influence in Eretz Yisrael. The German language was included in the curriculum. Soon thereafter (1869) the Mikveh Israel Agricultural School was founded by the *Alliance Israélite Universelle,* a French-Jewish society interested in spreading education among the Jews of Eretz Yisrael, North Africa and the Balkans. This was followed by the establishment of other schools under the same auspices, and the French influence began to predominate. French speech became the measure or badge of culture and refinement, and French manners came into vogue. The French influence remained entrenched and spread unhampered among the young of Eretz Yisrael until the eighties of the last century, when Ben Yehudah, with missionary zeal and fervor, launched his violent attacks against it.

Ben Yehudah issued his first blast against the influence of foreign languages in Eretz Yisrael in the Hebrew magazine *Habatzelet* of 1880. At that time even the most ardent of Hebraists, such as Ahad ha-Am, Grazovsky and others, could not conceive of dispensing with the European languages as a medium of instruction in the study of general subjects. But Ben Yehudah was of a different mind. With his characteristic fanaticism he declaimed against the use of these languages and urged that they be replaced by Hebrew, "for if we want our people to survive, if we want our children to remain Hebrews, we must train them in the Hebrew language . . . We must make our sons and daughters forget the corrupt foreign dialects which tear us to shreds and undermine our unity as a people, thus rendering us an object of scorn among the nations."

His Efforts Bear Fruit

Ben Yehudah's words did not go unheeded, although they did not fail to elicit also a good deal of criticism and ridicule. Ben Yehudah was challenged to demonstrate the feasibility of his proposition and to translate his ideas into practice. In 1883, he was offered a teaching position in one of the *Alliance* schools in Jerusalem; and he accepted. Although he had to give it up after a few months because of poor health and inadequate pedagogic training, he succeeded in breaching the Chinese Wall.

Both the school authorities and the teachers began to realize the possibilities and advantages of using Hebrew as the medium of instruction. The Sephardic community, although constituting a majority, could not provide pupils in large enough numbers to fill the schools; the Ashkenazic community also had to be attracted. But the Ashkenazic parents refused to send their children to a school where the Bible was translated into Ladino or Arabic, the languages familiar to the Sephardic pupils. Hence, the use of Hebrew as a means of instruction appeared to be an acceptable solution.

Ben Yehudah's short-lived teaching experience produced two staunch disciples who pursued his work with zeal and persistence: David Yellin and Joseph Meyouhas. The idea of Hebrew as a medium of instruction caught fire and the movement grew apace. By 1888, all subjects were taught by means of Hebrew in the colony Rishon le-Zion, and four years later a resolution was adopted at a teachers' gathering in Jerusalem advocating the exclusive use of Hebrew in the teaching of all subjects in the schools of Eretz Yisrael.

The restless and dynamic Ben Yehudah, however, was not satisfied with the progress made in the use of spoken Hebrew among school children only. His aim was to have the Hebrew language gain currency among the adults as well, so that it should become *the* language of Eretz Yisrael. "The day will come in the not distant future," he wrote. "Israel will yet abandon the foreign languages employed in our land, and will return to the language of his ancestors. . . . On that day there will be one language for the whole nation, which will instill in it one heart and one spirit. Israel will be one and his language will be one. This wonderful day we envisage in the near future; we see it coming in the next few years."[1]

That same year he founded an organization called *Safah Berurah* (A Pure Language) whose object was to spread the study of Hebrew and its use for conversational purposes among the adults as well as among the children in the schools. But even previously, in the year 1883, a secret organization with the same objectives, entitled *Tehiat Yisrael* (The Revival of Israel), was organized by Ben Yehudah and Y. M. Pines. Among the purposes of this organization were: "to revive the Hebrew language in the mouths of the people living in Eretz Yisrael. The members living in Eretz Yisrael are to converse with one another in Hebrew, in social gatherings, in clubs, and even in market places and in the streets without being ashamed. They are also to give their attention to the teaching of the language to their sons and daughters. . . . The organization should also endeavor to make Hebrew the vernacular of the schools."

Obstacles on the Way

The task of Ben Yehudah and his collaborators was not easy. Their efforts were hampered by serious obstacles from various quarters.

There were, in the first place, the skeptics and scoffers, the hidebound "realists" and "practical" people, who always resist new ideas as "fantastic dreams." These maintained that Hebrew is primarily a "bookish" language, that it had been "dead" too long to be revived as a vernacular, and that it lacked the vitality and virility required for daily self-expression by a modern man. The language, they held, lacked many essential conversational words, which would have to be coined artificially, while its constructions did not possess the necessary suppleness for colloquial use.

Then there were the vested interests of the French-speaking officials, representing Baron Rothschild of Paris or the Alliance, of the English-speaking authorities connected with the Evelina de Rothschild or Agudat Ahim school sponsored by the Anglo-Jewish Association, and of the German-speaking staffs of the Lämel and, later, the Hilfsverein schools. The use of Hebrew as a vernacular and medium of instruction, they felt, would jeopardize their authority and prestige in the Holy Land.

There were also those who, on the one hand, refused to part with their respective native dialects, such as Ladino and especially Yiddish, and who, on the other hand, regarded the use of the sacred tongue for secular everyday purposes as a sacrilege. They therefore viewed the efforts of Ben Yehudah and his associates with misgivings and even condemned them as heresies.

Furthermore, in accordance with the attitude then in vogue in Eretz Yisrael, women were not permitted to study Hebrew. As late as 1889, the editor of the Hebrew magazine *Ha-Tzebi* asserted, there was not a single girl in Jerusalem who knew Hebrew. Some of the wealthy, "modernized" Jews taught their daughters French, but, God forbid, not Hebrew, nor Jewish history, nor anything about Jewish literature. Such studies, they feared, might contaminate their daughters and might identify them with the "heretical" nationalists. It was perfectly obvious to those interested in the revival of Hebrew that their aims could not be achieved so long as the women, the mothers in Israel, remained ignorant of the Hebrew language. A movement was therefore launched to establish schools for girls, where Hebrew was to be given the major emphasis. The first such school was opened in Safed in 1891. But this act stirred up a hornet's nest. The traditional *herem* (ban) in all its awesome details was proclaimed against the school. Ben Yehudah became the target of violent attacks. He was referred to as *Ben Amalek* (the son of Amalek, the traditional arch-enemy of the Jewish people). He was ridiculed, criticized and persecuted. Some rabbis denounced him in the synagogues, children occasionally threw stones at him in the streets, some of his neighbors cursed and scolded him. All this failed to shake him. Undaunted, he persisted in his activities.

Ben Yehudah Sets the Example

Ben Yehudah practiced as well as he preached. Even before his arrival in Eretz Yisrael, while still a student at the Sorbonne, he had reached the conclusion that the revival of the Hebrew language was an essential requisite for the renascence of the Jewish people. He was not certain at first whether such a revival was possible. Could a "dead language" be revived? History did not provide the answer; it could point to no parallel. He decided to experiment. He began using Hebrew in his con-versation with acquaintances. He encountered, of course, serious difficulties. Hebrew was deficient in terms for modern concepts, objects and ideas. He was stumped every once in a while for want of a term that would express exactly what he meant. Yet, we have such a vast literature, he thought, so many untapped linguistic resources in the Bible, Talmud, Midrash and later sources. Much of the needed vocabulary would be found there, since workaday occupations and pursuits were not foreign to those books. Thus was born the idea of a *Complete Dictionary,* comprising the vocabulary of all the ancient and modern sources. "There is no doubt," writes Ben Yehudah in the introduction to his dictionary, "that if I had envisaged the work involved . . . I would not have found the courage to start it."

Fortunately, Ben Yehudah did not then realize the magnitude of the project, and the result has been a 16-volume dictionary, which embraces every department of Hebrew literature, with all derivatives and definitions which the application of Hebrew to new branches of science and literature has rendered indispen-sable. The last of these volumes is already in the process of publication. It is hard to believe that this man, of frail physique, suffering from a malignant disease, who at the beginning of this scholastic career had had no interest in philological work, could have accomplished such a monumental task. Only a fanatical devotion, a mystic singlemindedness, and an iron will-to-live enabled him to survive to the age of 65, in the face of tremen-dous physical and economic difficulties. He lived to see five vol-umes of his *Thesaurus* published, and he left material for the rest of this great work which is now nearing completion.

Slow Progress

Despite the efforts of Ben Yehudah and his staunch disciples, the progress of Hebrew as a spoken tongue in Eretz Yisrael began rather slowly and haltingly. Here and there a group of farmers and colonists decided to adopt Hebrew as the medium of intercommunication. Now and then a school staff adopted a resolution to employ Hebrew as the language of instruction. But the implementation of such decisions and resolutions involved enormous difficulties. Such difficulties were particularly aggravated in the teaching of the sciences and technical subjects. There were no textbooks and no terminology. Each teacher had to exercise his own ingenuity in coining terms. The diversity in the coinages resulted in confusion and misunderstanding. Furthermore, a variety of pronunciations was in vogue in Eretz Yisrael. In Jerusalem itself one could hear all kinds of spoken Hebrew: Lithuanian, Sephardic, Yemenite, Polish, Persian, Ukrainian, and what not. In order to remedy this situation and to bring unity out of this diversity, a committee was organized in Jerusalem in 1890 under the title *Vaad ha-Lashon* (Language Committee), consisting at that time of four members: E. Ben Yehudah, David Yellin, Hayyim Hirschenson and A. M. Luncz. This committee was in the nature of an offshoot of the society *Safah Berurah,* organized by Ben Yehudah during the same year, to which reference has already been made.

Vaad Ha-Lashon Begins to Function

The committee was rather short-lived. After a year's existence both the Safah Berurah Society and the Vaad ha-Lashon ceased to exist as a result of dissension among its members. It was not until 1904 that the Vaad ha-Lashon was reorganized under the auspices of the Agudat ha-Morim (Teachers' Organization). The new Vaad ha-Lashon was composed of a number of philologists in Jerusalem, as well as representatives of the Agudat ha-Morim. The reorganized committee was charged with the responsibility of fixing the pronunciation, determining the proper orthography, and the coining of new terms. It was also suggested that the Committee publish a series of classified dictionaries of terms for the use of both school and home. The Committee was to be recognized as the supreme authority over all new word-coinages, spelling and pronunciation.

The Committee's first task was to fix the pronunciation of Hebrew. It decided that the oriental Sephardic pronunciation be adopted as the official pronunciation of Hebrew in Eretz Yisrael. To this effect a circular letter was sent out in 1907 to the principals and teachers of all schools and kindergartens, exhorting them to train the children in the accurate sounding of the vowels and consonants in accordance with the accepted pronunciation. The Committee further concerned itself with the coining of new terms and the publication of the technical dictionaries, the first of which included terminologies for wearing apparel, mathematics, botany, calisthenics, and the like. This Committee, which was reorganized after the establishment of the State of Israel as the Hebrew Language Academy, has been active ever since, serving both as a motor and as a rudder, providing both stimulation and direction for the development of the Hebrew language.

Counter Forces at Work

Slowly but surely Hebrew advanced to occupy new positions. But the counter-forces were also at work. The glamour of the Parisian Boulevard emanating from the Alliance schools, the constantly growing German supernationalism of the Hilfsverein, the assimilative tendencies of the Anglo-Jewish Agudat Ahim school in Jerusalem—all these cooperated consciously and unconsciously in halting the swelling tide of Hebraism. The linguistic dualism in each of these types of school was a constant irritant, which continued to gall the more Hebraic-minded teachers. Would Hebrew become *the* language of Eretz Yisrael, or would the Holy Land be constantly plagued by a babel of tongues? A showdown was due. Hebrew was still to face its supreme test.

The Hilfsverein on the Educational Scene

The Hilfsverein der Deutschen Juden (founded in 1901) came rather late upon the educational scene in Eretz Yisrael. It started its activities there in 1903, but it soon succeeded in outstripping all the other educational agencies in the Holy Land. By 1914 it had under its complete or partial auspices a network of fifty schools the country over, catering to some 7,000 pupils, and ranging from kindergarten to teachers' training schools. Although the German language occupied a prominent position in these schools, major emphasis was laid upon Hebrew studies. The schools of the Hilfsverein thus contributed greatly toward the improvement of education in Eretz Yisrael and toward the promotion there of the Hebraic spirit.

As a matter of fact, during its early educational career in Eretz Yisrael, the Hilfsverein, in marked contrast to the Alliance Israélite, was clearly and unmistakably in favor of using Hebrew as the medium of instruction. In the report presented at the general convention of the Hilfsverein on March 20, 1908, great concern was voiced over the educational evils entailed by the use of the babel of tongues current in Eretz Yisrael. A single language, this report stressed, must be employed as the medium of instruction. "And that language is Hebrew. Hebrew, be it understood, is no longer a dead language in Jerusalem. . . . The problem of converting this newly arisen language into an instrument capable of use in literature and science will in time be solved by the same forces that have led to the revival of the language."

Such was the tone of the Hilfsverein with regard to the place of Hebrew in Eretz Yisrael in the year 1908. Whether this attitude toward Hebrew stemmed from deep-seated convictions or was merely a stratagem calculated to draw away support from the competitive educational agencies, the Alliance Israélite and Agudat Ahim, cannot now be determined. But it cannot be denied that the Hilfsverein had acquitted itself creditably in the field of education in Eretz Yisrael. No less an authority than Ahad Ha-Am wrote glowingly, as late as 1912, of the achievements in the Hilfsverein schools regarding the further- ance of the Hebrew language and the Hebraic spirit.[2]

But during the years immediately preceding World War I, events began to take a new turn. A wave of German patriotism swept through the Hilfsverein schools. The new German spirit was particularly conspicuous in the Teachers' Seminary in Jerusalem. New teachers from Germany, some of them Christian, were imported. The use of Hebrew as the medium of instruction was discarded, except in the teaching of Hebraic subjects. German patriotic songs, German history and folklore, and German literature were gradually displacing and eclipsing the Hebraic subjects and the Hebrew spirit. The Hebraic-minded students chafed and fretted under these provocations. Clashes between the students, teachers and administrative authorities began to occur. Matters were building up to a crisis.

The Projected Technicum in Haifa

The crisis was not long delayed. It came in the year 1913-14. The projected Technicum, since renamed Technion, in Haifa was nearing completion. The greater portion of the sums raised toward this project was contributed by Russian and American Jews. The establishment of the school attracted a great deal of attention. It was just the kind of institute the country needed. There was a serious shortage of technological workers in the entire Turkish empire, especially in the Middle East. An Institute of Technology would open up a vast field in professions and industry for Jewish young men in Eretz Yisrael and in the Diaspora, and it would accelerate the development and industrialization of the country. Eretz Yisrael would occupy a focal position in the economic and cultural life of the Turkish empire, and Jewish prestige would gain immensely. The whole *Yishuv* (Jewish settlement) was agog about the possibilities.

Particularly encouraging was the fact that the Zionist Organization was a party to this project and was represented on the Board of Governors by two members of the Zionist Executive Committee: Dr. J. Tschlenow and Dr. Shemaryah Levin, and Ahad Ha-Am. The presence of these three prominent Zionist leaders was a sure guarantee that the Hebraic character of the institution would be safeguarded.

But there appeared a fly in the ointment. Rumors began to be current that the German language, not Hebrew, would be the medium of instruction in the new institute. These rumors were soon confirmed by the announcement that a director had been invited to head the institute who knew no Hebrew and to whom Judaism was totally alien. Then the official pronouncement appeared: "The natural and technical sciences should be taught in the German language, in order that this most cultural language may serve as a bridge to the development of modern science."

This pronouncement struck at the heart of the spiritual unity of the Jewish people. If the German language was to be predominant in the one and only Jewish institute for advanced professional studies in the "spiritual center," then the prospects of Hebrew as the language of the Jews in Eretz Yisrael and as a unifying bond among the Jews of the world were dim indeed. The elementary and intermediate schools in the *Yishuv* would take the cue from this highest educational institution and would deem it necessary to stress, likewise, "this most cultural language."

The "War of the Language"

This, the Teachers' Organization in the *Yishuv* decided, should never come to pass. The Technicum would either be Hebraic or it would not be at all. The whole *Yishuv* concurred in this decision. Furthermore, it was felt that this was the crucial moment to strike the death-blow at the linguistic multiplicity and confusion in Eretz Yisrael.

Things began moving with dramatic swiftness. The three Zionist representatives resigned from the Board of Governors of the Technicum in protest against its decision. Teachers in the Hilfsverein schools demanded that the German language be banned as the language of instruction. When the demand was rejected, a general strike of teachers in all the Hilfsverein schools was declared. All the elements in the *Yishuv* banded and rallied around the banner raised by the Teachers' Organization in defense of the Hebrew language and its central position. A strike fund was established. New schools were organized to replace the schools on strike. Protest meetings were held

1

4

2

5

3

Ancient Hebrew Writing. Coins dating from the end of Second Commonwealth and stamps of modern Israel.

1. *First Revolt Against Rome: Jerusalem the Holy*

2. *Second Revolt Against Rome: Jerusalem*

3. *Second Revolt Against Rome: Jerusalem the Holy*

4. *Israeli Stamp: Of the Redemption of Israel, Yr. 1*

5. *Israeli Stamp: Of the Freedom of Israel, Yr. 2*

The Nash Papyrus. Hebrew Writing of about the First Century of the Common Era. See page 90.

Early Yiddish Writing. An Aramaic and Yiddish Version of the "Song of the Kid" (Had Gadya). See page 88.

Eliezer ben Yehudah. See pages 204, 233.

Ancient Hebrew Writing. The Gezer Calendar. Inscribed potsherd. See page 64.

←

Sinaitic Writing. Inscription for a goddess (l-b'lt). Carving on stone. See pages 83, 288.

↓

Ancient Hebrew Writing. The Siloam Inscription. Carving on stone. See page 62.

Ancient Semitic Writing. The Mesha Stone. Carving on stone.
See page 6?.

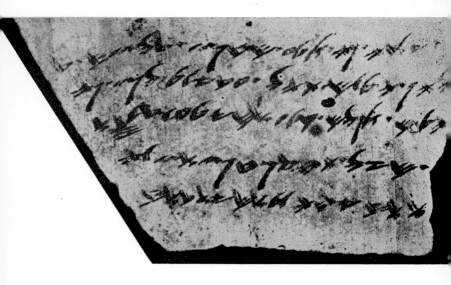

Ancient Hebrew Writing. Two Lachish ostraca. Inscribed potsherds. See page 63.

throughout the country. Children joined the battle with their natural zeal and enthusiasm. A small number of parents were lukewarm about the "War of the Language" and continued to send their children to the Hilfsverein schools, but the children rebelled and refused to go to the "German" schools.

The authorities of the Hilfsverein employed all sorts of stratagems to break the strike and "bring the *Yishuv* to its senses." They tried persuasion, cajolery, promises and threats. They did not even hesitate to avail themselves of the aid of the German consul and the Turkish police force. But it was all in vain. The *Yishuv* remained adamant and refused to yield. It reacted as if there were involved in this struggle a vital organ, which must not be allowed to be touched by unfriendly hands. The struggle for the Hebrew language was converted into one for the spiritual freedom of the Jewish people.

Repercussions among the Jews of the Diaspora

The "War of the Language" had its repercussions among the Jews of the Diaspora. American Jewry was particularly outspoken. Spurred by Hebraists and the Zionists of America, the American members of the Board of Governors of the Technicum urged the Board to reverse its decision and put an end to this destructive struggle, and they appealed at the same time to the Zionist representatives to withdraw their resignation. Consequently, the Board met on February 22, 1914, and decided that mathematics and physics be taught in Hebrew from the very outset, and that in the other technical and scientific subjects the teachers be asked to equip themselves, within a period of four years, with a sufficient knowledge of Hebrew to be able to teach these subjects entirely in Hebrew.

Little did the world dream, during the first months of the year 1914, that in this "War of Languages" Germany was beginning its bid for world domination. In another few months a war erupted on a scale then unprecedented in the annals of world history.

The Hebrew Victory

The battle for Hebrew in Eretz Yisrael was fought and won. The cause of Hebrew gained tremendously. The enthusiasm generated by the "War of the Language" gave a fresh and powerful impulse to the spread of Hebrew and to its use among the Populace of the *Yishuv*. New schools were organized under the auspices of the *Yishuv,* in which the language was no longer an issue. The World Zionist Organization, which up to that time had refused to engage in educational work in Eretz Yisrael, now deemed it advisable to change its policy, and it began to concern itself with educational pursuits and projects. The place of Hebrew as the vernacular of the *Yishuv* and as the national language of the Jewish people was now unchallenged.

No sooner was the Balfour Declaration issued (November 2, 1917), than plans were being made for the establishment of the Hebrew University, the cornerstone for which was laid on July 24, 1918. The regeneration of the Jewish spirit and the return to Jerusalem were to symbolize the return of the Jews to their ancient homeland.

What was to be the language of instruction in the Hebrew University? The question was no longer in order. It was, of course, to be Hebrew; this was now taken for granted.

CHAPTER THIRTEEN
HEBREW IN AMERICA

The Relationship Between Hebrew and English

Hebrew and English, the one being a Semitic language and the other belonging to the Indo-European linguistic family, naturally differ in structure, word-formation and inflection. Yet, through the channels of the Bible in King James' "authorized" version, Hebrew exercised great influence upon English. We should, of course, bear in mind the fact that Shakespeare, the other major factor in the development of English, was in turn likewise influenced to a considerable extent by the Bible. This is obvious to any student of both English and Hebrew. Indeed, if we were to "deprive modern Europe and America of the Hebraic heritage . . . the result would be barely recognizable."[1]

When, for example, we speak of "people arising as one man," "making war," or "making peace"; when "our heart goes out" toward "those who go down to the sea in ships," or those who "escaped by the skins of their teeth" and "drained the cup of misery to the dregs"; when our "heart breaks" for them and we "raise funds" on their behalf, but feel that this is merely "a drop in the bucket"—in all such instances we employ Hebraic mental patterns encased in English words. One could readily add a host of similar Hebraic idioms and expressions that have become an integral part of the English language. "Generation after generation of Englishmen heard the Bible read in church and studied it at home. In many cases it was the only book; in all, the principal book. At last its cadences, its music, its phraseology, sank into his mind and became part of his being . . . Hence by slow degrees his daily speech was not merely enriched, but to some extent molded by its influence."[2]

But this influence is not limited to translated Hebrew expressions and idioms; it also embraces a considerable number of words borrowed directly or indirectly from Hebrew and incorporated into the English language. To mention but a few of these words—some of which are clearly Hebraic, while others can be traced to a probable Hebrew or Semitic origin—used in common everyday speech and with which English could hardly dispense, we have: "alphabet," "amen," "ape," "ass," "balm" (from "balsam"), "bedlam" (from Bethlehem—a hospital for lunatics in London, its full title being St. Mary of Bethlehem), (sons of) "Belial," "camel," "cane," "cherub," "cotton," "gause," "horn," "Hallelujah," "jubilee," "jubilation," "lamp," "leviathan," "mammon," "manna," "nard," "niter," "paschal," "sack," "sapphire," "shekel," "Sabbath," "sabbatical," "seraph," "shibboleth," and many more. Some of these words may not be traceable to Hebrew directly, but their origins bear a striking resemblance to the respective stems in that language.

It may also be interesting to add here that a considerable number of famous or popular books bear titles that are either direct translations or paraphrases of biblical words or expressions: Grapes of Wrath (cf. Deuteronomy 32.32), That Day Alone (Isaiah 21.11), Green Pastures (Psalm 23.2), As a Driven Leaf (Leviticus 26.36), Valley of Decision (Joel 4.14), The Good Earth (Deuteronomy 6.18), The Way of All Flesh (Genesis 6.12), A Little Lower than the Angels (Psalm 8.6), Little Foxes (Canticles 2.16), The Woman Thou Gavest Me (Genesis 3.12), A Peculiar Treasure (Exodus 19.5), East of Eden (Genesis 4.16), My Son, My Son (2 Samuel 19.1), The Stray Lamb (Psalm 119.176), Song of Songs (Canticles 1.1), A Time To Be Born (Ecclesiastes 3.2), Valley of Darkness (Joshua 7.25), The Green Bay Tree (Psalm 37.35), City of God (Psalm 46.5), Hind Let Loose (Genesis 49.29), Man is not Alone (*ibid.* 2.18), etc.

It is, of course, well-known that the Liberty Bell contains the inscription "And proclaim liberty throughout the land unto all the inhabitants thereof" (Leviticus 25.10). The writings of Abraham Lincoln and, in our own days, of Franklin Delano Roosevelt, Winston Churchill, and Henry W. Wallace, display traces of a profound influence of biblical style and diction.

Hebrew Among the Early American Settlers

Thus, Hebrew cannot be regarded as an entirely foreign language to English-speaking people. Unwittingly, a certain number of Hebrew words and expressions are employed in everyday English speech. Hebrew is certainly far from being an alien tongue on American soil. As a matter of fact, many of the early American settlers were good Hebraists and were deeply rooted in the original biblical literature. They knew the language, they loved it, they wrote it, and some even spoke it. "Not only was Hebrew considered the foundation for an exact understanding of the Old Testament, but it was then as later thought to be the mother of languages, a knowledge of it was therefore believed to advance learning in the best sense."[3]

Samuel Johnson, the first president of King's College, now known as Columbia University, declared in 1759 that "Hebrew was a gentleman's accomplishment." He further asserted that "as soon as a lad has learned to speak and to read English well, it is much the best to begin a learned education with Hebrew . . . the mother of all languages."

In the writings of Cotton Mather (1663-1728) we find interspersed a number of Hebrew words and expressions such as איה (the acrostic abbreviation for אם ירצה השם) *if God pleases,* בעלי נפש *men of refinement,* חסידים ראשונים *the first good men,* אנשי מופת *wonder men, Sefer Jereim* (the book of God-fearing men), etc.[4] His writings include also a dissertation on Hebrew punctuation; while his younger brother, Nathanael, at the age of sixteen "entertained the auditory with a Hebrew oration which gave a good account of the academical affairs among the ancient Jews. Indeed the Hebrew language was become so familiar with him, as if . . . he had apprehended it should quickly become the only language which he should have occasion for. Rabbinical learning he had likewise no small measure of."[5] Their father, Increase (Hebrew Yosef) Mather, delivered discourses in Hebrew and his writings contain quotations from the Talmud, Midrashim, Kabbalah, Saadia, Rashi, Ibn Ezra, Bahya, Maimonides, Kimhi and others.

The first book printed in the colonies was the *Bay Psalm Book,* which was an English rendition in verse and rhyme of the Psalms from the Hebrew by Richard Mather, John Elliot and Thomas Welde in 1640. In 1781 Ezra Stiles, president of Yale University, delivered a Hebrew oration at the public commencement, in which he used as his text the verse from the book of Ezra 7.10: "For Ezra had set his heart to seek the laws of the Lord, and to do it, and to teach it . . ." At Harvard, a Hebrew oration was delivered annually at the commencement until 1817. It is hardly likely that this practice would have been continued if there had not been in the audience some people capable of understanding the addresses.[6] According to Charles Seymour, former president of Yale University, Stiles "was a thorough master of the Hebrew language, which he wrote and spoke with fluency and grace unusual even for those days . . . He regarded it (the Hebrew language) as an important element in a liberal education, as the key to a vast storehouse of knowledge which could make possible an understanding of a highly significant aspect of human culture."[7]

Little wonder then that Stiles, when he became president of Yale in 1777, assigned to Hebrew a predominant place in the curriculum of the college. In his diary, Stiles records: "From the first accession to the presidency, 1777-1790, I have obliged all the Freshmen to study Hebrew . . . This year I have determined to instruct only those who offer themselves voluntarily . . . Accordingly, of thirty-nine freshmen, twenty-two have asked for instruction in Hebrew . . ." It may also be added that on the seal of Yale University are engraved the Hebrew words *urim we-tumim.*

Yale College was not alone in including Hebrew in its curriculum. Hebrew likewise ranked high in the curriculum of Harvard, the oldest American college, from its very beginning. There too Hebrew was regarded, not only as the key to the study of the Bible, but also as the mother of all languages. One day each week for a period of three years was devoted by Harvard students to the study of Hebrew and allied tongues, and the Hebrew text of the Bible was the principal one used. "The famous Dutch Hebraist, John Leusden, received at one time an order for fifty copies of the Hebrew Psalter for the use of Harvard College students."[8]

The study of Hebrew was not restricted to the colleges. The lower schools also made attempts to provide instruction in the language. The early Puritan settlers were deeply rooted in Scriptural literature, and they realized only too clearly that it was only through the channels of the Hebrew language that the inspirational messages of the Bible could be received directly, pure and unadulterated. Thus it is said of Governor Wm. Bradford (1590-1657), one of the *Mayflower* Pilgrims and second governor of Plymouth Colony, that he studied Hebrew most of all languages "because, he said, he would see with his own eyes the ancient Oracles of God in their native beauty."[9]

The Bible was to the Puritan not merely a book for recitative reading; it was a rule of life. Since the Bible was regarded by them as the revealed will of God, it constituted for them, as it did for the Jews, a guide in every aspect of faith and practice. In fact, they identified themselves and their destiny within the focus of biblical history: King James I was their Pharaoh, America was Canaan, and the Atlantic Ocean was the Red Sea. They named their colonies after cities mentioned in the Bible, such as Salem and Bethlehem. They chose biblical names for their children. It is not impossible, therefore, that upon the

break with England in 1776 there may have been some sentiment among the colonists in favor of adopting Hebrew, the
original language of the Bible, as the language of the new-born
country.[10] One is very strongly tempted to speculate what effect
the adoption of Hebrew as the language of the United States
might have had on the history of the Jewish people, the Hebrew
language and Hebrew literature.

First Attempts of American Jews in Hebraic Scholarship

Hebrew was not adopted as the language of the new country,
although it continued to be, until about a century ago, a required course in most American universities. The Hebrew language had to pursue its precarious course as the vehicle of a
minority group struggling for its economic, political and spiritual existence, its members few and thinly scattered before and
long after the Revolution. In the year 1800, of a total population in the United States of less than four million, the Jewish
group numbered about 2,500. Most of them lived in Philadelphia and New York, while many were completely cut off
from any Jewish contacts.

The first Jewish settlers in colonial America were in the main
of Spanish-Portuguese origin. They had arrived in 1654 in New
York, which at that time was called New Amsterdam. They
were largely Marranos or descendants of Marranos, who had
suffered a great deal for their Jewish beliefs and practices,
which they cherished dearly. But having had little, if any, direct
contact with Jewish communal and spiritual life for a long
period of time, these immigrants possessed little Hebraic learning. Hence, they were primarily interested in transmitting to
their children the rudiments of the beliefs and observances of
Judaism, while their attempts to teach Hebrew and go to Hebraic
sources were few and feeble.

To be sure, the earliest American Jewish settlers were not
all of Spanish-Portuguese or Sephardic origin. They included a
considerable proportion of Central-European or Ashkenazic
Jews. The social and cultural influence of the Ashkenazic

minority was, however, insignificant. Even as late as the beginning of the nineteenth century, after they had become a minority, the Sephardic Jews still maintained their predominant influence in the social and cultural areas.

The situation did not improve much in this regard after Jewish immigrants from central Europe, especially Germany and Hungary, began to gravitate to the shores of the United States during the nineteenth century. These immigrants were likewise so situated as to be able to exercise little zeal for Hebraic scholarship. Those arriving later in the nineteenth century were in the main inclined toward Reform Judaism, in which the Hebrew language was then reduced to a minor role. Whatever interest Hebrew did hold for the immigrants of that day was limited to the prayerbook; and, in the case of the Reform Jews, it was minimized even there.

Moreover, they were preoccupied with the struggle for economic and social readjustment, and they lacked the foresight, perhaps also the time and the energy as well as the teachers, to concern themselves with problems such as Hebraic education. Nor could they look for guidance and stimulation in this respect to their more prosperous and socially better adjusted Spanish-Portuguese brethren.

Nevertheless the German Jewish immigrants included also some scholars who mastered the Hebrew language and even made important contribution to Hebraic scholarship. Outstanding among these were Isaac Leeser (1806-1869) and Benjamin Szold (1827-1902). Szold's Hebrew commentary on Job may still be regarded as an outstanding scholarly achievement.

The first attempt by an American Jew to write a Hebrew textbook and grammar was made by Emanuel Nunes Carvalho, minister of Mikveh Israel Congregation in Philadelphia and "Professor of the Hebrew and Chaldee Languages."[11] Carvalho was a Sephardic Jew, born and educated in England. He came to New York in 1806, where he taught Hebrew and other languages privately and was later (1808-11) engaged as teacher in the Polonies Talmud Torah school, which subsequently became part of the Public School system. In 1811 he went to Charleston, S. C., where he served as minister of congregation Bet Elohim and as teacher in a school of ancient and modern languages which he established. He came to Philadelphia in 1814 and assumed there the ministry of Mikveh Israel Congregation, a post which he held until his death (1817).

Carvalho's textbook, entitled *Mafteah Leshon Ibrit, A Key to the Hebrew Tongue,* published in 1815, comprises a chrestomathy and grammar. The chrestomathy consists of Hebrew vocabularies and their English translations, arranged generally in an alphabetical order, followed by selected passages from the Bible. The interesting feature of this chrestomathy is that, unlike similar textbooks in Hebrew published during this period and throughout the first half of the nineteenth century, this text did not restrict itself to biblical Hebrew but included also a goodly number of talmudic words, as well as some interesting original coinages, such as *se'adot* (pins), *tartzan* (respondent).

Carvalho must have been a fairly good Hebrew scholar. He was certainly conversant with the Bible, some Talmud, and probably with David Kimhi's commentaries and grammatical works. But his scholarship was undisciplined and unmethodical. His textbook, judged by modern standards, is quite inadequate from the standpoint of both method and grammatical science. It is inconceivable how anyone could have acquired from such a textbook any appreciable measure of Hebraic knowledge. The book is significant, however, as the initial stage in the process of teaching Hebrew as a language, without exclusive reference to the Bible, on American soil.

Another Hebrew textbook by an American Jew appeared in 1834. Its author was Joseph Aaron, "Hebrew Professor and Teacher of Hebrew Grammar." The book is small in size and meagre in content and it bears the title *Sefer Mafteah el Lashon Ibri we-Hokhmat ha-Dikduk Meforash im Nekudot. Sha'ar ha-Rishon.* (A Key [or Beginners'] Book of the Hebrew Language and the Knowledge of Grammar, with Vowels. First Part.)

The little book consists of three parts: (a) a series of phonetic and grammatical rules, especially related to nouns; (b) a dictionary comprising some three hundred words, all monosyllables and stemming from the Bible, with English translations, and (c) reading exercises drawn from the liturgy and translated into English. The author was confident that this vocabulary of monosyllables would furnish the pupil "with a good stock of words" essential to the language which "he will acquire by an imperceptible gradation, if his master assigns him a daily portion as a task, to be learned by rote."

The author, probably of East European or German origin, must have adopted, in part, the Sephardic pronunciation which was then fashionable among American Jews, and, consequently, his transliterations suffer from considerable confusion. Thus, he transliterates *Chataph pausuch* (*hataph patah*), *Shivo Nang* (*shewa na'*, vocal *shewa*). He pronounces the *tserei i* as in "mine" and the *kametz o* as in "go," but the consonant *ayin* is pronounced by him *ng*, in accordance with the vogue among the Sephardic Jews of America.

In his preface the author promised to publish a second part, in which he intended to discuss "Verbs with their conjugations." But this part apparently never appeared.

Four years after the publication of Aaron's grammar, two more books by Jewish scholars appeared. One was a Hebrew grammar in two volumes, by Isaac Nordheimer, and the other was a dictionary of biblical Hebrew and Aramaic, entitled *Imrei Shefer* (Goodly Words), by M. Henry. Nordheimer was a European trained scholar, who received his Ph.D. in Oriental Languages at the University of Munich in 1834. Shortly after his arrival to America (1835), he accepted the post of Acting Professor of Arabic, etc. in the University of the City of New York (1836). With the encouragement and assistance of his friend William W. Turner, of whose "constant and essential aid in both literary and typographical execution" he makes acknowledgment, he published his *Critical Grammar of the*

Hebrew Language (New York, 1838, 1841). This was the most thorough and most scientific Hebrew grammar published in America before the present century.

The First Primers for Jewish Schools in America

All these scholarly efforts were designed primarily for adult beginners or advanced students of Hebrew in the colleges and universities. The first attempt to meet the needs of young pupils in the elementary grades of the Jewish schools, which began to be established during the second quarter of the nineteenth century, was made by that indefatigable worker on behalf of Jewish education in America during that period, Isaac Leeser. His text-book, entitled *Moreh Derekh le-Lammed et Na'arei Benei Yisrael Darkhei Leshon Ibrit. The Hebrew Reader Designed as an Easy Guide to the Hebrew Tongue for Jewish Children and Self-Instruction. No. I. The Spelling Book,* was first published in 1838, and its fourth edition was issued in 1856.

This book, the author writes in his Preface, was to be the first of "a whole series calculated for the acquisition of the Hebrew, if proper encouragement had been extended." He complains, however, that although the book "has met with approbation, still the sale has been very slow, the demand for the various schools being quite small." Yet, the author drew comfort from the fact that "additional efforts are made to erect schools for the spread of the Hebrew language," and, consequently, he feels that he might be encouraged to proceed with the publication of "Hebrew Reader No. II, containing easy lessons for translations from Hebrew into English."

It is regrettable that Leeser did not carry out his plan for the publication of the subsequent readers of the series. The "Speller" merely pays attention to the phonetic aspect of Hebrew. It provides exercises, as well as a few simple grammatical rules of pronunciation. Liturgical selections, with the English translations, are appended at the end of the book.

The "Speller" also includes directions to the teacher, designed to guide him in the proper use of the lessons in the text. These directions are interspersed among the lessons, which is, from a pedagogic point of view, unsatisfactory. However, both in the construction of the reading exercises for the pupils, as well as in his suggestions to the teachers, the author evinces fine pedagogic insight and acumen.

A much more ambitious primer was that by Reverend G. M. Cohen, published in 1850, bearing the endorsement of Dr. Max Lilienthal, among others. This book is entitled *The Hebrew Language Demonstrated on Ollendorf's Method.* It consists of two parts; a theoretical part containing comprehensive grammatical rules concisely presented, and a practical part comprising reading and Hebrew exercises. The latter are modelled on the pattern of the Ollendorf method in teaching foreign languages, according to which each lesson exemplifies a certain specific principle of grammar or usage and operates with a limited new vocabulary, which is given at the beginning of the lesson. The sentences are generally disconnected, although toward the end of the book there are some original stories and connected discourse, incorporating biblical materials. Translation activities from English into Hebrew are also given at the end of some of the lessons.

The author was undoubtedly a good Hebraist and a fine pedagogue. His Hebrew is, in the main, accurate and, in the spirit of the time, biblical; but it is simple and direct, without the periphrases and flourishes characteristic of the Haskalah style then in vogue. Some of his pedagogic ideas may sound revolutionary even today. How many of our modern Hebrew educators in America would subscribe, for example, to the following recommendation made by our author?

"As soon as the scholar knows the letters well, and is able to combine them with some alacrity, nothing should be read by him without the meaning thereof being given immediately. He ought never to imagine that a word could be read without understanding it."

Yet, it is doubtful whether the author had any direct experience in teaching children. He managed to compress within the framework of some thirty pages the fundamental principles of the entire Hebrew grammar, and, within a little over fifty pages, a vocabulary of some six hundred words in various formations. It is inconceivable that children in the primary grades could be expected to master all this material in one year, or in two years, even taking into consideration the fact that the Hebrew instruction at that time was given in all-day schools.

The mechanical make-up of Hebrew textbooks in those days was, of course, far below the modern standards for such books. They were drab and unattractive in appearance. The print was small, and no pictures or illustrations were employed to relieve the monotony and drabness of the texts. This may be one reason why Jewish education was then so unpopular, though the public schools had not yet come into vogue to claim the major part of the time and attention of the child.

The Struggle for Jewish Education

Sporadic attempts to remedy this situation were made by various religious and communal leaders, notable among whom was Isaac Leeser who, although an immigrant from Germany, associated himself with the Sephardic communities in Richmond, Virginia, and later in Philadelphia. Efforts were made to organize all-day Jewish schools in such large communities as New York, Chicago, Philadelphia, Baltimore and Cincinnati. But all these schools had a brief, precarious existence. Among them was the Hebrew Education Society of Philadelphia and the Maimonides College. The latter, organized by Leeser toward the end of his life (1867) for the purpose of offering extensive and intensive Jewish training, closed after six years. All these schools had to contend, on the one hand, with the indifference of Jewish parents, who refused to make any sacrifices for the Jewish education of their children, and, on the other hand, with the super-sensitiveness of those who feared that the Jews would be accused of clannishness. To those active in Jewish education in modern times the situation has a familiar ring.

The only Jewish educational institution that took root and survived was the Sunday School. This school, founded by Leeser with the cooperation and sponsorship of Rebecca Gratz (1838), developed into the Hebrew Sunday School Society of Philadelphia. It was modeled after the Protestant type of school, in which religious education was given only on Sundays, and gradually evolved into a system of Jewish education which spread all over the country and attracted large numbers of pupils. The limitations of this type of Jewish education were recognized by Leeser himself, who regarded it merely as "a necessary evil." He deplored the fact that the school could give no attention to the study of Hebrew, essential to an understanding of the Bible. He might have added that its meager curriculum laid no adequate foundation for future cultural development.

Nevertheless, owing to the direct influence of, and personal contacts with, men like Leeser, Szold, Bernard Illoway, Bernard Felsenthal, Sabato Morais, Isaac Mayer Wise and others, a number of Jewish scholars and ardent Jews emerged on the American scene to labor zealously on behalf of Hebraic culture and education. Because of their efforts the spark of Hebraism was kept alive until such time as it could be fanned into a greater flame under more favorable circumstances.

Indeed, the second half of the nineteenth century witnessed the appearance of a number of Hebrew essays, poems and books in America. The *Occident,* founded by Leeser in 1844, published Hebrew essays by Rabbis Illoway, Wise, and Joseph Levy; as well as Hebrew verses by Sabato Morais. Other Anglo-Jewish magazines during that period, such as the *Jewish Messenger,* the *Hebrew Leader* and later the *American Hebrew,* also included Hebrew material.

The first Hebrew book on American soil, apart from textbooks, grammars and dictionaries, saw publication in 1860. Entitled *Abnei Yehoshua* (The Stones of Joshua), a homiletical commentary on the *Sayings of the Fathers,* it was written by Rabbi Joshua Falk ha-Kohen, an immigrant rabbi from Poland.

The first volume of American Hebrew poetry by Jacob Zevi Sobel, entitled *Shir Zahab li-Khbod Yisrael ha-Zaken* (A Golden Song in Honor of Ancient Israel), appeared in 1877. Part of it recounts the trials and tribulations endured by scholarly Jewish immigrants in the process of adjustment to an unfriendly and unsympathetic American environment.

It should be stated parenthetically that these were not the first attempts at Hebrew composition in the New World. As early as 1642, the first Hebrew author and rabbi, Isaac da Fonseca Aboab, had accepted a call to a newly established Jewish congregation in Pernambuco, Brazil, where he stayed until 1654. While there he wrote a book of Hebrew poems in paytanic style describing his experiences during the protracted war between the Portuguese and the Dutch.

Among the valiant workers for the revival of Hebrew in America during the latter part of the nineteenth century was Wolf Schur, who made several attempts during its last decade to publish a Hebrew periodical. His weekly *ha-Pisgah* (The Summit), later followed by *ha-Tehiah* (The Revival), was published intermittently in New York, Baltimore, Boston and Chicago successively. He also produced a volume, entitled *Netzah Yisrael* (The Glory of Israel), which appeared in 1897, in which he endeavored to defend Judaism against the attacks of Christianity and other religions, on the one hand, and against the anti-religious views of the socialists, anarchists and extremists of the Reform movement on the other hand.

The end of the nineteenth century and the beginning of the twentieth century marked a definite turning point in the history of the Jewish people in general and in the development of Jewish education and the Hebrew movement in the United States in particular. This was the period of awakening in Eastern Europe from the dream of Haskalah (enlightenment) and emancipation. It was also the period of the realization by a large number of thinking Jews that salvation for the Jewish people in Russia lay in emigration and auto-emancipation. While a trickle of Jewish immigrants wended its way to

Eretz Yisrael for the purpose of rebuilding the ancient homeland, an avalanche of immigrants went to the United States.
Immediately after the Civil War, the Jewish population had
numbered 275,000. Between 1881, the year of the pogroms
in some one hundred and sixty Russian towns and villages,
and 1907, more than 1,200,000 Jews arrived in the United
States, while 600,000 more were added during the subsequent
six years. This large influx of immigrants from Eastern Europe
was bound to effect a transformation in American Jewry, especially in its cultural aspects.

Beginnings of Hebraic Activities and Literary Efforts in America

The third wave of Jewish immigrants, stemming from Eastern Europe, began about the year 1870. A number of Hebrew
scholars and writers arrived around that time, among whom
were Zvi Hirsh Bernstein, Zvi Gershoni and Judah David
Eisenstein. In 1871, one year after his arrival in the United
States, Zvi Hirsh Bernstein (1845-1907) launched the first
Hebrew weekly in the United States, called *Ha-Tzofeh ba-
Aretz ha-Hadashah* (The Observer in the New Land), which
survived for a period of five years. Similar ventures in Hebrew
journalism followed with varying success in permanence and
quality. About thirty Hebrew periodicals appeared over a
period of thirty-seven years (1871-1908), some of them ap-
pearing only once, while the longest-lived weekly, *Ha-Ibri,*
edited by Gershon Rosenzweig (1861-1914), epigrammatist
and versifier, lasted ten years (1892-1902). The contributors to
these magazines included some leading writers, scholars and
poets, such as Wolf Schur, J. D. Eisenstein, G. Rosenzweig,
A. H. Rosenberg, M. M. Dolitzki, N. H. Imber (the author
of *Hatikvah*), M. D. Rodkinson. But the journalistic level of
the magazines of this period was not high. The Jewish *milieu*
was not responsive or stimulating, while the economic struggle,
the pains of adjustment and a feeling of rootlessness and
defeatism, drained the mental energy and stunted the growth

of these talented writers. The nostalgia for the pulsating, vibrant and spiritually rich Jewish life in the ghettos of Russia, despite the political and economic handicaps experienced by these immigrant writers, prevented them from striking root in the inchoate and inane Jewish American scene. Yet they kept the Hebrew fires burning and prepared the ground for a more indigenous, more auspicious and creative period of Hebraic activity.

While spoken Hebrew was struggling to be reborn in Eretz Yisrael, there is evidence of sympathetic birthpangs in the American Diaspora during the early stages of this struggle. Even during the eighties of the last century, before the advent of Herzlian Zionism, organizations sprang up with the object of promoting Hebrew literature and culture, and of spreading the knowledge of the language among the young and old in both oral and written expression. The first such organization, named *Shohare Sefat Eber,* was organized in New York in 1880. This organization, incidentally the first Hebrew organization in the world, including Palestine, published a magazine *Ha-Meassef* (the Compiler), only one issue of which appeared. It also opened a library, containing periodicals and books chiefly in Hebrew, but also in other languages, provided they dealt with subjects of Jewish interest. On the opening day of the Library, on the second day of Passover, over two hundred people were gathered and speeches were delivered mainly in Hebrew.

The *Shohare Sefat Eber* of New York did not last long; it apparently disappeared after one year's existence. But another organization with a similar name and with the same objectives, was established in Chicago. The first Hebrew monthly in America, entitled *Keren Or* (Ray of Light), of which only two issues appeared, was published under the sponsorship of this society. Having survived for over thirty years, this organization ceased to exist during World War I, after having attained a creditable record of achievements in the field of Hebrew education and the promotion of Hebraic culture. A third organization under the same name was organized in Newark, New Jersey, in 1889, with the primary object of stressing the use of oral Hebrew and of promoting the reading of Hebrew.

Another important Hebrew organization, *Ohole Shem Association*, was founded in New York, October 8, 1895, with the object of promoting and fostering the study of Hebrew and other Semitic languages, and of encouraging the study of Jewish history. This organization, composed of leading Hebrew intellectuals, lasted over a decade and made a significant contribution toward the growth and development of Hebrew in America. It sponsored a series of lectures in Hebrew, German and English on Jewish subjects. It also published, during the first year of its existence, a Hebrew monthly, entitled *Ner Ma'arabi* (Western Candle), and again in 1901, under the title *Ha-Modi'a le-Hodashim* (The Monthly Announcer). In 1904 it issued an annual in Hebrew, entitled *Yalkut ha-Ma'arabi* (The Western Miscellany), dedicated to the Hebrew poet M. M. Dolitzki.

Modern Hebrew Takes Roots in American Soil

The renewed Russian pogroms following the debacle of the ill-fated revolution of 1905-6 resulted in a new migratory wave of Jews from Eastern Europe. The immigrants of this period included a number of young men and women who had been reared on the vibrant and dynamic literary traditions of the new "golden age" in Hebrew literature initiated by Mendele, Ahad Ha-Am and Bialik. They were also imbued with the resurgent spirit of modern Zionism. Some of them had already made their literary *debut* in the European countries from which they came.

These new arrivals were dissatisfied with the hackneyed themes and stereotyped style which characterized the literary and journalistic efforts of the American Hebraists at that time. They joined the *Mefitzei Sefat Eber* (Disseminators of the Hebrew Language), a society founded in 1902, but they soon took over the leadership of the American Hebrew movement and began experimenting with new literary forms and projects. A number of new periodicals made their appearance in quick succession, but were short-lived. Among the new ventures was a daily paper *Ha-Yom* (The Day), published by M. Goldman (1909-10 and 1913-14). A new Hebrew-speaking organization called *Ahieber* was formed (1909), to which these young Hebraists belonged, and which was destined to play an important role in the Hebrew movement in America. This organization lasted for about fifteen years and ably served the promotion of Hebraic activities in the country. It sponsored a number of Hebrew publications and aided in the distribution of Hebrew publications in Europe and in Palestine. It published two annuals entitled *Luah Ahieber*. One of its major projects was the publication of the *Ha-Toren,* which began under its auspices as a monthly (1913) and continued for a year and a half. It was subsequently (1916) changed to a weekly under the editorship of I. D. Berkowitz, famed author and Hebrew translator of Sholem Aleichem; and later (1921), with Reuben Brainin as editor, changed back to a monthly.

A flurry of excitement was occasioned by the arrival of Reuben Brainin in 1910 to the United States. Brainin was often referred to as the Georg Brandes of modern Hebrew literature. He was a veteran author, a critic of stature and one of the pillars of modern Hebrew literature in Europe. His arrival was hailed by American Hebraists as the beginning of a new era in American Hebrew letters. Indeed, immediately upon his arrival he undertook to publish and edit a new Hebrew weekly, *Ha-Deror* (The Swallow), which promised to blaze new literary paths. Enthusiasm ran high. Grandiose plans were in the making and were being publicized. The appearance of the first issue in August 1911 was celebrated at a mass meeting in New York. Three thousand subscribers had been secured, no mean beginning for a Hebrew newspaper in America. But after the appearance of fifteen issues over a period of about five months the publication was discontinued without leaving any marked impression on the progress of Hebrew journalism or literature in America. The disillusionment was a severe blow for American Hebraists from which they could not easily recover.

The American Hebraists, however, displayed excellent resilience and vitality. Their ranks were re-enforced by a new influx of immigrants from Eastern Europe and Palestine, especially toward the end of World War I and during the subsequent Russian Revolutions. The *Ha-Toren,* particularly during the five years of its appearance as a weekly under the able editorship of Berkowitz signalized the beginning of a new trend in American Hebrew literature. The editor, as well as many of the contributors to this magazine, were renowned and gifted writers. They included such famous names as those of David Ben-Gurion, Eliezer Ben Yehudah, Reuben Brainin, Shemaryah Levin, Nahum Slouschz, Isaac Ben-Zevi, second president of Israel. That was a critical period in world history as well as in Jewish history. Those were the days of the terrible pogroms in Russia and Poland resulting from the Russian revolutions and counter revolutions. Those were also the days preceding and following the Balfour Declaration. These famous writers and leaders found in the *Ha-Toren* a platform from which to address their readers during those critical years.

The *Ha-Toren* was not inferior, indeed, it was in many respects superior, to similar Hebrew magazines in Russia and in Palestine. Some complete outstanding works appeared in instalments in this magazine, such as Sholem Aleichem's autobiography, in Berkowitz's translation, David Neumark's *Shitah Yehudit be-Philosophiat ha-Bikoret* (A Jewish Method in the Philosophy of Criticism). Other contributors to the *Ha-Toren,* whose names have since become familiar to American Hebrew readers, were: M. Waxman, N. Syrkin, Yehudah Kaufmann (Ibn Shemuel), Israel Davidson, B. Z. Halper, S. Bernstein, Henry Malter, Menahem Ribalow, Daniel Persky and Zevi Scharfstein. Among the contributors from abroad were such famous names as those of Ahad Ha-Am, Nahum Sokolow, Rab

Tzair (Chaim Tchernowitz), A. A. Kabak, and Zalman Shneur. The *Ha-Toren* continued to exist until 1926, and it exercised a considerable influence on the development of Hebrew in America.

Simultaneously with the *Ha-Toren* appeared another magazine, the weekly *Ha-Ibri* (The Hebrew), under the editorship of Rabbi Meir Berlin, then president of the Mizrachi organization. This magazine had been previously published in Berlin. Its publication was resumed in New York in 1916 and continued for about six years. The *Ha-Ibri,* like the *Ha-Toren,* was conducted on a high journalistic level.

The *Ha-Ibri,* although a Mizrachi organ, did not bear a partisan character in its literary content. It reacted vigorously and liberally to all problems of Jewish life in America and abroad, and it was edited with fine literary skill and in an excellent lively Hebrew style. It succeeded in promoting the spread of Hebrew among the orthodox religious Jews and, after the first year of its existence, it made one important concession to orthodoxy—it excluded poetry from its contents, in order to avoid the possibility of offending the religious sensibilities of its orthodox readers by themes of love and poetic license. Among its contributors were some well-known writers, such as M. Lipson, the associate editor of the magazine, Rabbi J. L. Fishman (Maimun), David Pinski, J. Opatoshu, Israel Efros, Meyer Waxman, M. Ribalow, Ab. Goldberg, Simon Ginsburg, Gedaliah Bublik, Abraham Shoer, and others.

Another Hebrew publication worthy of notice during the same period was the monthly magazine *Miklat* (Refuge), edited by I. D. Berkowitz and sponsored by the Hebrew Maecenas, Abraham J. Stybel, which lasted only for a little over a year (Tishre 1919-Kislev 1920). It was designed to serve, as its name indicates, as a refuge for the European Hebrew writers who, because of the war and the Russian revolution, were left without any organ in which to publish their writings. This short-lived magazine has not been equaled in external appearance, in size and, in some respects, in the quality of its literary contents. Its one serious failing, from a journalistic standpoint, was its rootlessness. It failed to reflect the American Jewish scene adequately, and, consequently, it did not succeed in exerting much of an influence on the growth of modern Hebrew literature in America. A relatively small proportion of its contributors were American, among whom, especially worthy of mention, are the following: A. S. Orlans, Hillel Bavli, Morris Levine, Ben-Zion Halper, S. B. Maximon, David Neumark, B. N. Silkiner, E. Lisitzki, Simon Ginsburg, Daniel Persky, N. Touroff, and Jacob Z. Raizin and J. Ovsay.

The culmination of the journalistic attempts of the American Hebraists is undoubtedly the weekly *Ha-Doar* (The Post), which made its first appearance in November 1921, and has continued to appear without interruption. For the first eight months it appeared as a daily under the editorship of M. Lipson. During the early period it reached a daily circulation of about 9,000. However, owing to shortage of funds it was changed to a weekly, and its editorship was taken over by Menahem Ribalow, who was its editor until his death in the Fall of 1953. *Ha-Doar* includes also, on alternate weeks, a youth supplement and a children's supplement, both vocalized. Its literary level compares favorably with that of weeklies in Eretz Yisrael or elsewhere. Its present editor is M. Maisels.

Another Hebrew magazine that has displayed a capacity for survival is the monthly *Bitzaron* (Stronghold), edited until recently by Rab Tzair (Chaim Tchernowitz). After the death of its editor, May 15, 1949, an editorial board, consisting of prominent writers, took over the editorship. This magazine has been in existence over ten years. Its general tone is semi-scholarly, but it reacts vigorously also to current national and international problems.

There are also a few other Hebrew magazines that appear periodically, such as the scholarly quarterly *Talpiyyot* (Academies), edited by Prof. Sh. K. Mirsky; the pedagogic quarterly *Shebile Ha-Hinnukh* (The Paths of Education), edited by Prof. Z. Scharfstein; and the medical journal *Ha-Rofe ha-Ibri* (The

Hebrew Physician), edited by Dr. D. Einhorn. All of them stand on a high scholarly and literary level.

Spoken Hebrew Gains Vogue

At the same time the movement to promote Hebrew as a spoken language has been gaining momentum. Spurred by the growth and development of Hebrew as a vernacular in Eretz Yisrael and in Eastern Europe, a number of Hebrew teachers in America began introducing in the Jewish schools the *Ivrit b'Ivrit* method, by which Hebrew is employed as the medium of instruction and as the language of the classroom and the school. The organization of the Bureau of Jewish Education in New York in 1910 under the dynamic leadership of Dr. Samson Benderly gave Jewish education in America a new lease on life. Dr. Benderly and his disciples endeavored to modernize Jewish education, to organize it on a firm community basis, and to encourage emphasis on conversational Hebrew in the Jewish schools. Hebrew-speaking clubs dedicated to the promotion and cultivation of Hebrew literature and language were organized in many parts of the country, numbering about a dozen in New York City alone. A need was felt to organize a nationwide federation to coordinate and to stimulate the Hebrew activities in the United States. After several abortive attempts in this direction, the Histadruth Ivrith of America (National Organization for Hebrew Culture), "an organization dedicated to the dissemination of the knowledge of the Hebrew language and literature in this country," was organized in the spring of 1916.

The Histadruth Ivrith has been growing steadily in influence and scope of activities. It publishes the *Ha-Doar,* together with its bi-weekly vocalized supplements *Musaf la-Kore Ha-Tzair* (Supplement for the Young Reader) and *Ha-Doar La-Noar* (The Post for the Youth). It also maintains a publishing house, *Ogen* (Anchor), devoted to the publication of the works of Hebrew writers in the United States. More than fifty

Hebrew works of Hebrew writers have been published to date, all of them reflecting the contributions of American Hebrew writers in the fields of creative art, philosophy, sociology and kindred subjects. Among its noteworthy publications are: *The Anthology of American Hebrew Poetry,* a work representing sixty years of Hebrew poetry in this country, a translation of Shakespeare's *Tempest* by E. E. Lisitzky, a translation of *Hamlet* by Israel Efros, a volume of Judah Halevi's *Complete Poems,* edited and annotated by Dr. S. Bernstein, and an English translation of Bialik's poems edited by Dr. Israel Efros. Recently the Histadruth has also embarked upon the publication of a Hebrew series of junior books, written within the framework of a controlled Hebrew vocabulary. Four books in this series have already appeared and several books are in the process of preparation. A similar project is being sponsored by the United Synagogue of America, under whose auspices nine books have thus far appeared. More recently the Jewish Education Committee of New York City has undertaken to carry on the publication of a Junior Hebrew Library, with the object of publishing four books annually.

The Histadruth also publishes the *Sefer ha-Shanah,* an American Hebrew yearbook. Six issues of the yearbook have appeared to date. Each volume in large format contains 450 pages of varied types of literary materials, dealing with all phases of Jewish religious, social and cultural life in America. Outstanding American Hebrew poets, scholars and writers are the contributors.

Mention should also be made of the significant publication *Ha-Tekufah* (The Era), which was founded in 1918 in Moscow by the Hebrew Maecenas, Abraham Joseph Stybel, with David Frischman as editor. The last five volumes appeared in New York under the editorship of Aaron Zeitlin and E. Silberschlag. Some of the most distinguished Hebrew writers have contributed to this periodical. Thirty-five volumes have been published thus far, and some of the most outstanding contributions in modern Hebrew literature have appeared there.

In 1955, an American Hebrew Academy was established under the auspices of the Histadruth Ivrith. Its object was to encourage Hebrew-speaking scholars to pursue their researches and to publish them in Hebrew. The Academy publishes a periodical, *Perakim* (Chapters), in which its proceedings are recorded.

Development of Hebrew in America as Compared with Israel

The course of development of Hebrew in America is, of course, different from that in Eretz Yisrael, both in form and in content. Since Hebrew is not the vernacular of American Jews, it is not conditioned in its development by the changing needs and exigencies in the same degree as is the language in Eretz Yisrael. In vocabulary and in style Hebrew in America is more bookish and classical; it is less susceptible to change, modifications and innovations than Hebrew in Eretz Yisrael.[12] Similarly, American Hebrew writers do not generally deal with such themes, commonly found in Israeli Hebrew literature, as farming and farmers, chicken and cattle raising, road-building and labor, and the like. They are more inclined to follow, with few exceptions, the traditional classical patterns initiated by Mendele, Perez, Ahad Ha-Am, Bialik, and their disciples.

Hebrew Youth Movements

An especially promising and encouraging phenomenon in the development of the Hebrew movement in America is the growth of the Noar Ivri (Hebrew Youth Movement), also sponsored by the Histadruth Ivrith. Branches of the Noar Ivri exist in New York, Philadelphia, Chicago and other cities in this country. The mainspring of the Noar Ivri are the consistently increasing number of Hebrew-speaking summer camps, five of which are already in existence in the United States, besides two in Canada. The demand far exceeds the supply; and more camps, combining recreation and Hebrew education, are being planned.

Hebrew in the Public Schools and in the American Colleges and Universities

In recognition of the growing importance of Hebrew as a living language, a number of public high schools in the country have admitted Hebrew as one of the modern languages in the curriculum. In 1955 there were close to 7,500 students pursuing Hebrew courses in some sixty-four high schools and junior high schools and in ten colleges in the city of New York. During a period of sharp decline in both total high school population and in the study of all foreign languages, with the exception of Spanish, the enrollment in Hebrew classes has been constantly rising. Courses in Hebrew are also offered in fourteen public high schools of twelve cities outside of New York.

There are about two thousand students taking Hebrew in ten colleges in New York City. In all, there are some eight thousand students studying Hebrew as a modern or academic language in New York. Close to five hundred courses are offered. Over fourteen hundred colleges and universities accept Hebrew as meeting the modern language requirement.[13]

Now, with the State of Israel accepted as an established reality, there is little doubt that the study of Hebrew in the high schools and colleges of the country will gain momentum. There is also good reason to believe that interest in the study of Hebrew among the Jews of America in general will increase. Witness the constantly growing number of students attending the adult classes in Hebrew sponsored by the various Hebrew Teachers' Institutes, Jewish Community Centers, Zionist Organization districts, B'nai B'rith lodges, and synagogues.

EPILOGUE
HEBREW FOR AMERICAN JEWS
Changing Jewish Attitude Toward Hebrew

We have attempted to trace the history of the development of
the Hebrew language from its beginning to this day. As long
as the Jews were in their own land they took their language
for granted. No particular significance, religious or national,
was attached to it. It was then the "language of Canaan,"
spoken by other Semitic peoples, such as the Moabites and the
Phoenicians.

After the Jews lost their political independence, and the
language of the predominant environment began to intrude
as a rival, their emotional attachment to the Hebrew language
emerged and manifested itself. It gradually grew upon them
and became the vesture of their inmost thoughts and emotions.
Form and content amalgamated and became inextricably inter-
dependent. Torah, in its broader aspects, Eretz Yisrael, the
people of Israel, and Hebrew—all fused into a compound
and were intimately blended as one and indivisible in the traditional Jewish mind. In order to preserve the one, the others
must likewise be preserved. Hebrew thus became the "Holy
Language," the language of the Torah, of the Jewish religion
and civilization, so much so that the rabbis frowned upon any

attempts at translation, and they asserted emphatically that the Torah must not be read in any other language than Hebrew (Sofrim 1.6). Instinctively, the rabbis must have realized that a translated Torah tends to become stereotyped and ceases to be a dynamic living tradition, constantly adapting itself to the changing conditions and needs of the times, but within the framework of its original intent and basic character. The fates of Alexandrian Jewries during the talmudic period and of German Jewry during the Haskalah period bear ample testimony to the correctness of the rabbinic attitude toward a translated Torah.

When the Jewish people were robbed of their physical fatherland they turned to the Hebrew language as a refuge of faith and a citadel of strength. In time of stress and danger and in the face of death they sought to vent their feelings in the words of their sacred tongue. In periods of joy and exultation their heartstrings vibrated to the rhythm of the Hebrew sounds. Jewish thinkers, poets and singers throughout the ages eulogized it in the most touching terms. "The people of Israel were delivered from Egypt," said the rabbis, "because they did not change their names . . . and they continued to speak in the Holy Tongue." Hebrew, according to Bialik, "may be compared to a gem for which one exchanges all his wealth, and which then, for fear of robbers, he swallows." Such was the significance of Hebrew for the Jewish people. It became for them a symbol of Jewish unity, distinctiveness, hope and renascence.

Significance of Hebrew in Jewish Life

What does all this mean to American Jews? What should be their attitude toward the study of Hebrew and toward the promotion of Hebrew culture in America?

Hebrew is the language of our past. It was the instrument employed by the creative genius of our people throughout the generations. It is the master key whereby one may unlock the storehouse of original literary sources. Without a knowledge of Hebrew it is impossible to attain ready and direct access to the bedrock of the Jewish soul, or to study its evolution and embodiment in the writings of the Bible, the Talmud, the medieval and modern philosophers and poets.

Hebrew is the nerve-center which unites and integrates the Jewish people in time and in space. It serves as an intellectual and emotional bond among all Jews throughout all generations, and throughout all the lands of dispersion. Its granite syllables are personal links to the timeless message of Moses or Isaiah. And by means of the Hebrew Bible and prayerbook, Jews of the remotest corners of the earth are bound together. As the universal language of study and prayer, Hebrew is a major unifying force of the people of Israel. It is not difficult to imagine what would happen if, for example, the Jews of America would use only English as the language of worship, the Jews of China would employ Chinese, and the Jews of France would worship in French. This would very likely mean the end of the unity of the Jewish people.

Hebrew is the symbol of regeneration and self-assertion in Jewish life. The Jewish will to live, and the undying faith in the creative destiny of Judaism in the face of all difficulties, are symbolized by the revival of Hebrew as a spoken language in Eretz Yisrael and elsewhere. Hebrew is now the official language of the State of Israel. It has thus regained its position among the modern living languages. By means of this language only can we identify ourselves with the vibrant, creative life of modern Israel. Through Hebrew alone can we experience, even if only vicariously, the birthpains and the creative joy of the rejuvenated people.

Hebrew is a potent medium for revitalizing the Jewish community of America, for rendering it dynamic and creative, and it is a source of spiritual satisfaction and security for the individual American Jew. By means of it, channels are established leading directly to the fountainhead of Jewish creativity throughout the generations. Through these channels the living stream of the accumulated Hebraic wisdom of the past and the new creative resources of modern Israel will flow pure and undefiled, constantly refreshing and regenerating.

The Present Spiritual Crisis in Diaspora Jewry

Those of us who are watching alertly the trend of the times and events in Jewish life are cognizant of the fact that the Jews of the Western World are, at the present time, living through a grave spiritual crisis. A dream and an aspiration which had been a source of courage and endurance for the Jewish people, which had given wings to their imagination and meaning to their lives in the face of untold persecutions and sufferings over a period of two thousand years, has apparently come true. The hope for the deliverance and restoration of Zion and for *kibbutz galuyot* (ingathering of exiles), which had been cherished for centuries, has at last become, in large measure, a reality. The dream having been realized, a powerful motive and purpose for the continuity of Jewish life in the Diaspora seems to have been lost. The result is drifting and perplexity.

Particularly affected by this crisis is the Jewish youth of America and probably of other western countries. The elation which marked the period of emergency in the Jewish State had, of necessity, to be followed by an emotional let-down. The realization is never as roseate as the anticipation. The "prosaic" problems and difficulties which followed in the train of the dramatic appearance of the State and the heroic struggle of the "War of Liberation" have served to dampen further the enthusiasm of our idealistic youth. The question confronting us now is "where do we go from here?" We are in need of a new, or renewed, vision and goal, a fresh compass and cynosure.

Are we to liquidate and terminate the *Galut* by means of assimilation as suggested by some, or through immigration to Israel as recommended by others? Should we endeavor to maintain and promote our cultural identity in the Diaspora independently of Israel or in intimate relationship with Israel? Can we find an adequate rationale and a sufficiently powerful motivation for persisting in our cultural self-fulfillment in the Diaspora?

A culture is, in the final analysis, a way of life—a complex of attitudes, practices and general outlooks on life, that follow a distinct and consistent historical pattern, which lend the particular people a distinctive place in the world. Can we, in the light of this definition, envisage the possibility of our distinctive cultural self-fulfillment in America? Can a Jewish culture be maintained and thrive alongside the predominant American culture?

The answer to these questions cannot be easily supplied. The solution is obviously difficult. The impact of the majority culture is too overwhelming. In order to survive and to maintain our creative identity in America we must achieve a synthesis of American and Jewish cultures, as well as a dynamic motive and purpose which should grip our heart and fire our imagination, such as the Messianic hope of the preceding generation or the upsurging nationalism which marked the "War of Liberation."

Needed—A Dynamic Source of Motivation for Jewish Life in the Diaspora

What are the sources from which we can ̶ ̶ ̶ ̶ ̶ ̶ motives? How can we recapture the imagination of ̶ ̶ ̶ ̶ ̶ ̶ win their hearts for the purpose of active ̶ ̶ ̶ the building and preservation of a cr ̶ ̶ ̶ ̶ ̶ in America?

In order to retain active members ̶ ̶ ̶ up and to be a vibrant participant in a mi ̶ ̶ ds a strong sense of identification with the ̶ ̶ ̶ d faith in its destiny, as well as deep-se ̶ ̶ ̶ e and tenacity. All these can stem only ̶ ̶ ̶ ̶ program which has its roots deep in the ̶ ̶ ̶ of the group, and which provides outle ̶ ̶ ̶ life-program of creative and dynamic ̶ ̶ ̶

The Real Meaning of Historic Culture

All this implies the need of a re-evaluation of emphasis of traditional, as contrasted with political, "Zionism," the origins of which are imbedded in the ancient Messianic ideal. We must recapture and re-emphasize the elements of cultural, as well as those of cosmic and individual salvation, implied in this Messianic ideal, in the term *geulah shlemah* (complete deliverance) as articulated by our prophets, poets and sages, both ancient and modern. Political rehabilitation and security may, of course, be necessary prerequisites and basic steps in the process of historical Zionism, but only as the means of achieving the *geulah shlemah,* not as its end. The end is, in effect, a process, not a product—an ideal that can never be fully or completely achieved. Like all genuine ideals, it recedes as we get closer to it, but it constantly serves as a beacon of light that stimulates and lifts the soul to grandeur.

Those of us who were raised on traditional Hebraic sources and on the literary traditions of the Hebrew classics know only too clearly that Zionism is not merely a matter of settling in Eretz Yisrael a number of Jewish refugees or victims of persecution. Nor is it only the establishing of a Jewish State in Palestine in order that the Jews might be "like all the nations." This in and of itself would be, to paraphrase Ahad Ha-Am, far from adequate to compensate the Jewish people for two thousand years of untold sufferings and afflictions.

The primary need is for a regeneration of the Hebraic spirit, a revival and resurgence of the prophetic genius of the Jewish people, and an opportunity to revitalize the Hebraic civilization on its native soil in consonance with that genius. This means the establishment of an ideal society, the object of which is "to perfect the world under the kingdom of God"—a society based on social justice, democracy, humanity, universal brotherhood and peace. It means likewise a restoration of Jewish self-respect, as well as of a feeling of personal integration and mental poise for all Jewish individuals who identify themselves with Hebraic culture, whether they live inside or outside of the State of Israel. In brief, the State of Israel is to be a homeland not only for the Jews living there, but also for a vital and burgeoning world Judaism—a center from which dynamic forces of creative Jewish living will radiate to the circumference of the entire diaspora; or, to use Ahad Ha-Am's metaphor, Eretz Yisrael is to be the heart from which fresh bloodstreams will flow into the body of Diaspora Judaism, constantly revitalizing and energizing it.

However, the Diaspora must not be on the receiving end only; it also has something to contribute to the development of the spiritual center. In the first place, to pursue Ahad Ha-Am's metaphor consistently, the heart cannot function effectively unless the blood vessels in the body likewise function normally and are capable of promoting and facilitating the blood circulation. In the second place, the Diaspora can safeguard the State of Israel from turning in the direction of narrow nationalism. There is a strong temptation for a small people that has regained power, after having suffered for a long time from oppression and persecution, to become over-aggressive and chauvinistic. A strong international-minded Diaspora would serve as a brake and would induce Israel to resist such temptation. Then, again, the Jews living in the Diaspora might acquire and create, under the cultural influence of the various countries where they reside, spiritual values which, in the process of interaction with the culture of the Jewish State, would produce a deeper and broader general Jewish culture. Both the State of Israel and the Diaspora would thus benefit spiritually from the interaction of the culture of Israel and the cultures of the various countries of the Diaspora.

But in order to accomplish these purposes and to facilitate this mutual interaction it is necessary to have the hearts of the Jews in the Diaspora attuned to the rhythm of Jewish life in Israel, as well as to the historic Jewish ideals which dominate and motivate this life. It is, likewise, necessary that the Jews of Israel be sensitized to the needs and problems of the Jews in the Diaspora. Indeed, the reconstruction and revitalization of the Hebraic civilization in Israel will of necessity be conditioned, to a considerable extent and for many years to come, by the human material as well as by the spiritual influence of the Diaspora. In other words, the fulfillment of the Hebraic cultural ideal is, in effect, a cultural two-way passage, and the effectiveness of his fulfillment will be determined by the establishment of proper and efficient channels of intercommunication. Thus, there is no real dichotomy of Israeli and Diaspora Judaism. Judaism is one and indivisible, with its center or nucleus in Israel and its "field" or sphere and cultural influence over the whole Diaspora.

The Role of Hebrew in Diaspora Judaism

The role of Hebrew education and the Hebrew language in the light of all this is, of course, obvious. It is its function to establish these channels of transmission and to facilitate the process of intercommunication. Education is a slow process, lacking glamor and flourish, but it is the only effective means of bringing Zion's ideal to full fruition. Young people, and adults too, who possess the proper Hebraic orientation will be not only the builders of Israel, but also the backbone of a meaningful Judaism in the Diaspora, which will integrate itself with the revitalized Judaism of Israel and model itself to some degree on the ideal patterns evolved there, while evolving and creating at the same time values and life patterns indigenous to their particular locale.

There is no intention in this discussion to overidealize the Hebrew language per se and to exaggerate its significance as a mere language, without reference to the culture and literature to which it is a symbolic guide. The mere knowledge of Hebrew does not make one a better Jew any more than the mere knowledge of English makes one a better American. Judaism without Hebrew is a disembodied soul. Hebrew without Judaism, without an interest in the study of Torah in its broader implications, especially in the Diaspora, is an empty shell, a devitalized corpse. To worship either one without the other partakes of the nature of idolatry.

We are, of course, compelled, under the present circumstances, to resort in varying degrees to translations of Hebrew sources and to languages other than Hebrew in the study of Judaism, and a great deal may be said in favor of such works. The cultivation of reading interests on Judaism and its culture, even in translation or in a non-Hebrew language, is certainly preferable to a mere knowledge of spoken Hebrew devoid of interest in reading and study of Jewish literature and culture. But let us recognize the inadequacy of a translation or of the non-Hebrew language as a symbolic guide to Judaism, and let us refrain from making a virtue out of necessity. We must endeavor gradually to strengthen our Hebraic program, in order to make the original resources of Judaism increasingly accessible to our children. Let us remember the lesson learned from our history to the effect that any Jewish community which has divorced itself from the original Hebraic sources, however sumptuous and magnificent the architecture of its temples and schools, will not survive. To quote Professor Solomon Schechter, "If history has anything to say in the matter, the lesson it affords us is that the disappearance of the Hebrew language was always followed by assimilation with their surroundings, and the disappearance of Judaism. The Hebrew language is not a mere idiom; it is in itself a religious symbol of history, a promise and a hope."[1]

The only guarantee for the survival of the Jewish community as a creative force in Jewish life is an effective, functional, Torah-centered and Hebraic type of education.

This, therefore, is the direction, and this is the challenge to American Jews and to American educators.

NOTES AND BIBLIOGRAPHY

INTRODUCTION

1. Jespersen, Otto, *Mankind, Nation and Individual,* p. 5.
2. *Ibid.,* p. 11.
3. Hasidism is a religious movement among Jews which originated in Poland in the middle of the eighteenth century and spread throughout Europe. It stressed the elements of joyous faith, enthusiasm, conviviality and comradeship in religion, thus serving to relieve the gloom and misery of Polish and Russian Jewry. The movement still has its adherents in Europe, America and Israel.
4. Kuzari I, 27.
5. See below, Chapter IX, Note 3.
6. J. Hagigah I, 76d.
7. Erubin 14b.
8. J. Baba Metzia 7a.

CHAPTER ONE

1. This is based on popular etymology. Actually the stem of אִישׁ is אוש, while that of אִשָּׁה is אנש.
2. Genesis Rabba 18,6 and 31,8.
3. Pirke d'Rabbi Eliezer, 26.
4. Cf. Jespersen, Otto, *Language,* 1921, p. 21.
5. See L. Ginzberg, *Legends of the Jews,* I, p. 173.
6. Wm. Wright, *Comparative Grammar,* p. 9.
7. Quoted by De' Rossi, *Me'or Einayim,* p. 456f.
8. In modern times other factors co-operate in diffusing a unified or Standard Language, such as the growth of big cities, the radio, television, theater, newspapers, and other modern means of intercommunication. But in ancient days all these factors were not in operation. Nevertheless, the process of differentiation still persists even in modern times, and complete agreement is never attained. The urge for variety and the tendency toward idiosyncrasies is as

widespread in language as it is in dress, in furnishing and the like.

CHAPTER TWO

1. Only here and there do we find some typical Aramaisms in the early portions of biblical literature. Compare the relative pronouns *zu* (Exodus 15.13, 16), for the Aramaic *di*, and *-ti* (for *-t*) as in *shakamti* (Judges 5.7). The verb *ramah* (threw, Exodus 15.1, 21) is another example of Aramaic origin. Later portions of the Bible are, however, replete with Aramaic influences due to the increasing spread of this language as the *lingua franca* of the Middle East.

2. See A. Sh. Yahudah, *Eber wa-Arab*, pp. 1-25. Some of Yahudah's etymologies are challenged by modern scholars.

3. *Ibid.*, pp. 8, 15-25. Another example of Egyptian influence on Hebrew, via midrashic interpretation, may be found in the words *abrekh* (a learned young man) and *pi'nah* (discovered). When Joseph was appointed Prime Minister of Egypt by Pharaoh, the word shouted before his chariot was *abrekh* (Genesis 41.43), which is composed of two Egyptian words *ab* (heart) and *rekh* (to you), meaning "take heed," "watch out." The rabbis, however, interpreted this word as a composite of *ab* (a father, or elder, with respect to wisdom) and *rakh* (tender, as regards age), and it has been used in this sense in modern Hebrew. Similarly, the title *tzafnat pa'neah* was conferred upon Joseph by Pharaoh upon his appointment as Prime Minister (Genesis 41.45). The meaning of this title in Egyptian is, according to Yahudah (*op. cit.*, 10), "this living (person) is the (source of) provision for the land," which is the equivalent of the term *mashbir* (provider), by which Joseph is described elsewhere (*ibid.* 42.6). The rabbis, however, construed this title to mean "the discoverer of hidden things," since the word *tzafnat* seems related to the Hebrew stem *tzafan* (hid). Consequently, the word *pi'nah* has come to be employed in later Hebrew in the sense of "discovered."

4. This language is also called Akkadian because the Assyrians and Babylonians are supposed to have inhabited

the northern alluvial section of Mesopotamia known as Akkad (cf. Genesis 10.10).

5. See Genesis 21.22-34 and 26.26-32.

6. Cf. Gordon, Cyrus H., *Old Testament Times,* p. 109, note 16.

7. These letters were discovered in Tell-El-Amarna in 1887; see below, chapter III.

8. The identification of the *Habiru* or *Apiru* (in Egyptian and Ugaritic documents, as well as, according to Albright, in cuneiform inscriptions) with the Hebrews is still a moot problem, although the preponderance of evidence seems to favor it. The etymology of the name is, likewise, still a matter of dispute. It should be pointed out, however, that the transition from *Habiru* or *Apiru* to *'Ibri* presents no special phonetic or grammatical difficulty. The Hebrew sound ע is generally rendered in the cuneiform script employed in Akkadian, by *h*; while the change from *p* to *b* in early Hebrew, especially under the influence of a following ר sound, is not unique; cf. the Ugaritic ערפת an equivalent of the Hebrew עֲרָבוֹת (clouds). Similarly the development of the form *'Ibri* from *Habiru* is in keeping with the principles of Hebrew grammar; cf. Chomsky, Wm., *David Kimhi's Hebrew Grammar (Mikhlol),* p. 235; also p. 249, note 397.

9. S. Zeitlin, *JQR,* 1939, 8ff.; also Albright, *From the Stone Age to Christianity,* pp. 266f.

10. Meg. 18a.

11. *Antiquities,* III, 10, 6.

12. John 5. 2.

13. Dalman, *Grammatik des Jüdisch-Palestin-Aramaisch,* p. 1.

14. An analogous example is the name *Yiddish* by which the Judeo-German dialect is designated. Originally the Hebrew word *Yehudit,* of which *Yiddish* is a corruption, applied only to Hebrew, that is, the language spoken by the Jews (Judeans). Since the Judeo-German dialect was employed by the Jews of Eastern Europe; the term *Yehudit* or *Yiddish* came to be applied to this dialect also. Similarly the Yiddish translation of the Bible and other sacred books is generally referred to as *Ivri-Taitsh,* a corruption of *Ivri-Deutsch* (Hebrew-German).

15. Modern scholars are of the opinion that Philo knew Hebrew and had access to the original biblical sources. But the evidence adduced by them is not entirely convincing (cf. Wolfson, H. A., *Philo,* I, 88f.). All one can say in this regard in the light of the available evidence is that if Philo did know Hebrew, his knowledge of the language was meager and he made little use of it in his works. While he was thoroughly conversant with the Greek version of the Bible, his familiarity with the original Hebrew text was very slight and he probably referred to it rarely, as evidenced by some of the gross errors into which he occasionally fell; cf. Azariah de' Rossi, *Me'or einayim,* 108ff.

16. That literary dialects do not reflect the actual dialects spoken by the people has long been recognized by linguists. Indeed, "Standard Language" is an artificial dialect resembling none of the dialects employed in any particular locality. To quote Henry Sweet (*Sounds of English,* p. 7), "The best speakers of Standard English are those whose pronunciation, and language generally, least betray their locality." The tendency among writers, and this is particularly true of ancient writers, was to transcend the distinctive characteristics of the local dialects and to write a language which cannot be identified with any of these dialects, since the writers addressed themselves to all the people and not to those of any particular locality, and adopted instead an artificial language, which should represent, as it were, the "standard" or "best" language. "Every branch of literature evolved its special language, coloured by that of the district in which it first sprang up. But in the 5th and 6th centuries (B.C.E.) educated Greeks understood literary texts though written in dialects widely apart. Greek literary language has its 'style' like all Greek art; it is no mere exact copy of the reality. The Homeric language, an Ionian stratum laid over an Aeolian, is extremely artificial." (Otto Jespersen, *Mankind, Nation and Individual,* 1946, p. 54.)

CHAPTER THREE

1. An analogous case may be found in the phonetic transition from Anglo-Saxon *ham* (compare "hamlet"), *stan*, etc., to "home," "stone," and the like; while in Middle English or Scotch these words are pronounced *hoom* and *stoon*. This change from Anglo-Saxon *a*, when accented, to modern English *o* is a basic phonetic law (cf. Sturtevant, *Linguistic Change*, p. 69f.), which seems to operate with equal consistency in the case of the transition from Semitic *a* to Hebrew *o*.

2. The possessive or genitive ending in modern English (e.g., "father's house") is not the original case ending, but is derived from the possessive pronoun "his," e.g., "father his house."

3. In his book, *Mi-Sitrei he-Abar*, pp. 337ff., Dr. S. Feigin cites numerous examples in the Bible which may be plausibly explained as remnants of these case-endings. Stereotyped forms of these case-endings may also be seen in such instances as *rabbati 'am . . . sarati ba-medinot* (for *rabbat 'am*, "full of people," and *sarat* (or, *sarah*) *ba-medinot*, "princess among the provinces") Lamentations 1.1; *shokhni seneh* (for *shokhen seneh*, "of him that dwelt in the bush") Deuteronomy 33.16.

4. In English as well as in other European languages a separate personal pronoun is employed in verbal forms to indicate person, gender and number relative to the verbal status or activity. This is not the case in Hebrew and in the other Semitic languages. In these languages the personal pronoun is absorbed in the verbal form by means of suffixes and prefixes, composed of certain specific letters, added to the verbal stem. The past tense is signalized by suffixes, the future tense, by prefixes, as well as suffixes in certain forms. In Hebrew, as well as in Aramaic and Ethiopic, the vocalization of the prefixes in the future tense of the simple verbal forms is *i* (*hirek*), except in the first person singular, when it is vocalized *e* (*eshmor* in place of *'ishmor*), probably in order to distinguish it from

the phonetically similar form of the third person (*yishmor*).

But the original vocalization of these prefixes in the Semitic languages was really *a* (*patah*) as in "far." This vocalization is still retained in Arabic, as well as in the Canaanitish glosses of the Amarna letters. Thus we find there the forms *yazkur* (Hebrew *yizkor*) "he remembers," *tanshuku* (Hebrew *tishshokh*) "you bit or bite." In Hebrew the sound *a* of the prefixes reasserts itself in verbs that begin with one of the throat-letters *aleph, he, het, 'ayin,* e.g., *ya 'amod* "he will stand." The attenuation or transition from *a* to *i* in the prefixes of the future tense must accordingly have taken place in Hebrew after the Amarna period, probably long thereafter. During the time of Abraham, or even Moses and the Judges, these prefixes were undoubtedly sounded *a*.

This change from unaccented *a* in a closed syllable to *i* is not uncommon in Hebrew also in nouns. Thus, for example, the biblical name Miriam is derived from Mariam. The Greek translation of the Septuagint still transliterates this name as *Mariam,* from which we get the English *Mary.* Compare *mirzah* (Amos 6.7), from *marzeah* (Jeremiah 16.8) "house of feasting." There are a number of such forms, which in ancient transliteration, as well as in the Babylonian vocalization, are rendered with patah (*a*), but are vocalized with hirek (*i*) in our system of vocalization.

5. In JQR, N.S., XXXIX, 4, a new interpretation of this letter is given by Professor H. Tur-Sinai (Torcyzner).

6. Other examples are: *dr* (for *dor*) "generation," in the Ugaritic poems; *bnti* (for *baniti* "I built," and *'asti* (for *'asiti*) "I made" in the Mesha inscription; *tzr* (for *tzoor*) "rock" and *'sh* (for *'ish*) "man" in the Siloam inscription; and *w't* (for *we-'ata*) "and you," *hnb'* (for *ha-nabi'*) "the prophet," and *'tt* (for *'otot*) "signs" in the Lachish letters.

7. Compare Latin *amat* and French *aime*; Aramaic *malkhu* from *malkhut* (kingdom).

8. One of the problems with which Hebrew grammarians,

both medieval and modern, have had to grapple is the peculiar character of the verbs whose stem ends in the letter *he* (e.g., בנה "he built," presumably from the stem *bet, nun, he*). However, this final *he* disappears or changes to *yod* when it is due to occur in the middle of the word in the inflected forms. What may account for the disappearance of this *he?* Why does it not remain in the inflected forms like the other root-letters? Some medieval Hebrew grammarians already discerned the answer about eight centuries ago. They suggested that not the *he,* but a *yod* or a *waw* (which passed into *yod*) is the original final root-letter. But because of the weak consonantal value of the *waw* and *yod,* their sounds drop off at the end of the word, while the preceding vowel is retained. An analogous example is the dropping, in English, of the equivalent sounds in such words as "saw," "grow," and in the southern pronunciation (in the United States) of such words as "my" and "by" (pronounced *ma* and *ba*). However, before our vowel-system was established in Hebrew it was necessary to employ some sign to indicate the existence of the preceding vowel, otherwise the final consonant might be regarded as silent. Hence the *he* was placed there to serve this purpose, but in the middle of the word the original *yod* reasserts itself.

The Mesha inscription corroborates this theory. We find there two forms in which the original *waw* is retained also at the end of the word; namely, אענו (I shall afflict), ויענו (and he afflicted), which would correspond to the normal Hebrew forms אֲעַנֶּה and וַיְעַנֶּה (or וַיְעַן).

On the same principle we could explain the two "peculiar" forms in the Bible which have been puzzling the grammarians; namely, וַיְשַׁנּוֹ 1 Samuel 21.14 and וַיַּכּוֹ 2 Samuel 14.6, where we should expect the regular forms וַיְשַׁנֶּה (or וַיְשַׁן) and וַיַּכָּה (or וַיַּךְ). But quite plausibly we simply have here further instances of the restoration of the original root-letter, the final *waw,* and these forms should be read וַיְשַׁנּוּ (and he changed) and וַיַּכּוּ (and he struck).

9. See Tur-Sinai, N. H., *ha-Lashon we-ha-Sefer,* II, p. 14.

On the function of the ‫כ‬ in all these instances, see also my *David Kimhi's Hebrew Grammar*, §85 J.

10. It is interesting to note that the Rashbam, with his usually keen insight, sensed the correct meaning of the passages in Genesis. The word *ka-yom* there is interpreted by him as *le-alter, mi-yad* (on the spot, immediately).

CHAPTER FOUR

1. Sturtevant, E. H., *An Introduction to Linguistic Science*, p. 42.
2. Bloomfield, L., *Language*, p. 283.
3. The *a* ending of the Greek names (with the exception of a few) is not to be interpreted as evidence of their Aramaic origin, but rather as due to the aversion of the Greek language to final consonants (see Nöldeke, Theo., *Beitraege zur semitischen Sprachwissenschaft* (1904), p. 135.
4. Albright, Wm. F., *Archaeology of Palestine and the Bible*, 50. This potsherd is badly damaged, and the decipherment of its text is still a matter of dispute among scholars. Another potsherd, however, of the same period, found in Tell-el-Hesy bears an inscription "with two perfect letters and one damaged letter of somewhat Sinaitic appearance . . . ; these may be read ‫בלע‬ *bl'* as the name of the owner of the object of which it is a fragment." (G. R. Driver, *Semitic Writing*, revised edition, p. 100). Moreover, recent discoveries of diverse scripts seem to point to experimental attempts at alphabetic writing in Canaan, which may be traced as far back as "the second half of the third millennium B.C." (*ibid.*, 191).
5. Yadayim IV, 5.
6. See above, Chapter III. As a matter of fact, variation of Ugaritic writing may have been employed in Palestine as early as the second millennium B.C.E., as attested by recently discovered inscriptions from Beth Shemesh and Mt. Tabor; cf. Gelb, I. J., *A Study of Writing*, p. 130.
7. Clodd, E., *The Story of the Alphabet*, 177.
8. On the authenticity of the Dead Sea scrolls, which are

presumed to antedate the Nash papyrus; see below, Chapter VII, note 2.

9. See Landau, J. L., *Short Lectures on Modern Hebrew Literature*, pp. 17-18.

10. See Zunz, *Zur Geschichte*, p. 206, and Profiat Duran, *Ma'aseh Efod.*, p. 21.

11. The head of the ox may be visualized in this picture.

12. The top of this letter represents the ancient house resembling a tent, while the bottom is merely a ligature, a little "tail" connecting this letter with the one next to it.

13. Both forms were employed, depending on whether the writing was from left to right or the reverse.

14. This represents the hump of the camel or the long neck of the camel and its head.

15. The form resembles the door of a tent.

16. The palm of the hand can easily be identified here.

17. The picture of the goad may be seen in the old Hebrew form, while in the square script the bottom part of this letter constitutes the ligature.

18. Here is the picture of the waves ending in a ligature.

19. See above, p. 78.

20. According to Prof. N. H. Tur-Sinai (Torczyner), the names of the letters of the alphabet stem from Greek, rather than from Canaanitic or Jewish sources. Ancient Jewish tradition had, according to him, no fixed names for the letters. The so-called traditional names (*aleph, bet,* etc.) of the letters were borrowed, he maintains, from the Greeks at a late talmudic period and adapted in form to the Hebrew or Aramaic dialect then in vogue. Furthermore, the order of the letters was based, in his opinion, on didactic principles and was designed to teach the pupils the ways of God, which are to be emulated. See *ha-Lashon we-ha-Sefer*, II, 150-194. Tur-Sinai advances some cogent arguments, but his views raise more questions than they solve. The whole issue is far from settled. Further investigation into these problems is needed.

21. Cf. Psalms, chapters 9, 10, 25, 34, 37, 111, 112, 119; Lamentations, chapters 1-4; Proverbs 31. 10-31; also Ben Sira, 51. 13-30.

22. Mo'ed Katan 16b. The same Hiyya, who was a favorite pupil of Judah ha-Nasi, once told Simon, the son of the Nasi, that had he been a Levite he would have been disqualified from participating in the Levitical chants, because of his gruff voice. When the offended Simon reported Hiyya's observation to the Nasi, the latter advised him to retort to Hiyya's criticism of his voice with the reminder that when he recites the verse וְחִכִּיתִי לַה' (Isaiah 8.17), he is guilty of the most flagrant blasphemy, since Hiyya pronounced the *het* like the letter *he,* in which case the word was read by him וְהִכִּיתִי (I struck). He accordingly made no phonetic distinction among the letters ה, ח and ע.

23. Ber. 32a; J. Ber. 4d.

24. Shab. 104a and J. Meg. 71d.

25. There are a number of forms in Hebrew where these consonants are spirant even when not preceded by a vowel, as, for example, in *malkhei* (kings of) and *radphu* (they pursued). The reason for the spirantization of the consonants *k* and *p* in these instances is the fact that the vowel which had preceded these consonants was dropped after having effected their spirantization. Thus the original forms *malakei* and *radapuh* evolved into *malakhei* and *radaphu* by a process of spirantization, and this pronunciation persisted even after the medial vowel had been discarded. The grammarians generally assume a sort of semivowel preceding these spirant consonants, reading such as the above-given forms *malekhei* and *radephu,* but there is no valid basis for such an assumption. Cf. below, Chapter VI, n. 10.

CHAPTER FIVE

1. One must accordingly assume that the vocalization and subdivision of words in our masoretic text is in a certain sense an interpretation or commentary, albeit a traditionally accepted one. Other vocalizations or readings are not, therefore, precluded. Thus, for example, in place of כֻּלֹּה מְקַלְלַוְנִי (a grammatical monstrosity), in Jeremiah 15.10, a better reading כֻּלָּהֶם קִלְלוּנִי has been sug-

gested; instead of אֶת־מַה־מַּשָּׂא, *ibid.*, 23.33, the reading אַתֶּם הַמַּשָּׂא rendered in the Septuagint and the Vulgate makes better sense. In a great many instances, the masoretes, leaving the text as it is, direct the reader to substitute the correct division of words. A full list of such examples is given by S. R. Driver in his *Notes on the Book of Samuel*, second edition, Introduction xxviii-xxx. See also preceding chapter, p. 86.

2. Cf. *Mahzor Vitry*, ed. Hurowitz, p. 91.
3. See *Dikduke ha-Te'amim*, p. 16.
4. Cf. *Tzahot*, p. 7.
5. Introduction to *Moznayim*.
6. Cf. *Me'or Einayim*, pp. 473-477.
7. Quoted in Ginsburg's Introduction to Levita's *Masoret ha-Masoret*, p. 47.
8. See Erubin 21b, Ber. 60a, Ber. Rabbah 36, 12. Other designations mentioned in the Talmud are *piske te'amim* (Meg. 3a) and *pissuk te'amim* (Ned. 37b). It is often assumed that these terms refer to accents or cantillation signs. This is, however, highly improbable. It seems fairly certain that the "signs" alluded to by these terms constituted some experimental system of reading-aids or vocalism. This is borne out by Jerome's use of the term *accentus* both in reference to the pronunciation and to the signs denoting pronunciation (cf. Gesenius, *Geschichte der Hebr. Sprache und Schrift*, p. 198). It is quite improbable that these terms applied to accents or cantillation signs, in the present acceptation of these terms in Hebrew, for Jerome, in his introduction to Isaiah, definitely asserts that he used his own independent judgment in the syntactical grouping of the words. Had there been any accents in the Hebrew texts before Jerome, he would certainly have made reference to them.
9. Cf. Baba Batra 21b and Canticles Rabbah 1, 17. The Rabbis are uncertain as to the exact reading of such words as זכר עֲמָלֵק in Deuteronomy 25.19 (זָכָר or זֵכֶר), or דודיך Canticles 1.2 (דּוֹדַיִךְ or דּוֹדֶיךָ?).
10. Cf. such examples as: נִירִי, הִשְׁלִיךְ, גְּבוּל, שׁוֹמֵר (2 Samuel 22. 29).
11. See *Masoreten des Westens*, I, p. 33f.

12. Cf. below, p. 106f.

13. The meaning of this word in Syriac, from which language the term was probably borrowed, is "the piercer"; hence the connotation of "pointing," that is, putting a point in the middle of the letter; compare the English "puncture" and "punctuate."

14. There are only a few instances left in our masoretic text where the long pronunciation of a consonant is represented by doubling the consonant instead of putting a *dagesh* in it, e.g., יִשָּׂשכָר Genesis 30.18; קִלְלַת Deuteronomy 21.23; רְנָנַת Job 20.6; מְחַצְצרִים 1 Chronicles 15.24. The unvocalized שׂ in יִשָּׂשכָר and the צ in מְחַצְצרִים are not to be pronounced, according to Ben Asher.

15. For example, גָּבַה "was high," כָּמַהּ "languished," נָגַהּ "shone," תָּמַהּ "wondered," הִתְמַהְמַהּ "lingered," וַתֵּלַהּ "languished" (Genesis 47.13, stem להה); also the nouns אֱלֹהַּ "God" and יָהּ "Lord."

16. See Pinsker, S., *Mabo*, 177.

17. See above, p. 91.

18. The absence of a *dagesh* where one is expected, in consonance with the above-mentioned conditions, is often designated in biblical texts by a horizontal line above the letter entitled to a *dagesh*. This sign is known as *rafe* "soft" or "weak," e.g., מְקָצֵה Genesis 8.3 (for מִקְצֵה). The *rafe* sign likewise goes back to the prevocalic period when it was used in contradistinction to *dagesh*, to indicate the spirant pronunciation, or the absence of a vowel in the letter on which it is placed. In this latter capacity it accordingly served as the predecessor of our *shewa* sign (ַ֯), which is employed for the same purpose.

19. To these regular or full vowel-signs were added the following special signs:

   1. The *shewa* (ְ). This sign was designed by the founders of the vowel-system to indicate that the consonant under which it stands is vowel-less. Hence its name *shewa* or *shaw'* (nothingness). However, at the beginning of a syllable, the vowel-less pronunciation of a consonant is phonetically difficult. The *shewa* in such instances

is, therefore, partially sounded and is termed by Hebrew grammarians *shewa na'* (vocal *shewa*), in contradistinction to the silent *shewa* (*shewa na*). For example, in a word like יִשְׁמְרוּ "they will watch," the first *shewa* is silent, the second is vocal.

2. Composite or half-vowels. When the weak consonants, or throat-sounds אהחע had lost their vowels and were consequently entitled to *shewa,* they were likely to be lost in pronunciation. For example, in words like נַעֲרָה "girl" (on the analogy of יַלְדָה "little girl"), אֶעֱשֶׂה "I shall do" (compare אֶבְנֶה "I shall build"), אָהֳלִי "my tent" (analogous to אָזְנִי "my ear"), etc., a vowel was added to the *shewa.* Otherwise, these throat-consonants would lose their sound-values and would become totally inaudible. The vowel to be added may be *patah, segol,* or *kametz,* depending on the preceding vowel. These vowels are to be pronounced hurriedly and are, therefore, denoted as *hateph* (hurry) vowels: *hateph-patah, hateph-segol,* and *hateph-kametz.*

20. See p. 149.
21. *Ma'aseh Efod,* p. 21.
22. *Ibid.,* p. 149.
23. See *Me'or Einayim,* p. 475.
24. See *Masoreten des Westens,* I, p. 28.
25. See above, end of Chapter IV.
26. Comp. Abba Ben David, *Leshon ha-Mikra 'o Leshon Hakhamim,* p. 142f.

CHAPTER SIX

1. Thus, the rabbis observe that the ending *ah* (הָ‬) in such forms as *mitzraimah, midbarah,* etc. indicates direction and stands in place of a prefixed *l* (to), as *l'mitzrayim* (to Egypt), *la-midbar* (to the desert), etc. (Yeb. 13b). In another instance it is pointed out that the particle *ki* has four different meanings: "if," "lest," "indeed," "because" (Git. 90a).
2. רֹאשׁ הַמְדַבְּרִים בְּכָל מָקוֹם (Introduction to *Moznayim*).
3. Comp. *Teshubot Dunash* against Menahem, p. 30.

4. The tense-idea in biblical Hebrew was, as will be pointed out later completely different from that in the European languages and modern Hebrew.

5. The tendency to drop a vowel-less *n* and to assimilate it to the next consonant with the result of doubling it is evident also in English. Note, for instance, such words as "immoral" (for "inmoral") and "irreligious" (for "inreligious"). The doubling of the letter is, of course, represented in Hebrew by a *dagesh*; see above, p. 105. In Hebrew an unvocalized *n* is consistently dropped, and the *dagesh* in the subsequent letter, signifying doubling, compensates for the loss of the letter.

6. Comp. *Yesod Mora,* Chapter 1 and introduction to *Moznayim.* However, the term "book" was employed in the Middle Ages for essays or sections of a book.

7. Comp. *Opuscules d'Abou'l-Walid,* ed. Derenbourg, pp. 344ff.; also Ibn Barum, *Kitab al-Muwazana,* ed. Kokowzoff, p. 12.

8. See *Sefer ha-Shorashim s.vv.* ‏לקח, ילד, יכח, התל‎, ‏אהב, צפן, פשט, נתן‎.

9. Abot 3, 21. The actual translation of this dictum is "where there is no flour (bread), there is no Torah." By a play on the word *kemah* (flour), it came to be applied to Kimhi.

10. According to the Kimhian vowel-theory, there are five long and five short vowels. The five long vowels are *kametz* (ָ), *holem* (וֹ), *shurek* (וּ), *hirek* followed by a *yod* (ִי), and *tzere* (ֵ). The five short vowels are *patah* (ַ), short or hurried *kametz* (ָ), *kibbutz* (ֻ), *hirek* (ִ), and *segol* (ֶ). The short vowels normally occur in a closed syllable, i.e., in a syllable ending in a consonant, e.g., ‏בַּרְזֶל‎ "iron." The long vowels regularly occur in an open syllable, that is, a syllable ending in a vowel, e.g., ‏בָּאתִי‎ "I came." Under the influence of the accent, the case may be reversed; that is, short vowels may occur in open syllables (e.g., ‏מַיִם‎ "water," ‏מֶלֶךְ‎ "king") and long vowels may be found in closed syllables (e.g., ‏יוֹם‎ "day," ‏שִׁיר‎ "song").

But what about the *shurek* in ‏וּבוּלְךָ‎ "your boundary"

and the *hirek* in שִׁירְךָ "your song"? Those two vowels are apparently in a closed syllable, since they are followed by a consonant with a *shewa* (־ְ). Yet they are unaccented and have only a little perpendicular stroke to the left designated as *meteg* (bridle). In all such cases, the Kimhians asserted, the *shewa* is vocal, and the vowel preceding it is, therefore, in an open syllable. The *meteg* serves to attest to the vocalic character of the following *shewa* and is, therefore, to be regarded as a secondary accent.

This principle has been generally adopted by the grammarians, who, since the day of David Kimhi, have regarded every *shewa* following a long vowel with a *meteg* as vocal. This is, however, an artificial and erroneous theory, and there is ample evidence to disprove it. Indeed every *shewa*, preceded by any of the vowels, regardless of whether they bear or do not bear a *meteg,* is silent, except when it occurs under a throat-letter, or under the first of the same two consonants in succession, in which case it is designated by an additional vowel (*hatef*), e.g., וְהַשֹּׁעֲרִים הַמְשׁוֹרְרִים Nehemiah 12.45, נַהֲרִי, נַחֲלַי Job 20.17, etc. The *meteg* in all these instances was merely intended to warn the reader to give these vowels their full value and not to shorten them because of the subsequent vowel-less consonant (cf. Chomsky, Wm., *David Kimhi's Hebrew Grammar,* note 19). It therefore occurs in unaccented long vowels in a closed syllable, even where the possibility of a vocal *shewa* is inconceivable, e.g., בָּתִּים, שָׁת־לִי Genesis 4.25, שֵׁם־יוֹסֵף *ibid.,* 41.45, לְבָעֶרְקָיִן Numbers 24.22.

11. For example, in the יִפְעֹל formation of verbs beginning with the radical *nun,* this radical is never dropped in the imperative, in biblical as well as in modern Hebrew. In the Talmud, however, we find such "ungrammatical" forms as *pol* (for *nephol,* imper. of the verb *naphal,* "fell") and *dor* (for *nedor,* imper. of *nadar,* "vowed"). The talmudic forms were, of course, suggested by the future forms *yippol* and *yiddor.* Since the imperative is ordinarily formed by removing the prefixes, the forms *pol*

and *dor* are normal analogical developments, which Kimhi, with his evolutionary sense of language, sanctioned.

12. Comp. Hayyuj, ed. Nutt, p. 2, where Menahem is called to task for using the forms צָרוֹתוֹ for יָצָרוֹ (his creating) and לְעוּד for לַעֲדוֹת (to adorn).

13. See *Shorashim* s.v. בְּלל. Very likely Ibn Janah is referring here sarcastically to his opponent, Samuel ha-Nagid.

14. *Bet Yehudah,* commentary on Kiddushin, chapter 1, Mishnah 1.

15. Comp. S. Asaf, *Mekorot le-Toldot ha-Hinukh be-Yisrael,* I, p. 80. A similar tirade is voiced by Samson Bloch against the rabbis of Poland in the nineteenth century; cf. Klausner, Joseph, *Ha-Sifrut ha-Ibrit ha-Hadashah,* II, p. 355.

16. See also Baron, Salo, *Sefer Turoff,* 1938, p. 178.

17. Comp. Asaf, S., *op. cit.,* p. 277.

18. See above, p. 112f. According to Ab. N. Polack (*Kazariah,* 1951, p. 255f.), East-European Jewry, especially that of Ukraine, actually stems, in the main, from the early medieval Jewish state of the Khazars, where the Jewish inhabitants were largely composed of immigrants, or their descendants, from Hellenistic countries. Under the influence of Greek, where the *u* is a phonetic blend of *oo* and *ee,* the Jews of the land of the Khazars are presumed to have employed the *waw* to represent the *oo* as well as the *ee* sounds (see *ibid.,* p. 122f.). The Yiddish pronunciation in Poland was influenced, Polack maintains, by that in the Ukraine.

It may be interesting to note that ample evidence is available to prove that a phonetic distinction between *shurek* and *kibbutz* existed during the Middle Ages among the Jews of France, Germany and parts of Eastern Europe. The *shurek* was pronounced by them *oo,* while the sound of the *kibbutz* resembled that of the *hirek.* In fact such a pronunciation is still in vogue among the Yemenite Jews (see Yitzhak Damati, *Kontresim,* II, 7, ed. Yalon, H., p. 7f.). In the course of time, however, probably not before the end of the seventeenth century, the less conservative Jews of Western Europe assimilated the *kibbutz* sound to that of *shurek,* probably under the influence of the Sephardic pronunciation. But the Jews of Poland and Ukraine persisted in pronouncing both the *shurek* and the *kibbutz* like *ee*.

19. See *Sefer Yesod Mispar*, attached to *Mabo*, p. 153f., note 103.

20. Cf. מְחוּיָאֵל and מְחִיָּיאֵל: Genesis 4.18; פְּנוּאֵל and פְּנִיאֵל: *ibid.*, 32.31, 32; פִּינוֹן *ibid.*, 36.41 and פּוּנוֹן: Numbers 33.42. Similar examples from the Talmud are too numerous to mention; see Dalman, *Grammatik des Jüdisch Palestin.-Aramaisch*, p. 53f.

21. See *Mabo*, p. 6.

CHAPTER SEVEN

1. Canon, a Greek term which means "rule" may be derived from the Hebrew *kaneh* (measuring rod). It is employed to designate the books included in the Bible, which are regarded as sacred by both Jews and Christians. These books are known as "canonical." Other books written during the biblical period, which failed to gain admittance into the Canon, were termed "apocryphal" or "non-canonical." The process of canonization extended over a period of several centuries. The books of the Pentateuch were accepted quite early, perhaps during the period of Ezra and Nehemiah (5th century B.C.E.), while the final canonization did not occur until late in the second century C.E.

2. Recently a number of tattered leather and papyrus scrolls were discovered in the cliffs above the spring of Ain Feshkha, ten miles south of Jericho, containing, among others, the complete book of Isaiah. These are generally referred to as "the Dead Sea Scrolls." This discovery raised a storm of controversy among scholars. Some of them hold that these manuscripts antedate the Nash papyrus and were written during the Maccabean period, while others vigorously challenge the extreme antiquity of the scrolls and date them from the medieval period. In the light of the orthography in the biblical texts and, particularly, of the artificial and corrupt Hebrew style in the original non-biblical texts, the possibility of their belonging to the period of the Second Commonwealth is extremely doubtful. The sopheric

tradition, guided by the injunction of *lo toseph alaw*, which was then, most likely, already in effect (see below, pp. 144f.), would have prevented copyists from interpolating such a plethora of vowel-letters in the biblical texts. There must have been at that time a more or less accepted pattern of orthography in biblical texts intended for use in synagogues or schools, from which scribes would hardly have dared to deviate. Furthermore, the writers of the original texts in these scrolls would have employed, during that period, either Aramaic, or a much more natural mishnaic Hebrew, as a medium of self-expression. There is, to be sure, evidence of ignorance of Hebrew during the Second Commonwealth, as is proved by some isolated inscriptions of the Bet-She'arim necropolis. It is conceivable that a person ignorant of Hebrew would nevertheless prefer a Hebrew inscription on a tombstone. But it is quite inconceivable that such a person would undertake to write an important document in Hebrew, with which he was unconversant, in a style different from the one in vogue among the circles employing the language.

These scrolls are, accordingly, more likely to be dated from the early medieval period and to be traced to Karaitic sources. The Karaites were not influenced by the rabbinic interpretation of the injunction *lo toseph alaw*, and they had no qualms about adding vowel-letters in the biblical texts. Similarly, the Karaites, as well as the early *paytanim*, were wont to write in this loose style characteristic of the original *Megillot* (scrolls), coining new words and constructions arbitrarily, without regard to rules of grammar and syntax. On the basis of the available evidence, one is led to conclude, with Prof. S. Zeitlin, that these scrolls were written, in the main, by ignorant scribes, from memory or dictation, as far as the biblical texts are concerned, during the early medieval period. Cf. S. Zeitlin, *JQR*, XLVI, 1-3. In any event the great ado about the importance of these scrolls is probably unwarranted. Their significance for biblical studies and philological research may have been exaggerated. Since the language of the non-biblical scrolls is, in any event, a sectional dialect, which did not affect standard Hebrew, it is not within the province of our discussion.

3. The *Targum* of the Pentateuch, which goes under the name *Targum Onkelos,* and the Targum of the Prophets, ascribed in the Talmud to Jonathan the son of Uziel, a disciple of Hillel, date back to the talmudic period. These are the traditionally authoritative *Targumim.* There is, however, another *Targum* of the Pentateuch, to which authority was denied, which goes under the name *Targum Yerushalmi* or the "Palestinian Targum." This *Targum* consists of two versions, one a complete text, the other a parallel recension in a fragmentary condition. The complete text used to be known erroneously as *Targum Jonathan* and is now referred to as "Pseudo-Jonathan." The editing of this *Targum* must have taken place at a relatively late date, since we find there the name of the city of Constantinople (Konstantini, Numbers 24.19), founded in 330 C.E., as well as the names of one of the wives and a daughter of Mohammed ('Adisha and Fatima), as the names of the wives of Ishmael (Genesis 21.21).

4. See Tosefta Shabb, 13 (14), 2.

5. J. Meg. 4, 1.

6. Kiddushin 30a.

7. Sofrim VI, 4 and J. Ta'anit IV, 2.

8. The normal spelling in the Bible of the feminine pronoun, third person, singular is הוא, which is vocalized with *hirek* under the *h.* According to a masoretic note to Genesis 38.25, there are only eleven instances in the Torah where this feminine pronoun is written היא. The interchange of *waw* and *yod* is not at all uncommon in the Bible and is quite widespread in the Talmud. The reason for this is either the resemblance in the forms of these two letters in the square script, or the phonetic similarity of the sounds *u* and *i* in ancient Hebrew. There was at that period no clear *u* sound, but rather one resembling the Greek or French *u,* which is composed of both the *u* and the *i* sounds. The *waw* and the *yod* therefore served interchangeably to indicate one or the other of these two vowels.

9. See M. Z. Segal, *Mebo ha-Mikra,* 867-8.

10. Erubin 13a:

בני הוה זהיר במלאכתך שמלאכתך מלאכת שמים
היא שמא אתה מחסר אות אחת או מייתר אות אחת
נמצא מחריב את כל העולם כולו.

"My son, be careful in your work, for your work is of heavenly character. If you subtract or add one letter you may destroy the whole world."

11. See examples in the following verses: Genesis 33.4; 37.12; Numbers 3.39; 10.35-36; 21.30; 29.15; Deuteronomy 29.28; 2 Samuel 19.19; Isaiah 44.9; Ezekiel 41.20; 46.22; Psalms 27.13; 80.14; Judges 18.30; Job 38.13, 15.

12. Abbot d'Rabbi Nathan, Chapter 34.

13. כך אמר עזרא אם יבא אליהו ויאמר לי מפני מה כתבת
כך אומר לו כבר נקדתי עליהן, ואם יאמר יפה כתבת
אעביר נקודה מעליהן

14. Shab. 115b-116a.

פרשה זו עשה לה הקב"ה סימניות מלמעלה ולמטה
לומר שאין זו מקומה.

15. Rashi *ad loc.,* also Sof. 6:1.

16. The term *masorah* is either derived from the Hebrew stem *masar* (to hand over, transmit), or, which is more likely, from the stem *'asar* (to bind); cf. *masoret ha-berit* (the bond of the covenant), Ezekiel 20.37. This term, therefore, probably indicates that the reading of the text is binding or obligatory by tradition.

17. See *Mishneh Torah,* Hilkhot Sefer Torah, Chapter 8.

18. Cf. Kahle, *Masoreten des Westens,* I, pp. 45ff.

19. Different versions of parallel texts were in existence even in the biblical days. Compare the following examples and note the variant versions 2 Samuel 22 = Psalms 18; 2 Kings 18 to 20, 19 = Isaiah chaps. 36-39; 2 Kings 24. 17ff. = Jeremiah 52; Isaiah 2. 2ff. = Micah 4. 1ff.; Psalms 14 = Psalms 53; Psalms 40. 14ff. = Psalms 70, and many others.

20. *Against Apion,* I, 8.

21. Cf. Ch. D. Ginsburg, *Masorah,* p. 25.

22. Men. 29b.

23. Mordecai Obadiah, *Mi-Pi Bialik,* p. 37.

24. Abot, V, 25.

CHAPTER EIGHT

1. San. 38b.
2. Pes. 87b.
3. Sota 49b and Shabb. 12b.
4. Shabb. 12b.
5. B.M. 104a. See also *JQR*, XLII, 3, 329f. As to Prof. Zeitlin's objection to my interpretation of the term *hediot*, I desire to refer to a passage in *Sifre*, Num. 103, p. 102, ed. Horowitz, which was called to my attention by the late Prof. Louis Ginzberg, "where the coupling of 'people slight of knowledge and *idiots*' makes it quite clear that idiots (*hediotot*) are people having no knowledge at all." (From a letter by Prof. Ginzberg, dated Febr. 11, 1952.)
6. The Perfect is characterized by suffixes, the Imperfect by prefixes, and, in some cases, by suffixes as well. For example, in the stem *gdl* (grow) with suffixes indicating second person singular, masculine and feminine, the Perfect is respectively, *gadalta* and *gadalt*; the Imperfect is *tigdal* and *tigdeli*.
7. Hullin 137b.
8. Abodah Zarah 58b.
9. J. Nedarim VI, 1; also Bab. Nedarim 49a.
10. Shab. 115a.
11. See Daniel 2.18, etc.; Esther 1.20; Ezra 1.8.
12. This word is actually a blend of the words אִם לֹא (or אִן לֹא), and it is found in this sense in Genesis 24.38.

CHAPTER NINE

1. Comp. the English term "quiddity" from the Latin *quid* (what), employed in scholastic philosophy. Incidentally, the formation of nouns ending in *ut*, signifying abstract ideas, was widely employed by the medieval Hebraists. They also coined numerous nouns of this type from the *hitpa'el* conjugation, of which type there are only two examples in the Bible (Daniel 11.23 and Ezra 7.13). It was probably coined under Aramaic influence and is used extensively in modern Hebrew. Yet, despite the

strong affinity of mishnaic Hebrew with Aramaic, this type is entirely lacking in mishnaic Hebrew.

2. See Klar, Binyamin, *Mehkarim we-Iyyunim,* p. 31ff.

3. In Midrash Rabba, Esther 7, the expression והחזיקו ביהודתן occurs, in which the word ביהודתן is emended by some to read ביהדותן. This emendation is, however, questionable. The word יהדות is also found in Jossipon. But since this book contains numerous late interpolations, it cannot be relied on as a source for the dating of the occurrence of this term. The term *Judaismos* was coined, according to Prof. S. Zeitlin (*JQR,* XLIII, 4, p. 372f.), by the Jews of the Hellenistic Diaspora to denote the distinction between their faith, or way of life, and Hellenism. The term occurs for the first time in the *Fourth Book of Maccabees* and in the *Epitome* of the *Second Book,* both of which were composed in the city of Antioch.

4. Quoted in Joseph Klausner's *Ha-Sifrut Ha-Ibrit Ha-Hadasha,* III, p. 384.

CHAPTER TEN

1. *Mas'ot Biniamin ha-Shelishi.*
2. *Ba-Yamim ha-Hem.*
3. *Sefer ha-Kabtzanim.*
4. *Shor Abus.*
5. *Tikwat 'Ani.*
6. *Oniyyah.*
7. Comp. Leviticus 19.3: *tira'u . . . tishmoru* (ye shall fear . . . ye shall keep), Isaiah 18.3: *tir'u . . . tishma'u* (see ye . . . hear ye), and numerous other examples.

CHAPTER ELEVEN

1. This date is erroneously identified with *Seder 'olam Rabba,* chapter 30, as that of Nehemiah's arrival in Jerusalem, where he chastised those who had been neglecting the use of the Hebrew language (Nehemiah 13.24).

2. Introduction to *Agron,* p. 54f.

3. Cf. Gesenius, *Geschichte der Hebr. Sprache,* chap. 13; Schürer, *Geschichte des Jüdischen Volkes,* II, 19 (3rd

edition); Dalman, *Die Worte Jesu*, p. 7; Frantz Delitzsch, quoted by Ben Yehudah in *Millon, ha-Mabo ha-Gadol*, p. 215; S. Zeitlin, *JQR.*, XXXIV, 3, p. 336.

4. It may be interesting to note in this connection that when the mother exhorts her seven sons to endure the torture at the hands of Antiochus, during the Maccabean struggle, and to refuse to eat the forbidden food, she does so in "the language of the Fathers," most likely, Hebrew (Maccabees, II, VII, 24.27).

5. Prof. S. Zeitlin, however, rejects the possibility of dating these coins from the Hasmonean period. The use of the term *Yisrael* on these coins, he maintains, proves them to be of a later date, since this term was not in vogue in reference to the Jews during the Maccabean period. The Jews at that time were designated, according to him, exclusively *yehudim* (*JQR.*, April, 1936). We do, however, find the term *yisrael* in *Tosephta*, Yeb. XIV, 7; Er. VIII, 2; Git. V, 4; etc. But even if we were to accept Zeitlin's view, the argument with regard to the mishnaic word *herut* would still be pertinent, for it would demonstrate that mishnaic Hebrew was a living language even as late as the Bar Kokhba period.

6. See Miller, George A., *Language and Communication*, p. 121.

7. Probably the most cogent evidence demonstrating the mishnaic Hebrew as a vernacular is to be drawn from the organic structure of that language. It is an established fact that the progress of a living language is marked by slight mistakes that become accepted in the course of generations. Dead or purely literary languages are static and grammatically "correct," they permit of no deviations from the rules. The capacity for coining "erroneous" grammatical forms which are eventually sanctioned by usage is one of the hall-marks of a vernacular. Mishnaic Hebrew clearly displayed such a capacity. One series of "mistakes" in mishnaic Hebrew stems from the principle of assonance. On this principle, biblical Hebrew yields such "erroneous" forms as מוֹבָאֶךָ (for מְבוֹאֶךָ) under the influence of the preceding מוֹצָאֶךָ 2 Samuel 3.25; מְחָאֶךָ ... וְרָקְעֶךָ

304   *Hebrew: The Eternal Language*

(for וְרָקְעֶךָ) Ezra 25.6; צָאנָה (for צָאֶינָה) due to the subsequent וּרְאֶינָה Canticles 3.11. In mishnaic Hebrew we find numerous "errors" of this type, e.g., מְצֻלָּתָה חמתה מרובה (for מְצֻלָּה, Suk. I, 1), חָבִין . . . זָכִין (for זוֹכִין, Git. I, 6), etc., also such forms as הֵיתֵּר, הָבְדֵּל, הֵיזֵק, הַבְדֵּל הַזַּק, הַשְׁמֵד (for הַתֵּר cf. הַתֵּר, Isaiah 14.23, הַמְשֵׁל: Job 25.2). The principle of assonance is operative only in spoken languages, where changes are governed by sounds and articulation. In a dead or literary language such changes are inconceivable.

8. Ket. 66b.
9. See Philo, *Embassy to Caius*, §36.
10. Further evidence of the close correlation between the retention of the Hebrew language and the survival of Jewish communities is adduced by R. Patai in his book, entitled *Israel Between East and West*, p. 119.
11. Sanh. 5b; Jer. Shebi'it VI, 1. In Acco, Galilee, the sound of the *ayin* was no longer articulated during that period.
12. Pes. 42a.
13. Ned. 66b.
14. In Palestine this word was employed in the sense of candles or candlesticks.
15. See, however, above, p. 167, where it is suggested that the term *leshon hakhamim* may mean merely the language of the Talmud, and the possibility that this language was also the vernacular of the people is not thereby excluded.
16. Erubin 53a.
17. For a more elaborate discussion on the use of Hebrew during the Second Commonwealth see my article on this subject, *JQR.*, XLII, 2.
18. See *Dikduke ha-Te'amim*, p. 7.
19. *Sefer ha-Shanah li-Yehudei Eretz Yisrael*, I, p. 114f.
20. See A. Yaari, *Iggerot Eretz Yisrael*, p. 141.
21. *Matzref la-Kesef*, attached to *Me'or Einayim*, p. 108, note.
22. *Personalities and Events*, chapter 9.
23. See A. Yaari, *op. cit.*, p. 214.
24. See quotations from his will cited by I. Rivkind in *Shebile ha-Hinukh*, 1946, p. 299.
25. See *Millon, ha-Mabo ha-Gadol*, p. 3f.

26. *Ha-Toren,* IV, p. 43.
27. *Op. cit.,* p. 5.

CHAPTER TWELVE

1. Ha-Tzebi, 18, 1889.
2. Cf. *Al Parashat Derakhim,* IV, p. 176. The organization of the *Hilfsverein* occurred not long after the return of Kaiser Wilhelm from his visit in Palestine (in the Fall of 1898). It seems quite probable that the Kaiser was jealous of the French influence exerted by the *Alliance Israélite* and its educational efforts in Palestine. He accordingly sought to counteract this influence and to displace it. Soon after his return to Palestine he is said to have invited his friend James Simon and to have urged upon him to found a rival organization for the dissemination of the German influence in the Holy Land (see Hermoni, A., *be-Ikbot ha-Biluyim,* p. 163). The emphasis on Hebrew by this organization is therefore not to be attributed to a zeal for the language.

CHAPTER THIRTEEN

1. Cecil Roth, *The Jewish Contribution to Civilization,* p. 16.
2. Cecil Roth, *ibid.,* p. 12.
3. Miller, Perry and Johnson, Thomas, H., *The Puritan,* p. 698.
4. Cf. Pool, D. de Sola, *Hebrew Learning Among the Puritans of New England,* American Jewish Historical Society, No. 20; also Katsh, A. I., *Hebrew in American Higher Education,* p. 16, n. 41.
5. Cotton, Mather, quoted by Pool, D. de Sola, *ibid.,* p. 55f.
6. Harvard was not the only university where Hebrew orations were delivered at commencement exercises. A record is available of a Hebrew oration delivered at the commencement exercises of Columbia College, in 1800, by Sampson Simson. See *Publications of the American Jewish Historical Society,* The Lyons Collection, No. 27, pp. 373-5.
7. *Hadoar,* XXI, 12, Jan. 17, 1941, p. 189.
8. Neuman, A. A., *Relations of the Hebrew Scriptures to*

American Institutions, Jewish Theological Seminary of America, p. 10.

9. Cotton, Mather, quoted by Pool, D. de Sola, *op. cit.,* p. 32.

10. Mencken, Henry L., *The American Language,* p. 137f.

11. A Hebrew grammar in English was published in 1735 by Judah Monis, a converted Jew and instructor of Hebrew at Harvard University.

12. This is a normal historical phenomenon, a precedent for which may be found in the fact that during the talmudic period, the Babylonians were more conservative than the Palestinians in their use of Hebrew; cf. above, p. 115.

13. See *A Study of Hebrew in American Colleges and Universities* by A. I. Katsh, pp. 51 and 56.

EPILOGUE

1. Quoted by Norman Bentwich, *Solomon Schechter,* p. 291f.

AHAD HA-AM, Al Parashat Derakhim, Jüdischer Verlag, Berlin, I-IV, 1921

ALBRIGHT, W. F., Archaeology of Palestine and the Bible, Fleming R. Revell Co., New York, 1932-3

―――― From the Stone Age to Christianity, Johns Hopkins Press, 1940

ASAF, S., Mekorot le-Toldot ha-Hinukh be-Yisrael I, Devir, Tel Aviv, 1925

BARON, SALO W., Sefer Turoff, Bet Midrash Le-Morim, Boston, 1938

BEN ASHER, AHARON, Dikdukei ha-Teamim, ed. T. Baer and H. L. Strack, Leipzig, 1879

BEN DAVID, ABBA, Leshon ha-Mikra 'o Leshon Hakhamim, Mahbarot le-Sifrut, Tel Aviv, 1951

BENTWICH, NORMAN, Solomon Schechter, Jewish Publication Society, 1938

BLOOMFIELD, L., Language, Henry Holt, New York, 1933

CHOMSKY, WM., David Kimhi's Hebrew Grammar (Mikhlol), Dropsie College―Bloch, 1952

CLODD, E., The Story of the Alphabet, D. Appleton and Co., 1904.

DALMAN, G., Grammatik des Jüdisch-Palästinischen Aramäisch, Leipzig, 1894

―――― Die Worte Jesu, 3rd edition, 1930

DE' ROSSI, AZARIAH, Me'or Einayim, Vilna, Romm, 1894

DRIVER, G. R., Semitic Writing from Pictograph to Alphabet, revised edition, Oxford University, 1954

DRIVER, S. R., Notes on Samuel, second edition, Oxford, Clarendon Press, 1913

DURAN, PROFIAT, Ma'aseh Efod, Vienna, 1865

FEIGIN, SAMUEL, Mi-Sitrei he-Abar, Sefarim, 1943

GELB, J. H., A Study of Writing, University of Chicago, 1952

GESENIUS, WILHELM, Geschichte der Hebräischen Sprache und Schrift, Halle, 1814

GINSBURG, CH. D., The Masorah, London, I-IV, 1880-1905

GINZBERG, LOUIS, Legends of the Jews, I, Jewish Publication Society, 1909

GORDON, CYRUS, Old Testament Times, Ventnor Publishers, Inc., 1953

HALEVI, JUDAH, Sefer ha-Kuzari, translated by Judah ibn Tibbon, ed. A. Ziprinowitz, Tushiah, Warsaw

HAYYUJ, JUDAH, Shelosah Sifrei Dikduk, ed. John W. Nutt, London and Berlin, 1870

HERMONI, A., Be-Ikbot ha-Biluyim, Rubin Mass, Jerusalem, 1952

IBN BARUN, ISAAC, Kitab al-Muwazanah, ed. Kokowzoff, St. Petersburg, 1893

IBN EZRA, AHRAHAM, Sefer Tzahot, ed. Lippman, Fürth, 1827

——— Moznayim, ed. Heidenheim W., Offenbach, 1791

——— Yesod Mispar, attached to Pensker's Mabo, Vienna, 1863

——— Yesod Mora, ed. Lippman, 1834

IBN JANAH, JONAH, Opuscules et Traités d'Abou'-l-Walid Merwan Ibn Djinah, publiés par J. et H. Derenbourg, Paris, 1880

——— Sefer ha-Shorashim, ed. Wilhelm Bacher, Berlin, 1896

IBN LABRAT, DUNASH, Teshubot against Menahem, ed. Filipowski, London, 1855

JESPERSEN, OTTO, Mankind, Nation and Individual from a Linguistic Point of View, Oslo, Aschehouz & Co., 1925

——— Language, Its Nature, Development and Origin, London, G. Allen & Unwin, 1922

KAHLE, PAUL, Masoreten des Westens, Stuttgart, 1927

KATSH, ABRAHAM, Hebrew in American Higher Education, New York University, 1941

KLAR, BINYAMIN, Mehkorim we-'iyyunim, Mahbarot le-Sifrut, Tel Aviv, 1954

KLAUSNER, JOSEPH, Historiah shel ha-Sifrut ha-Ibrit ha-Hadashah, I-VI, Hebrew University, Jerusalem, 1930-50

——— Sefer ha-Shanah li-Yehudei Eretz Yisrael, I, 1923

LANDAU, J. L., Short Lectures on Modern Hebrew Literature, Edward Goldston, Ltd., 1938

LEVITA, ELIAH, Masoret ha-Masoret, Basil, 1538

MAHZOR VITRY (compiled by Simha ben Samuel of Vitry), ed. S. Hurwitz, Berlin, 1889-93

MENCKEN, HENRY L., The American Language, Alfred Knopf, 1952

MILLER, GEORGE A., Language and Communication, McGraw-Hill Book Co., 1951

MILLER, PERRY, and JOHNSON, THOMAS H., The Puritan, American Book Co., 1938

NEUMAN, A. A., Relations of the Hebrew Scriptures to American Institutions, Jewish Theological Seminary of America, 1938

NÖLDEKE, THEO., Beiträge zur Semitischen Sprachwissenschaft, Strassburg, 1904

OBADIAH, MORDECAI, Mi-Pi Bialik, Massadah, 1945

PATAI, RAPHAEL, Israel Between East and West, Jewish Publication Society, 1953

PINSKER, S., Mabo el ha-Nikkud ha-Ashuri 'o ha-Babli, Vienna, 1863

POLACK, AB. N., Kazariah, Mosad Bialik, Tel Aviv, 3rd edition, 1951

POOL, D. DE SOLA, Hebrew Learning Among the Puritans of New England, Publications of American Jewish Historical Society, No. 20, 1911

ROTH, CECIL, Jewish Contributions to Civilization, Macmillan and Co., Ltd., 1938

——— Personalities and Events in Jewish History, Jewish Publication Society, 1953

SCHÜRER, EMIL, Geschichte des jüdischen Volkes im Zeitalter Jesu Christi, 3 volumes, 3rd edition, Berlin, 1907.

SEGAL, M. Z., Mebo ha-Mikra IV, second edition, Kiryat Sefer, Ltd., Jerusalem, 1951

STURTEVANT, E. H., An Introduction to Linguistic Science, Yale University, 1947

——— Linguistic Change, University of Chicago, 1917

SWEET, HENRY, The Sounds of English, Oxford, Clarendon Press, 1910

TUR-SINAI, N. H., Ha-Lashon we-ha-Sefer, I-III, Mosad Bialik, Jerusalem, 1950-55

WOLFSOHN, H. A., Philo, I-II, Harvard University, 1947

WRIGHT, WM., Lectures on the Comparative Grammar of the Semitic Languages, Cambridge, 1890

YA'ARI, A., Iggerot Eretz Yisrael, Gazit, Tel Aviv, 1943

YAHUDAH, A. SH., Eber wa-Arab, Ogen, New York, 1946

ZUNZ, LEOPOLD, Zur Geschichte und Literatur, Berlin, 1845

INDEX

INDEX

Aaron, Joseph, 252f.
Abba Arikha (Rab), 214
Abnei Yehoshua, first Hebrew book in America, by Rabbi Joshua Falk-Ha-Kohen, 257
Aboab, Isaac da Fonseca, 258
Academy of Hebrew Language, 1, 204, 238f.
Accents, *see* Cantillation signs
Acrophony, 78, 88
Agnon, S. J., 13, 153
Agron, by Saadia, 302
Agudat Ahim School, in Palestine, 235, 239f.
Agudat Ha-Morim (Teacher's Organization) in Palestine, 238f., 242f.
Ahad Ha-Am (Asher Ginsburg), 153, 183, 188, 233, 240, 241, 261, 263, 268, 275-6, 305
Ahieber, Hebrew Organization, 262
Ain Fishkha Scrolls, *see* Dead Sea Scrolls
Akbar Khan, Mongol emperor, 18
Akhaneton, 39, 53f.
Akkadian, 24f., 39f., 53; influence on Hebrew, 39f., 131, 168f.; reason for designation, 283; script of, 54: See also Cuneiform
Al-Parashat Derakhim, by Ahad Ha-Am, 304
Albright, William Foxwell, 80, 141, 283, 288
Alexandrian Jewry, assimilation and disappearance of, 213; origin of, 211; political, cultural and economic status of, 213; vernacular of, 211f.

Alfred the Great, 29, 31, 115
Alliance Israélite Universelle, 233ff., 238, 304
Alphabet, 75ff.; borrowed by Greeks, 80, 99; dual forms of, 90f.; Egyptian, 78; meaning of names of, 88f.; order of, 89; origin of Hebrew, 78; twofold pronunciation of certain letters in, 91; use of, as numerical signs, 89; varied pronunciation of some letters in, 91f.
Amarna Letters, 24, 42, 286; Canaanite glosses in, 54; discovery of, 53; importance of, 54
American Hebrew Academy, 268
American Hebrew, Magazine, 257
American influences in modern Hebrew, 195f.
American Jewish Historical Society, *Publications*, 305
Amorite, 33, 34, 42
Ancient sources, use of, in meeting new language needs, 201
Anglo-Jewish Association, 235
Anthology of American Hebrew poetry, 267
Apocrypha, 140, 297
Arabic, 27, 55; influence of, in medieval Hebrew, 173ff.; in modern Hebrew, 185, 198ff.
Aramaic, as language of early Hebrews, 34, 157; during the talmudic period, 215ff.; influence of, in biblical Hebrew, 36f., 49, 168, 188f., 282, 301; in mishnaic Hebrew, 168, 170, 199f., 209; in later Hebrew, 131; traditional

313